SOCRATES

AN APPROACH

PHILOSOPHICA

EDITED BY
MARIO MONTUORI

VOLUME II

MARIO MONTUORI

SOCRATES

SOCRATES

AN APPROACH

BY

MARIO MONTUORI

J.C. GIEBEN, PUBLISHER
AMSTERDAM 1988

A choice of several essays from *Socrate. Un problema storico*,
Napoli, SEN, 1984. Translated by Marcus de la Pae Beresford, Oxford.

CONTENTS

INTRODUCTION

Forty years ago Olof Gigon, stressing more than had been the case previously the mythico-poetical nature of the so-called traditional Socratic sources, which he denied had any reliability for the purposes of an historically-based interpretation of Socrates, revealed with great vigour, and not a little scandal, the error into which Socratic historiography had finally fallen, exchanging the Socrates of legend with the Socrates of history.

But precisely the radicalness of Gigon's criticism which, by ruling out the very possibility of the positing and existence of the Socratic problem risked erasing the name of Socrates from the history of Western thought and, in general, of human civilisation, ought to have triggered off a fervent resumption of study and research into the historical persona of the son of Sophroniscus.

However, in the attempt to free the Socratic problem from Gigon's sceptical conclusions and restore to history the human and philosophical personality of the Athenian master, some people have conceded too much to Gigon's scepticism by abandoning the search for the historical Socrates in order to restate the Socratic problem as the historical problem of Socratism; others, too few in number, limited themselves to searching in those same traditional Socratic sources, refuted as such by Gigon, for new elements in confirmation of their historicity. The majority, however, have simply ignored Gigon's arguments either by restating the problem of the historical Socrates according to the ancient combinatorial criterion of Socratic texts expounded by Zeller, or subjecting the same texts to a structural or linguistic analysis which systematically ignores whether the Socrates who is the object of the investigation is the Socrates of history or the Socrates *dramatis persona* of Socratic literature.

There have been but very few who noticed the pressing problematic exigency which underlies Gigon's arguments and

1

therefore tried to overcome Gigon's scepticism, albeit taking as their starting point this very scepticism of his. On closer examination, this is nothing other than the radicalization of the thesis of the untenability of *a certain way* of stating and resolving the Socratic problem. Of that way which, by groundlessly or simplistically having faith in the essential reliability of Socratic sources, entrusted the solution of the problem of the historical knowledge of Socrates to the agreement of the sources amongst themselves or to the superiority of this or that over the others.

And so if Gigon's negative thesis, destructive and "provocative" as you wish, obliged historians, philologists and philosophers on the one hand to subject to a radical problematization all that one finally believed had accrued to the Socratic question, as if a century and a half of study and research and a huge literature had not had any effect; on the other hand, those who still wanted to study Socrates, having been warned finally to break with tradition and try another line of approach to the historical persona of Socrates that was different from the one theorized about and accredited by the authority of Schleiermacher, Hegel and Zeller.

Thus the Socratic problem was once again under discussion, but it was no longer the same.

The essays assembled in this volume are an example of this. An example, that is, of historical research which, over and above any scepticism and outside any historiographical schematism, aims at restating *the problem of the historical Socrates as a problem of historical method*: that is as an experiment of another line of approach to the historical persona of Socrates; another line of enquiry, in other words, capable of clarifying the reasons for that tragic link between Socratic cross-questioning and death by hemlock.

From this redrawing of the Socratic problem as a problem of historical method and from the related problematization of the texts of Socratism there will perhaps emerge a picture of Socrates which is less idealized but certainly more historically accurate; the picture of a Socrates, that is, who is not a model of wisdom beloved of the god of Delphi, and like Christ unjustly condemned, but of a man who thought of human things in a concrete world of men in a given moment in the civil history of Athens; the picture,

2

in fact, of that Socrates who in the Athens of the time of the Peloponnesian War found the conditions of his existence and the reasons for his fate.

The essays assembled here, though written in different and sometimes distant times, are all inspired by the same methodological criterion and all directed towards the same end.

The first, *Socrates, as a problem of historical method*, aims to be, over and above any scepticism, a restatement of the Socratic problem as a methodological problem, mindful of all the twists and turns of the Socratic question and of all the sources of Socratism: Plato and Xenophon no less than Aristophanes and Polycrates, the indictments and sentence of the Eliasts, which is the most explicit testimony of his contemporaries on the historical persona of Socrates and on the character of his teaching.

Socrates. From myth to history, is an exemplification of the criterion of enquiry theorized in the preceding essay, though chronologically the latter precedes the former.

If, as is alleged, all we know of Socrates is that he was charged, tried and condemned, the reason for his death ought to tell us something of the mode of being and thinking of that Socrates a citizen of Athens accused of impiety and corruption. An enquiry conducted along these lines tends therefore to reveal in the same reasons that motivated the charge of first Aristophanes, then Anytus, Meletus and Lycon, and lastly the sentence of the Eliasts, the essential and characteristic aspects of the teaching of Socrates, master of Alcibiades, Critias and Charmides, as well as of Antisthenes, Plato and Xenophon.

Socrates between the first and second Clouds and *On the trial of Anaxagoras* aim, each in its own way, to remove two errors which are serious and harmful to any possible solution of the Socratic problem into which modern Socratic historiography has fallen; the first error is that the *Clouds* gives grounds for distinguishing a "firstly" and a "then" in the intellectual life of Socrates, thereby giving grounds for believing in the existence of two different literary portraits of the same historical personage of Socrates: a physicist and master of natural science in the early years of his life, known to Aristophanes and unknown to Plato and Xenophon; a dissatisfied and problematic researcher in his maturity, known to Plato and Xenophon and so accepted by a long tradition of study.

The paper *On the trial of Anaxagoras* is intended to remove the second error confirming the argument of the preceding paper on the *Clouds*, demonstrating how the *psephism* named after Diopeithes, which had provided the juridical basis for the condemnation of Anaxagoras, would not have allowed Socrates, between 432-31, (the date of the publication of the *psephism*), and 423, (the date of the staging of the *Clouds*), to exercise that same profession of the science of nature for which the greatest natural philosopher of Clazomenae had been accused, tried and condemned.

Lastly, the essay *On Aspasia Milesia* broadens and develops a crucial point barely touched upon in the essay *On the trial of Anaxagoras*, examining for the first time the juridical presupposition and the reasons for the judicial charge, if indeed it really was a judicial charge, to which the fair Milesian was subjected with a view to clarifying the nature of the activity of those learned metics gathered round Pericles, amongst whom Aspasia was the most influential because she was the most loved, and the reasons for the trials by which they were affected and dispersed and Socrates' relations with Pericles' *entourage* and Socrates' friendship with Aspasia.

It might perhaps not be inopportune to conclude by adding that the collected essays were originally conceived and written in preparation for a larger volume, *Socrates. Physiology of a myth*, Gieben, Amsterdam, 1981, to which they are linked and to which they can provide, together with the complementary volume *De Socrate iuste damnato*, Gieben, Amsterdam, 1981, opportune clarifications and useful supplements.

Athens, Winter 1985   Mario Montuori

4

BIBLIOGRAPHICAL NOTES

Socrates as a problem of historical method, is the text of a paper given to Seminar in Classical Studies, promoted and organized by the International Research Seminar in Classics of the University of London, Birkbeck College, in conjunction with the Liberal League of Friends of Greece at the European Parliament in Strasbourg, where it was held on the 16-18 June, 1981.
It was published for the first time as the opening essay in the book of the same title *Socrate. Un problema storico,* Naples, 1984, pp. 7-23.

Socrates. From myth to history, Athens, 1967, pp. 68. Published as the first volume of a series promoted by the Italian Institute of Culture in Athens, it appeared in Greece shortly after the establishment of the military dictatorship, deliberately stressing the thesis, which had in fact already been advanced in the first French language draft *Socrate. Du mythe à l'histoire,* Beirut, 1963, pp. 43, republished in "Europe Sud-Est", 1964, I, pp. 39-47; II, pp. 27-33 according to which Socrates was justly condemned as an enemy of the Athenian democracy.
In November 1971, right in the middle of the military regime, *Socrates. From myth to history* appeared in modern Greek translation through the offices of Th. Joannidis, who published it in twelve episodes in the foremost daily of Thessalonica, "Thessaloniki". It has recently been published in a single volume in a modern Greek edition, Ο Σωκράτης, από τον μύθο στην ιστορία, Athinai, 1984.

Socrates, between the first and second Clouds appeared in the 'Atti della Accademia di Scienze Morali e Politiche della Società Nazionale di Scienze, Lettere ed Arti' of Naples, vol. LXXVII, 1966, and republished in *Socrate. Un problema storico,* Naples, 1984, pp. 95-151.

5

On the trial of Anaxagoras appeared in a collection of papers on ancient thought in "De Homine", nn. 22-23, September 1967, pp. 103-148, and republished in *Socrate. Un problema storico*, Naples, 1984, pp. 153-204.

On Aspasia Milesia, published in "Annali della Facoltà di Lettere e Filosofia" of the University of Naples, N.S. VII, 1977-78, pp. 63-85 and then in Corolla Londiniensis, Amsterdam, 1981, pp. 87-109, has been republished in *Socrate. Un problema storico*, Naples, 1984, pp. 205-230.

SOCRATES AS A PROBLEM OF HISTORICAL METHOD

More than a century ago, Antonio Labriola[1] concluded his essay on Socrates with the observation "questo soggetto tante volte trattato ha conservato, e conserva tuttora, l'attrattiva di una ricerca non mai esaurita".

It seems that no-one who studies Socrates today could conclude otherwise, despite the availability of a literature that appeared "erschreckend umfangreich" to Maier[2] as long ago as 1913.

The fact that Socrates wrote nothing, while much has been written about him, although historical information on the man and on the reasons for his fate is almost totally lacking, has transformed the study of Socrates into a borderline case of philosophical historiography, turning it into a problem which, it is said, there is no hope of solving[3].

Indeed it has seemed as though it is precisely this intangibility and indefinability of the historical person of Socrates, this perennial reformulation as a problem, this intrinsic problematic quality of Socrates the man, that constitutes his true essence and reality. However, the fact that, as has often been pointed out, the historical personality of Socrates has come down to us irredeemably lost among a bewildering array of literary images which, as such, fall outside the basic categories of historical interpretation, cannot, if we consider the matter carefully, persuade us to abandon the study of Socrates the man and to restrict

1. See A. Labriola, *Socrate*, Napoli, 1871; ed. by B. Croce, 4th ed., Bari, 1947, p. 165.

2. E. Maier, *Sokrates, sein Werk und seine geschichtliche Stellung*, Tübingen, 1913, p. 2.

3. Maier's introduction to his *Sokrates, op. cit.*, is as follows, p. 1: "Immer noch ist für uns die Gestalt des Sokrates ein Problem. Und fast will es scheinen, ein hoffnungsloses".

ourselves to the indefinite reformulation of a historical problem bound, in any case, to lead to a discouraging conclusion.

The observation of the multiplicity and inconsistency of the images of Socrates in the literary tradition should, in itself, be sufficient to convince us that a historical and cultural phenomenon of vast proportions occurred at a particular period in the political history of Athens, at the centre of which there must have been a certain historical personality to whom such radically differing interpretations, representations or simple connotations could convene.

Therefore, rather than abandon Socrates and transfer the problem of the historical Socrates to the historical field of Socratism[4], as though it were possible to carry out research which takes no account of its subject, or, in our case, research on Socrates which ignores the historical person of Socrates[5], we should carry our inquiry into the centre of that great upsurge of idealizing and legend-making that occurred in Athens on the death of Socrates and as a result of his death, in the attempt to discover thus the way in which the historical person of the man who was accused, tried and condemned was refracted in a multiplicity of contradictory literary images.

Consequently, instead of attempting to eliminate or evade the Socratic problem because of the proven impossibility of formulating it as a problem of historical knowledge, it will be useful to repeat once more that the Socratic problem, in the current state

4. This is, in fact, the operation attempted, at least in a programmatic way, or perhaps one should say enunciated, by De Magalães-Vilhena, *Le problème de Socrate, cit.*, p. 12 f. Cf. also F. Adorno, *Introduzione a Socrate*, Bari, 1970, which transforms the problem of the historical Socrates into that of the historicity of each of the interpretations of Socrates.

5. This is the implication of the statement by De Magalães-Vilhena, *Le problème de Socrate, cit.*: "si (...) la personalité réelle de Socrate nous échappe, la critique a encore à faire avec le socratisme", pp. 12-13.

However, the classic example of the abandonment of Socrates is given by N. Gulley, *The philosophy of Socrates*, London, 1968, *Preface*, who openly avoids Socrates, considering that it is sufficient to discover what Socrates, or the Socrates that he does not know, thought. Gulley's approach has been followed by G.X. Santas, *Socrates. Philosophy in Plato's early dialogues*, London, 1979, who, defining his essay, as did Gulley, as "a philosophical study", avoids formulating the historical problem of Socrates.

of research, can no longer be called a problem of historical knowledge, concerned with discovering what Socrates the philosopher thought and what his place in the history of Western philosophy should be; rather, it is a problem of historical method, concerned with finding a possible way of approaching Socrates the man, who found the conditions for his existence and the reasons for his fate in Athens at the time of the Pelopennesian war.

The question is therefore one of reformulating the problem of the historical Socrates in the context of the political history of Athens, before posing it in the context of the history of Greek thought, since if it is possible to discover why Socrates the man was condemned, it will also be possible to discover the true nature of his way of being and thinking, which, while it attracted to him young men sharing a strong inclination towards political life, also rendered him liable to the accusation of corruption and impiety which was eventually made against him.

It follows from this that the true object of our study can no longer be Socrates the philosopher, who is supposed to have formed the link between the relativism of the sophists and the idealism of Plato; rather, it must be Socrates the Athenian citizen, who was accused, tried, and condemned for ἀσέβεια; this will make it possible to try to grasp the tragic connection between Socrates' dialoging and his death by hemlock, which is, as will be seen on careful consideration, the real problem of the Socratic problem. Clearly, this method of studying Socrates, while implying the recognition and adoption of Gigon's conclusion regarding the impossibility of formulating the Socratic problem as a problem of historical knowledge[6], also implies the rejection of Gigon's scepticism as to whether it is even possible to formulate the Socrates problem in a valid way at all[7], setting against this a well-founded confidence in the relaunching of the problem as one of historical method.

For if, indeed, all we know of Socrates is that he was accused, tried, and condemned[8], the reasons for his condemnation must

6. O. Gigon, *Sokrates*, 2nd ed., Bern, 1979, p. 14.
7. Gigon, *op. cit.*, p. 64.
8. This is all that is conceded by Gigon, *op. cit.*, *loc. cit.*, to the *Sokratische Frage*.

9

themselves tell us something about his way of being and thinking, which, by confrontation with the traditions, values, and laws of the Athens of 399 B.C., made him appear ungodly and subversive and consequently rendered him subject to the accusation, trial, and condemnation.

The death by hemlock in the prison of the Eleven becomes thus the one undeniable historical event in Socratic biograpy; the event, that is, which contains the secret of the human and philosophical personality of the son of Sophroniscus, and the central point from which the numerous lines of Socrates research radiate and on which they converge.

Thus, while on one hand the Socratic problem can be finally set aside in its traditional formulation, on the other hand it now reappears in a new and different form, as a statement of a method for a re-reading of the texts of the literary tradition, which avoiding the old attractions of the myth of the just man condemned, become the search for those elements of Socrates' life and thought which lend themselves to the elucidation of the reasons for his death.

It is hardly necessary to add that research with this aim in view cannot be limited to the narrow field of the traditional sources, occasionally recording points of agreement between them, but must be extended to cover both the apologetic and the accusing texts, Plato and Xenophon as well as Aristophanes and Polycrates, along with the sworn accusation and the verdict of the heliasts.

To object that the heliasts were a clique ruled by vulgar political interests[9], and that those who approve of their verdict have no sense of justice[10], is, in practice, to deprive oneself of the contribution of the only historical testimony regarding Socrates the man supplied by 500 contemporaries[11], whose behaviour cannot be judged by the light of a contingent polemic[12] or through

9. P. Martinetti, *Socrate*, in *Ragione e fede. Saggi religiosi*, Torino, 1944, p. 443.

10. K. Hildebrandt, *Platon*, Berlin, 1933, p. 72.

11. All the 500 Athenian judges at the trial of Socrates recognized his guilt; 160 imposed a fine on him, while 340 imposed the death penalty.

12. As was the case with Martinetti, *Socrate, cit.*, p. 445, who, resisting the

the mists of a false moralism[13].

It should at least be clear from what has been said so far that it is precisely the sworn indictment and the verdict of the heliasts that provide the key to the reading of the traditional texts, a key that can be used to translate the literary transpositions of the opposing arguments of accusation and defence into reliable historical testimonies of contemporaries concerning Socrates the man and his works.

Aristophanes and Polycrates, Plato and Xenophon, have drawn radically different pictures of Socrates; the former two throwing the heaviest blame on Socrates, while the latter two completely exonerate Socrates and consequently denounce the monstrous injustice of the condemnation; Aristophanes and Polycrates accusing Socrates of ἀσέβεια and μισοδημία, while Plato and Xenophon celebrate the master's piety and his loyalty to the laws of his Athenian homeland; for the first, he is the worst of men, deserving to die; for the second, the best of men, worthy of the Prytaneum.

This irreducible contradiction between the accusing and defending texts had, however, been simply brushed aside; from time to time, either the accusing or the defending texts, and usually, the former, have been excluded, so that the problem of the historical Socrates has been formulated and resolved, not by grasping the opposing arguments of the prosecution and the defence, in other words finding the truth in the opposing representations of Socrates by his contemporaries, but by excluding in prejudicial way the accusatory texts and by finding a harmony and agreement between the apologetic texts, for which *"le testimonianze, concise è vero, ma del tutto degne di fede"*[14] of Aristotle would have supply a reliable guide.

facism that had deprived him of his chair, wrote, with clear implication, "a Socrate possono anche oggi appellarsi tutti quelli che, senza essere filosofi, sentono di dovere obbedire alla voce della coscienza anziché alla legge degli uomini".

13. This was the case with K. Hildebrandt, *Platon, cit.*, p. 72.

14. T. Gomperz, *Griechische Denker*, Leipzig, 1896-1909, Italian ed., v. 2, Firenze, 1953, p. 449: on the contrary "Aristotele, writes E. Garin, *Osservazioni a una storia della filosofia*, in *La filosofia come sapere storica*, Bari, p. 81, fu il più grande prevaricatore del pensiero a lui precedente che l'antichità abbia dato".

Thus Aristotle became the guarantor of Plato and Xenophon, and the reliability of the images of Socrates in the literary tradition was entrusted to the reliability of Aristotle, in other words of one who could not claim to be a witness of Socrates and who was an unreliable historian.

Aristotle should be replaced as the standard for comparison by the one certain piece of historical information that we have on Socrates, or, at least, the only historical testimony that allows us to continue to discuss him, namely the sworn accusation of Anytus, Meletus, and Lycon, confirmed by the judicial sentence voted for by the majority of the heliasts[15]; this is the point of reference against which the accusing and defending writings — Plato's *Apology*, Polycrates' *Kategoria*, Aristophanes' *Clouds*, and Xenophon's *Memoirs* — should be set and compared.

It is not, therefore, from the agreement between certain sources, but from the subtle play of the counterpoint between the accusing and defending writings, that we can still hope to obtain a reliable historical reconstruction of the personality of the Athenian master, whose place is not between the relativism of the sophists and the idealism of Plato, but in a particular period of Athenian political history in which the contents of the Socratic dialogues could lead to the tragic nature of the fate of the man.

At any rate, there must have been some reason why, when Socrates was alive, the Athenians knew him only as impious and a corrupter while, once Socrates was dead, his death was honoured by some as symbolic of the just man condemned; that is to say, there must have been some reason why the only testimonies of the contemporaries of the living Socrates that have come down to us all comdemn the man and his works, as seen in the derision of the comic poets, the accusation of Aristophanes (which is repeated point for point in the sworn accusation of Anytus, Meletus and Lycon), the verdict of the majority of the heliasts, and, lastly, the *Kategoria* with which Polycrates later replied to Plato's *Apology*.

---

15. 290 of the 500 judges voted for the death sentence in the first vote and 340 in the second; it should be remembered that the remaining 160 in the second vote did not vote against the sentence because of Socrates' innocence, but voted for a lighter penalty, namely a fine: see Plato, *Apol*, 36a, Diog. Laert. II V 41.

When Socrates was dead, the man accused, tried, and condemned for being impious and a corrupter became celebrated by others as one specially favoured by the god of Delphi and destined for a spiritual mission towards a whole people.

We must now ask, therefore, what could have caused such a radical change of opinion concerning the man condemned for ἀσέβεια, and if Socrates' death itself, or rather the reasons for his death, were not themselves at the origin of the legend which sprang up around his name, whereby the Socrates who, to the majority of Athenians, had appeared liable to accusation and condemnation was multiplied in a number of literary images which were the exact opposites of those which, in the eyes of his contempories, justified the counts of the indictment and legitimized the sentence.

It has already been said and repeated elsewhere that the accusation and condemnation of Socrates as a corrupter of the young were extended to include the young men who had associated with him, and that the court's sentence could be taken to imply that these young men were themselves corrupt.

The sentence, in fact, was legitimate inasmuch as the existence of young men corrupted by Socrates must have been proved to the jury of the heliasts, or to a majority of them.

If this had not been so, if, in other words, there had been some good reason for disbelief in, or simply suspicion regarding the good faith of the judges or the legitimacy of the sentence, then the death of Socrates would truly have been something to condemn as "Justizmord"[16] or as "una colossale ingiustizia"[17], for which the democrats who had returned to Athens would have been responsible.

It is difficult to believe that, in an Athens which was in the process of binding up the wounds inflicted on it by the long and disastrous Peloponnesian war and in particular, when Euclides' amnesty was in force[18], a politically prominent man such as Anytus, together with the majority of the heliasts, would have

16. Maier, *Sokrates*, *cit.*, p. 105.
17. Martinetti, *Socrate*, *cit.*, p. 443.
18. On the amnesty of Euclides, which provided for the disregarding of all that had been done in the past or before 404, see Aristotle, *Resp. Ath.*, 39.

13

deliberately become responsible for a sensational act of injustice perpetrated against a man who had been widely known for at least twenty-five years in Athens and beyond and was certain to be protected by influential friends; and this at a time when the city was implementing the policies of oblivion and reconciliation for which the restored democracy in Athens had made itself the guarantor.

If after Socrates' death his friends, or rather those disciples associated with him in the sentence, decided to leave Athens[19], it was certainly not because the city had lost the man who had given it a soul and a hope of salvation[20], but because the situation was becoming too hostile for the Socratics[21].

They had, in fact, become doubly hateful to the Athenian democrats, firstly because they were οἱ καλοί τε κἀγαθοί[22], "the sons of the wealthiest"[23], who had let themselves be corrupted by Socrates, of whose culpability they constituted the clear and certain proof; secondly because they had been incapable of preventing Socrates' death by making him flee[24].

This death represented a flagrant betrayal of the spirit of tolerant benevolence for which the restored Athenian democracy wished to take credit, and therefore it displeased everyone, both friends and enemies of Socrates, so that each group blamed the other for the tragic event that had occurred in the prison of the Eleven: the friends lamented the monstrous injustice of the accusation and condemnation and the enemies deplored the ineptitude of the others, of saving Socrates from his fate, given that this could have been done[25]; both groups were, at one and the same time, the avengers of and responsible for a death which was unwanted and yet as inevitable as Socrates' resolve in obedience to his law, namely the law of the just man, or the law of the man

19. Diog. Laer. II, 10, 106. It is probable that the Socratics who left Athens with Plato were those who are recorded in the *Apology* and the *Phaedo*.
20. This is the opinion of L. Stefanini, *Platone*, 2nd ed., 2 vols, Padova, 1949, p. 22, among others.
21. As correctly pointed out by Maier, *Sokrates*, cit., I, p. 107.
22. As Aristophanes, *Nub.*, 101, had already described the disciples of Plato.
23. οἱ τῶν πλυσιοτάτων, Plato, *Apol.* 23c.
24. Plato, *Crit.* 45a, 46a.
25. Plato, *Crit.* 45c.

who had a better knowledge than anyone else of the just and the unjust[26].

The Socratics, corrupt as they could be called on the authority of the court's sentence and inept, as the democrats called them for having been incapable of avoiding the legitimate and predictable condemnation of Socrates, cannot have been slow to realize that there was no longer any place for them in Athens and consequently to decide to depart for the house of Euclides in Megara, "for fear of the tyrants", as Hermodorus[27] says, or, rather, in order to flee from the hatred of the people who attributed the death of Socrates to them rather than to the sentence of the heliasts, since, if they had wished, Socrates would have been saved, which everyone in Athens expected to be the outcome of the hateful affair.

Thus it is legitimate to suggest that, once they were reunited around Euclides, in the safe refuge of Megara, the Socratics, far from mourning their lost friend and collecting their memories of him, would be engaged seeking arguments defending him against the accusations made against him, or, rather, to set against the accusations those arguments which would rescue Socrates from the oblivion of death and would rehabilitate the Socratics themselves as well as Socrates. For if the Socratics stood accused of corruption by the court's sentence and of cowardice by public opinion, their return to Athens was dependent on the possibility of a rehabilitation of themselves and of the man condemned for ἀσέβεια; on the possibility, in other words, of re-establishing in Athens an image of Socrates as free of all blame, yet determined not to evade the sentence by flight[28].

But it must have been precisely in this projection of an image of Socrates which would appease the people's aversion, while not betraying the spirit of the Socratic dialogues, that each of the Socratics came to find that he was the bearer of his own Socrates, the faithful interpreter of his thought, and the jealous guardian

26. Plato, *Crit.* 47d.
27. Diog. Laert. II x, 106. That "tyrants" is to be understood as referring to the democrats who had returned to Athens is confirmed by Aelianus, *var. hist.* III 17, who records that Socrates identified democracy with tyranny.
28. Plato, *Apol.* 37c, *Crito* 44c, 52c; this could have been done, see, E.U. Paoli, *Studi sul processo Attico*, Padova, 1933, p. 191.

of his moral message. In other words, the indomitable enmity among the Socratics[29] must have arisen and sharpened precisely when the Socratics were enquiring into the nature of the Socratic heritage and into the significance that Socrates' words had had for each of them. It must have been at that time, in the exile of Megara and with an uncertain future ahead, that the master of all became the Socrates of each one, and the singularity of his personality was multiplied by the number of the Socratics, being split into a disconcerting variety of contradictory images. It was in this particular historical and psychological situation that Plato took up his position and began his literary career, and that the legend which sprang up around the name of Socrates originated and developed.

Plato took up his position, responding to the double accusation of corruption and cowardice with the *Apology* and the *Crito*, and at the same time drawing an image of Socrates which, opposing all alterations and mystification, he intended to make acceptable as the only true one, that is, one with which the friends and disciples of the master would be able to identify.

Thus, in opposition to the old and new accusers, in other words in opposition to the old accusation of Aristophanes and the sworn deposition of Anytus, Meletus and Lycon, in both of which the counts of the indictment were exactly the same, and also in opposition to the sentence of the heliasts which found Socrates impious and a corrupter and condemned him, Plato transformed the accused into the accuser, the impious man into the favourite of the god of Delphi, the corrupter of the young into the man entrusted with a spiritual mission towards a whole people, and the enemy of the city into the religious missionary sent by a god to save it.

Moreover, since the Athenians had blamed the Socratics for not having tried to save such a man, Plato responded by making it clear, in the *Crito*, that it was Socrates himself who refused to escape from the condemnation[31], even though his friends had urged him to do so and had made preparations for his flight.

---

29. On the enmity among the Socratics, see Diog. Laert. VII, 7; VI 2, 21; III 34, 35, 36; II 7, 65; II 6, 57-58; Plato, *Soph.* 251bc.
30. Plato, *Apol.* 33b.
31. Plato, *Crit.* 44c.

The fact that the Socrates of Plato, the Socrates whom Plato and the Socratics had known and loved in life, could not have been the Socrates whom the Pythia of Delphi was said to have proclaimed the wisest man of all, thereby condemning him to an interminable elenctic exercise from which he himself emerged confuted, and that the Socrates accused of ἀσέβεια could not have been the Socrates of the *Apology*, evidently a construction based on the Platonic invention of the oracle of Chaerephon, nor the Socrates who refused to flee to safety, in order not to disrespect the laws of the city which were proposed and approved by men whom he himself had described as ill-bred, wordy and ignorant of the just and the unjust[32], has already been stated and proved elsewhere.

It is sufficient to point out that, from behind the Socrates constructed for reasons of apologetics, there clearly emerges the Socrates who fascinated Alcibiades, Critias, Charmides, the Theban Pythagoreans, Euclides of Megara, Antisthenes, Plato, and two generations of men, Athenians or not, who were all eager, like the pupil of Pericles[33], and Plato himself[34], to take up political life as soon as possible.

If indeed, the examination of men to which the Socrates of the *Apology* and of the first so-called Socratic dialogues was dedicated is rightly understood to be a reduction of each man to his own human condition, so that each man is what he does or the consciousness of his own capacity in the exercise of an art or trade, then it will be seen that Socrates' questioning reveals a hidden implication of radical criticism of the democratic system that ignores any specific skill where the government of the state and the administration of justice are concerned. Precisely in the *Crito*, the dialogue which, it has been claimed, provides the clearest evidence of Socrates' unwavering respect for the laws of the Athenian fatherland, Plato makes Socrates voice the most pitiless and corrosive criticism of Athenian democracy, denouncing without any reserve the ill-bred and ignorant nature of the people made sovereign, and the inability of the legislators to distinguish good

32. Plato, *Crit.* 44cd.
33. See Plato, *Alc. I*.
34. See Plato, *Letter VII*.

17

from evil and the just from unjust[35], rather than hiding actually displaying openly his contempt for the judgement of the people[36], and consequently concluding that there is no practical possibility of comprehension or dialogue between the few, οἱ ὀλίγοι, and the many, οἱ πολλοί in other words between the minority and the majority; between those people, or that one person, the single ὁ εἷς who has knowledge of the just and the unjust, and those who have no knowledge at all[37]. When dealing with this matter, in Socrates' conversation with Crito about the laws, Plato accentuates the ambiguity of political concepts, by which majority and minority, the many and the few, οἱ πολλοί and οἱ ὀλίγοι, and consequently democracy and aristocracy, are transformed into the terms good and evil, οἱ αγαθοί and οἱ κακοί, just and unjust, virtuous and wicked, and competent and incompetent.

It is certainly worth mentioning a fact that used to be entirely overlooked or ignored, namely that the interchange of political and ethical concepts is connected in Plato with the ancient doctrine of ἐπιμέλεια which Socrates took from Prodicus of Ceos[38] and filtered through the ἄνθρωπος μέτρον of Protagoras, according to which things are good or bad as a result of the quality of the agent, or whether the man who does them is good or bad[39].

If, therefore, it is the quality of the agent that determines and defines the quality of the act, then good men will do good works and make good laws and political constitutions, while bad men will make bad ones[40]. And just as, by this process of alternation and identification of moral with political concepts, οἱ κακοί and οἱ πολλοί are interchanged and confused, so "the many", "the majority", the people, in short, the democrats, will make bad laws and constitutions, while the few οἱ ὀλίγοι — οἱ καλοί will by their very nature be creators of good constitutions[41].

35. Plato, *Crit.* 48a.
36. Plato, *Crit.* 44cd; 48c.
37. Plato, *Crit.* 49d.
38. [Plato], *Eryx.* 397d = DK 84 B 8.
39. Plato, *Apol.* 30b.
40. Plato, *Apol.* 25cd: "The villainous (οἱ κακοί) do something bad (τι κακόν), while the good men do something good (οἱ ἀγαθοί ἀγαθόν)", *Gorg.* 507ac; Xenoph. *Mem.* IV 2, 25-27.
41. Plato, *Gorg.* 515c; 517c.

This makes it possible to understand why Socrates' political teaching took the form of a moral parenetics aiming to produce the ethical and political ideal of the καλοκἀγαθία[42] inasmuch as it was an education of good and virtuous men destined for political life, and how for Socrates, consequently, the art of politics was identified with the virtue of making others better. This is a virtue possessed by few and a profession for experts, a virtue possessed by good men who, being morally good, are therefore also good at the art of government and capable and expert in the administration of public affairs, which should therefore be taken away from the many, οἱ πολλοί, in other words from the majority, and consequently from the democrats, because they were κακοί and therefore incapable of governing well.

This clearly shows the significance of Socratic questioning as a parenetical exercise designed to bring everyone to a knowledge of himself, his own capacities and limitations, since only he who knows himself is good and virtuous[43], while the root of all evil is ignorance of one's self[44].

It is easy to recognize from this the antidemocratic intention of the Socratic interrogation of man, and consequently why it was the sons of the richest families, "those who have the most leisure"[45], who joined Socrates and followed his example, questioning and confounding others, as well as the reason for the favour shown by Socrates and the Socratics, to the extent of betraying their country at war, to cities with oligarchic governments and to aristocratic constitutions[46], whence their manifest

---

42. The fact that καλοκἀγαθία was the aim of Socrates' political teaching had already been noted by Aristophanes, *Nub.* 101, and was clearly demonstrated by Xenoph., *Mem.* I 2, 14, 18, 29, and Plato, in the *Apology*, the *Charmides*, the *Alcibiades I*, the *Protagoras*, and the *Gorgias*, to which may be added the *Symposium*, 209ab, and, in general, the speech of Alcibiades.

43. Plato, *Prot*, 343a; *Charm.* 167a; 169e; *Alc. I.* 133bc; *Gorg.* 406b; *Ep.* 344a; Xenoph. *Mem.* IV 4, 25-27.

44. *Alc. I*, 117d.

45. Plato, *Apol.* 23c 1c.

46. See Aristoph., *Vesp.* v. 475; *Av.* vv. 1281-1283; Plato, Alcib I, 120e-124a; *Crit.* 52e-53b; *Lach.* 182e-183a, 188d; *Prot.* 342a-343b; *Gorg.* 515e; *Hipp. M.* 283e, 285b; *Resp.* VII, 544c; *Minos.* 318b-321d; *Leg.* I, 624a-625a; *Epist. VII,*

preference for Sparta[47], the Persians[48], and consequently for the bright and harmonious Apollo, who was particularly worshipped in Sparta[49], as opposed to Dionysus, who was dear to the mass of the people who recognized themselves in and identified themselves with this intemperate and plebeian god[50]; a further consequence was the preference for geometry rather than mathematics, since the former was qualitative and selective, and therefore aristocratic, leading to the Pythagorean and Platonic assumption of a god who was a geometrician[51], whereas the latter was quantitative, levelling, and therefore democratic.

This ruthless critique of the democratic system in its obvious synonyms, which inspires and sustains the Socratic questioning in the first Platonic dialogues in which the examination of men, and therefore not of concepts, of conditions and ways of being and not of ways of knowing, is carried out, becomes more open and at the same time more acute and detailed in the *Protagoras* and even more so in the *Gorgias*.

While in the *Protagoras*, abandoning all reticence, Plato launched an attack with all his might on παρρησία[52], the most elementary, indispensable, constituent principle of democracy, in the *Gorgias* the celebrated champions of Athenian democracy are

336c; Xenoph., *Mem.* VIII, V, 15-17; IV, 15; *Symp.* 8, 35, 39; Aristot., *Pol.* II 1, 1260b; Isocrat., *Panath.* 41; Plutarch, *Dion.* 53, 2.

47. Plato, *Crit.* 52c, 53b; *Hipp. M.* 283e; *Lach.* 183ab; *Prot.* 342-343b; *Alc. I*, 120c; *Gorg.* 502d-503d; 513c-515d;*Men.* 93b-95a; *Resp.* VII, 544c; Xenoph. *Mem.* IV, 4, 15; *Symp.* VIII 15.

48. Plato, *Alc. i* 120c ff.

49. On the legend of Apollo the Spartan lawgiver, see Herodotus, I 65, 2-3; Plato, *Leg.* i 624a; 630d; 632d. On the favour shown by Apollo to Sparta, Pind. *Pyth.* V 69-73; *Thuc.* I 118, 123; ii 54; Plutarch, *Pyth. Orac.* 19; Suidas, *s.v.*

50. See. C. Pascal, *Dioniso. Saggi sulla religione e la parodia religiosa in Aristofane*, Catania, 1912; R. Pettazzoni, *La religione nella Grecia antica*, 2nd ed., Torino, 1953, p. 73 ff; W.K.C. Guthrie, *The Greeks and their gods*, London, 1950, pp. 145-182.

51. On the Pythagorean and Platonic assumption of a god who was a geometrician, see Plato, *Gorg.* 508a; *Leg.* 757a-c; cf. B. Farrington, *Science and politics in the ancient world*, 2nd ed., London, 1965, p. 26 ff; P.M. Schuhl, *Essai sur la formation de la pensée grecque*, Paris, 1949, p. 377.

52. Plato, *Prot.* 319d.

themselves attacked[53], revealing themselves to be, like the majority of Athenians, incapable and inexpert, not because they had not been able to make the city strong and rich[54], but because they had not been able to make the citizens, or even their own sons, into better people[55].

The condemnation of democracy, as compared with the oligarchic governments of Crete and Sparta[56] and with the Persian monarchy, must have provoked a strong reaction among the Athenian democrats, which was interpreted by Polycrates, who entered the field by making ὁ κατήγορος speak as anyone in Athens would have spoken, outside the terms of Euclide's amnesty, involving in the accusation against Socrates two generations of disciples, namely Alcibiades, Critias and Charmides, and those who went away to Megara after the condemnation of Socrates.

Socrates, said ὁ κατήγορος, "hates the people"[57], "hates democracy"[58], and "urges all those who associate with him to deride democracy"[59] and "to despise established laws"[60]; Socrates "is a teacher of tyrants"[61], just like "Critias and Alcibiades" compared with whom "none wrought so many evils to the state"[62]. Socrates, continued the accuser, "teaches his companions to despise the existing laws"[63]; insists "on the folly of appointing public officials by lot"[64]; "teaches sons to treat their fathers with contempt; he persuades them that he makes his

53. Plato, *Gorg.* 515d.
54. Plato, *Gorg.* 518e-519a.
55. Plato, *Gorg.* 516a ff.; *Alc. I* 118d-119a.
56. Nor is it necessary to add that both the *The Constitution of the Athenians* and the *Politeia of the Spartans* the first of which condemns Athenian government by "the many", while the second praises Spartan government by "the few", are attributed, rightly or wrongly, to Xenophon, or at any rate to the Socratic circle.
57. Polycr. in Lib. *Declam.* I, 53.
58. Polycr. in Lib. *Declam.* I, 48.
59. Polycr. in Lib. *Declam.* I, 53.
60. Polycr. in Xenoph. *Mem.* I, 2, 9.
61. Polycr. in Lib. *Declam.* I 1, 60; "master of evil deeds", *cit.*, I, 136.
62. Polycr. in Xenoph. *Mem.* I, 2, 12.
63. Polycr. in Xenoph. *Mem.* I, 2, 9.
64. Polycr. in Xenoph. *Mem.* I, 2, 9.

companions wiser than their fathers"[65]; and distorts the verses of the most celebrated poets and "used them as evidence in teaching his companions to be tyrants and malefactors"[66].

The anti-Socratic polemic being reopened, Plato replied with the *Gorgias*, which was evidently conceived and written under the impulse of a powerful emotion which caused the older stylistic features to be abandoned[67]. Against Socrates the ἀσεβής and μισόδημος accused by Polycrates, against Socrates the teacher of tyrants and subverter of the democratic homeland, against Socrates the teacher of disciples none of whom had distinguished himself by services rendered to the Athenian state which had been betrayed a thousand times, Plato set a Socrates who gave instructions, not in rhetoric in the form of an ability to seduce and gratify[68], but in truth in the form of a way of living an ethical life[69], which is another way of distinguishing and contrasting rhetoric and philosophy, lies and truth, demagogy and pedagogy, and, consequently, democracy and aristocracy. With the political profession of the *Gorgias* exalted by Socrates' declaration that he was the only man in Athens who correctly understood politics as the art of making others better[70], the rupture of Plato and "certain other Socratics" with the city became final and irremediable; between Polus and Socrates, between those who spoke as "the many", οἱ πολλοί, spoke, and those who spoke as "the few", οἱ ολίγοι, there was a difference in language, due to the difference in the way of life, and consequently, as had already been said in the *Crito*[71], there was no possibility of dialogue and coexistence: the former group could still threaten and kill, but the latter group would not cease to speak in their attempts to improve themselves and others[72].

65. Polycr. in Xenoph. *Mem.* I, 2, 49.
66. Polycr. in Xenoph. *Mem.* I, 2, 56.
67. Compare Lutoslawski's table of stylistic affinities, reproduced in Stefanini, *Platone*, *cit.*, I, p. LXX, and the comparison of the features of the *Euthydemus* and the *Gorgias*.
68. Plato, *Gorg. 463a-466a; 523de.*
69. *Plato, Gorg.* 463a-446a; 500ad; 502e-503a; 526d; 521a; 521b ff.; *Apol.* 28b; 527b, de; 515c; 521a.
70. Plato, *Gorg.* 521de.
71. Plato, *Crit.* 49d.
72. Plato, *Gorg.* 521a-522e.

The positions taken up by Polus and Socrates recall, in the sharpness of the contradiction between them, the two savage opposing oaths repeated annually by the popular assembly on the one hand, and by the aristocratic hetairiai on the other[73]. Thus, in the *Gorgias*, Plato's Socratic struggle is resumed and intensified, together with the hostility towards the city which had fallen into the hands of the "tyrants"[74], and the implacable aversion towards the Athenian demos which was certainly repaid with the same aversion, since Plato was again obliged to go into exile while awaiting the dying down of the controversy that the κατηγορία and the *Gorgias* had aroused once more in Athens.

To this controversy Xenophon, in idleness in distant Scillus, resolved to make his own contribution, with an *Apology* of the master which did not get beyond the two books later collected as the first two of the *Memorabilia*, books which, in all probability, remained outside the controversy and were put into circulation with the book of *Memoirs*, which was composed later and repeated or plagiarized the memoirs of others.

When Plato returned to Athens after his Sicilian adventure, the death of Socrates had become a matter of past history, and the controversy arising from his death was finally exhausted, so that the Socratic Plato who had fought his battle to redeem both Socrates and himself was completely replaced by Plato the scholarch, who had certainly not forgotten his former teacher but whose philosophy was now far removed from Socratic parenetics.

If, therefore, the sources of Socratism are re-examined in order to discover, not what Socrates the philosopher thought, but why Socrates the Athenian citizen was condemned — not, that is, in order to construct a Socratic philosophy, but in order to understand the reasons why Socrates appeared impious and corrupting

73. The oath threating with death anyone who subverted or attempted to subvert democracy in Athens is in Andoc. *de Myst.* 96-98. The oath of the oligarchs against the people is given in Aristot. *Polit.* V 9 1310a.

74. It was Hermodorus, in Diog. Laert. II X 106, who called the democrats who had returned to Athens "tyrants", because they were usurpers of the government of the city, which should have been in the hands of the few. Indeed, Aelianus, *var. hist.* III 17, notes that "Socrates never became reconciled with the Athenian constitution; indeed, he considered democracy to be no different from tyranny and absolute power".

to his contemporaries and thus made himself subject to the accusation and condemnation, then it will become clear that the accusing and defending texts from the Socratic controversy are in agreement in depicting a Socrates who was a political teacher and an implacable opponent of Athenian democracy.

A political Socrates, teacher of a form of speaking specially designed for gaining victories in the courts and in political assemblies, a Socrates who was an unbeliever and a corrupter, was already present in *Clouds*, and reappeared in Plato, from the *Apology* and *Crito*, to the *Protagoras*, and *Gorgias*, and from Polycrates' pamphlet to the first two books of Xenophon's *Memorabilia*, although the constant figure of a political Socrates was hidden, in Plato at least, beneath a variety of disguises which correspond to the various stages of the controversy.

The controversy was taken up again in a dramatic way in the *Gorgias* as the conflict of two opposing ideals of ethical life which pass, through their evident synonyms, from the ideal plane of the conflict between philosophy and rhetoric, truth and adulation, to the political level of the conflict between aristocracy and democracy.

We have wanted to make clear here the necessity to focus Socratic research on this ethical and political conflict that was present in all aspects of Athenian political life at the time of the Peloponnesian war, by a reading of the texts of the Socratic controversy, of the accusing no less than the apologetic texts, a reading intended to elicit the reasons for and the significance of the death of Socrates, defining the role of Socrates within this conflict and consequently the intention and aim of the Socratic dialogues as a method for a possible re-examination of the Socratic problem, beyond the reach of all scepticism, which would permit the integration of all the partial research that has been done.

SOCRATES. FROM MYTH TO HISTORY*

> *"He was not condemned unjustly — according to the law. And that is the intensity of the tragedy. There have been no better men than Socrates; and yet his accusers were perfectly right."*
>
> *J.B. Bury*

1. — Few personalities belonging to the history of philosophy seem to be so intimately familiar to us and so closely linked to our own cultural life as that of Socrates, yet no other personality of comparable importance proves, upon every attempt at historical interpretation, to be so remote and enigmatic, so impenetrably shrouded in mystery, so tenaciously irreducible in the face of every endeavour to strip away the layers of myth which envelop it and restore it to its true historical dimensions, to its real human stature. Hence the need, which generations of historians, philosophers and philologists have keenly appreciated, to establish a closer, spiritual relationship with this unique and extraordinary man Socrates, and the ensuing disheartening certainty that the secret of this personality will never be wholly revealed[1].

* This essay, which sets out to show that Socrates was justly condemned as one of the subverters of the Athenian democracy, was published in Athens during the military dictatorship.

In republishing it here after a long interval I am reminded with affection of my Greek friends, with whom I shared the pain of those days.

1. In the preceding passage, I have made use of the observation of P. Martinetti, *Socrate*, 1939, in *Ragione e Fede. Saggi Religiosi*, Torino, 1944, p. 409, which has previously been taken up by P. Rossi, *Per una storia della storiografia socratica*, in *Problemi di Storiografia filosofica*, ed. by A. Banfi, Milano, 1951, p. 85.

More than sixty years ago, Karl Joël[2], who had already dedicated three large volumes to the study of Socrates, noted, when he resumed his treatment of the Socratic question, that in reality all we know about Socrates is that we know nothing: "wir wissen, dass wir nichts wissen"[3]. Nor does it seem that our knowledge of Socrates has progressed very far since then. Indeed even recently, in spite of the vast quantity of critical literature which has been contributed over the last few decades[4], a Socratic scholar has come to the same Socratic conclusion as Joël[5], a fact which confirms that Socrates still remains a problem for us, and one without any apparent hope of solution.[6].

The fact is, however, that the Socratic problem, in so far as it concerns the attempt to understand and define the human and philosophical personality of Socrates, is a problem as old as Socrates himself.

Perhaps we would not be far from the truth if we said that it first posed itself among Socrates' own contemporaries, when, in

2. K. Joël, *Der echte und der Xenophontische Sokrates*, 3 vols., Berlin, 1893-1901.

3. K. Joël, *Geschichte der Antiken Philosophie*, Tübingen, vol. 1, 1921, p. 731.

Still on the subject of our knowledge of the historical Socrates, the same Socratic maxim was taken up by L. Brunschvicg, *Le Progrès de la conscience dans la philosophie occidentale*, I, Paris, 1927, p. 4, and by F. Romero, *Sobre la Historia de la Filosofía*, Tucumán, 1943, p. 13.

4. As long ago as 1913, the literature on Socrates appeared "paurosamente ampia" to H. Maier, *Sokrates, sein Werk u. seiner gesch. Stellung*, Tübingen, 1913, Ital. trans. *Socrate. La sua opera e il suo posto nella storia*, 2 vols., Firenze, 1943-44, I, p. 8.

An indication of the extent of the literature is provided by V. De Magalhães-Vilhena, in the bibliography in the last 70 pages of his book, *Le problème de Socrate. Le Socrate historique et le Socrate de Platon*, Paris, 1952, and in the supplementary material appended to his *Socrate et la légende platonicienne*, Paris, 1952. For the most important works on Socrates to have appeared between 1947 and 1957, see the useful survey by A. Capizzi, *Il problema socratico*, in *Sophia*, XX, 3-4, pp. 199-207.

5. Cf. A.H. Chroust, *Socrates. Man and Myth*, London, 1957, Preface, p. XI.

6. Maier, *Socrate, cit.*, I, p.l, agrees with this, and even J. Humbert, in his study *Socrate et les petits socratiques*, Paris, 1967, makes the opening statement: "S'il est un problème qu'il résulte à la fois téméraire et vain de poser une fois de plus, c'est bien celui qui fait l'objet de ce livre".

the course of the great Dionysia of 423, Aristophanes and Ameipsias brought on to the stage a character called Socrates, a parody of Sophroniscus' son[7]. It is possible to believe that the appearance of a *character* called Socrates on the stage may have led the Athenians to take up their own personal positions towards the real Socrates, so that, through the spontaneous reaction of each member of the audience. Socrates's personality ended up being multiplied, as it were, by the number of people present. In other words, Socrates ceased to be himself, and become the image of himself reflected in the minds of the Athenians. Consequently, from that moment he became a subject of controversy among his own contemporaries.

This controversy over Socrates has never been exhausted, and perhaps never will be, since the figure of Socrates which has come down to us via the different accounts of his contemporaries turns out to be irredeemably lost among a bewildering array of images so various and inconsistent that they appear to preclude any hope of coherent reconstruction. Indeed, when one considers the fact that the variety and inconsistency of the images offered us by literary tradition is matched by a serious shortage of historical data, one has to concede that any attempt at an interpretation of Socrates is destined to remain permanently at the level of a hypothesis[8].

2. — When, at the beginning of the last century, the Socratic problem emerged for the first time in all its breadth and complexity as a problem of historical knowledge[9], the only feasible solu-

---

7. At the Great Dionysia of 423, two of the three comedies in the competition had Socrates as their subject: Ameipsias' *Connus*, and Aristophanes' *Clouds*. In 421, Eupolis also attacked Socrates in *The Flatterers*. *Clouds* is only available in the second, incomplete redaction — see my *Socrate tra Nuvole prime e Nuvole seconde* — while only a few fragments remain of the *Connus* and *The Flatterers*; these have been collected by T. Kock, *Comicorum atticorum fragmenta*, Leipzig, 3 vols., 1880-1888.

8. The hypothetical nature of any attempt to portray the historical Socrates was pointed out by A. Banfi, *Socrate*, Milano, 1944, p. 159, and again by A. Levi, *Sul pensiero di Socrate*, in *Studi di filosofica greca*, ed. by V.E. Alfieri and M. Untersteiner, Bari, 1950, p. 219.

9. On the origin of the problem of Socrates as a historical problem, with

tion seemed to be to find an external criterion which would enable the enquiry to separate fact from fiction, the data of history from the elements of legend[10]. However, since the use of such a criterion was necessarily subjective, it failed to remove the suspicion that it was not possible to arrive at a clear-cut distinction between legend and reality, but that only a loose and tenuous boundary could be traced between them, and that the elasticity of this boundary led to a fatal tendency to attribute to Socrates either more than or less than what was properly his[11].

A more thorough investigation of the sources, which examined the intrinsic reasons for their historical reliability and their essential 'Socraticity', later led critics to ascribe a particular quality of pre-eminence to one or other of the sources or series of testimonies, and to suppose that they had discovered the true Socrates in Xenophon, in Plato or in Aristotle[12], or even in a har-

regard both to the methodological position and to the degree to which Aristophanes has been accepted as a source of evidence on Socrates, see further *Socrates, between the first and second clouds*, and in particular my longer work, *Socrates. Physiology of a Myth*, Amsterdam 1981.

10. At the outset, the problem of Socrates was posed in precisely these terms by F. Schleiermacher, *Ueber den Wert des Sokrates als Philosophen*, 1818, reprinted in *Gesamm. Werke*, Berlin, 1838, III, 2, pp. 285-308. The celebrated *regula aurea*, which is the first methodological definition of the problem: *ibid.*, p. 297, and in *Plato*, ed. by Smith, London, 1879, p. 14.

11. The elasticity of Schleiermacher's *regula* was pointed out by E. Zeller, *Die Philosophie der Griechen in ihrer geschichtlichen Entwicklung*, II, I, *Sokrates und der Sokratiker*. English trans., *Socrates and the socratic schools*, New York, 3rd ed., 1962, from which I shall quote from now on, pp. 101-105. J. Burnet, *Plato's Phaedo*, 1911, Oxford, 1956, p. XXXVIII, attributed to Schleiermacher the merit of having been the first to see the question of Socrates "in the proper light", whereas Maier, *Socrate, cit.*, I, p 13, observed that Schleiermacher's celebrated *regula* permitted the arbitrary choice of any combination of historical facts.

12. The fact that Hegel, *Vorlesungen über die Geschichte der Philosophie*, 1833, Ital. trans. *Lezioni sulla storia della filosofia*, Firenze, 1932, II, p. 72, relied on Xenophon as the essential source for the reconstruction of Socrates' thought, naturally influenced some of the leading interpreters of Socrates. Xenophon was accepted as an authority by many scholars, in particular G. Grote, *A History of Greece*, London, 1850, vol. VIII, p. 545 ff.; A. Labriola, *Socrate*, 1871, 4th ed., Bari, 1947, ed. by B. Croce, who, finding in Grote "la caratteristica più completa e più perfetta della personalità di Socrate", p.l, n.l, believed that we should attribute to Socrates "nessun principio, massima o opi-

monizing blend of one source with another[13]; or that he was to be found by focussing on that common Socratic ground in the sources wherein even their diversity might be justified[14]; or, finally, by emphasizing the many-sidedness of Socrates, so that each

nione che non sia, o semplicemente riferita, o indirettamente accennata da Senofonte", p. 24; A. Fouillée, *La Philosophie de Socrate*, Paris, 1874; E. Boutroux, *Socrate*, 1883. Ital, trans., Milano, 1929, according to whom "lo storico [...] ha il diritto non solo di invocare le testimonianze di Senofonte accanto a quelle di Platone e di Aristotele, ma anche di porlo in prima linea poiché, unico dei tre, Senofonte è storico di professione", p. 15; A. Döring, *Die Lehre des Socrates als soziales Reformsystem*, München, 1895; also, we might add to the list the historian of Greek literature, A. Croiset, *Histoire de la Littérature grecque*, 1900, Paris, 1947, vol. IV, pp. 205-206.

Confidence in Xenophon was severely shaken by the detailed and penetrating analysis by L. Robin, *Les "Mémorables" de Xénophon et notre connaissance de la Philosophie de Socrate*, in *Années Philos.*, 1910, XXI, p. 1-47, reprinted in *La Pensée Hellénique des origines à Apicure*, Paris, 1942, p. 81-137; this was followed by the no less radical enquiry by Maier, *Socrate, cit.*, I, p. 17-80.

The change in the historians' view of Xenophon is expressed succinctly in the contrast between the affirmation of Labriola, *cit.*, p. 25: "I *Memorabili* sono scritti senza riserve e senza restrizioni, e sono un documento insigne della pietà e reverenza dello scrittore verso il Maestro. E in essi solamente deve cercarsi la dottrina di Socrate", and the judgement of M. Valgimigli, in Platone, *Apologia di Socrate*, Bari, 1950, *Introduzione*, who goes to the opposite extreme in defining Xenophon as a "grande raccoglitore e descrittore di ciarle al cospetto dei Secoli", p. 46. An attempt to rehabilitate Xenophon by a comparison with Plato and with the historical facts was made by L. Stefanini, *Platone*, 2nd ed., 1949, p. 10 ff., in a note in which he reassesses Xenophon's writings as a "preziosa fonte del socratismo"; this was followed up by J. Luccioni, *Xénophon et le socratisme*, Paris, 1953, who pointed out the essentially Socratic character of Xenophon's writings and their exact correspondence with those of Plato. A more valuable contribution to the re-assessment of Xenophon as a source was made by J. Humbert's study, *Le Pamphlet de Polycrates et le Gorgias de Platon*, in *R. Phil.*, V, 1931, pp. 20-77, and by the more recent volume by A.H. Chroust, *Socrates — Man and Myth. The Two Socratic Apologies of Xenophon*, London, 1957, both of which make clear the documentary value of the first two books of the *Memorabilia* in relation to the κατηγορία Σωκράτους of Polycrates and the apologetic literature produced in response to it. For a discussion of the literature on Socrates which used Xenophon as a source before 1952, cf. De Magalhães-Vilhena, *Le problème cit.*, p. 194 ff.

On the other hand, it is Aristotle who is relied on by K. Joël, *Der echte und der Xenophontische Sokrates, op. cit.*, and *Geschichte der Antiken Philosophie, cit.*, and especially by T. Gomperz, *Greek Thinkers*, Eng. trans., London, 1905, vol II, who defines his methodological standpoint with regard to this problem

representation of him in the sources could be said to express only a partial and insufficient aspect of him[15]. However, the reconstructions of Socrates which resulted from the application of these interpretative criteria betrayed strong traces of the particular character of the source or the testimonies on which they were based.

as follows: "The second of the criteria we have referred to is supplied by the curt but thoroughly trustworthy statements of Aristotle", p. 64. In fact, it was only for a limited time that Aristotle was accepted as an essential source for the thinking of Socrates. Even Maier, *Socrate, cit.*, I, p. 81, admitted that he found it "incomprensibile come mai si siano potute dare tanta importanza e tanta fiducia alle sue scarse osservazioni". These observations were, however, studied and made use of with regard to the question of Socrates by T. Deman, *Le Témoignage d'Aristote sur Socrate*, Paris, 1942, and, in a more cautious way, by A.H. Chroust, *Socrates in the light of Aristotle's testimony*, in *The New Scholasticism*, 26, n. 3, 1952, pp. 327-365. On the whole question, De Magalhães-Vilhena, *cit.*, p. 231 ff.

Taking up the challenge of Gomperz's appeal to the authority of Aristotle, E. Taylor, *On the alleged distinction in Aristotle between Sókrates and ò Sokràtes*, in *Varia Socratica*, Oxford, 1911, pp. 40-90, declared his intention of establishing "the direct opposite of such a view", p. 40. Aristotle was then replaced by Plato as a historically reliable source, and, in the historiography of Socrates. Socrates as the discoverer of the concept was replaced by Socrates the metaphysician and creator of the philosphy of the Ideas, cf. J. Burnet, *Plato's Phaedo, op. cit., Introduction; Greek Philosophy, Thales to Plato*, 1914, London, 1953 ed., p. 126; A.E. Taylor, *Socrates*, London, 1932. But the excessive extension of the Socratic period to include Plato's metaphysical *Dialogues*, with the recent exception of E. Turolla, Platone, *I Dialoghi, L'Apologia, Le Epistole*, 3 vols., Milano, 1953, on which see Montuori, in *Giornale Critico della Filosofia Italiana*, 4, 1954, pp. 539-549, has been fully criticized and decisively refuted. The most coherent view of Plato as a source appears to be that adopted by Maier, *Socrate, cit.*, I, p. 106 ff., who restricts his interpretation of the philosophical character of Socrates to the early works, from the *Apology* and *Crito*, p. 125, to the *Protagoras*, p. 132. Even to list the titles of works interpreting Socrates on the basis of Plato's evidence would be to run the risk of extending this note to an unreasonable length. Once again, therefore, I shall simply refer the reader to De Magalhães-Vilhena, *cit.*, p. 186 ff., p. 305, and to the book by the same author, *Socrate et la légende platonicienne*, Paris, 1952, which re-examines the literature on Socrates inspired by Plato.

13. Zeller's well-known criterion, *Die Phil. d. Griech., cit.*, II, I, p. 94 f., more concisely expressed in *Grundriss der Geschichte der Griechischen Philosophie*, Leipzig, 1914, p. 105, is again proposed by G. Zuccante, *Socrate*, Torino, 1909, p. 17: "Completare Senofonte per mezzo di Platone e temperare Platone per mezzo di Senofonte [...] Ricorrere ad Aristotele quando si tratti di

Hence the proliferation in modern Socratic historiography of those images of Socrates either as a moral philosopher and social reformer, based on the recollections of Xenophon; or as a philosopher of the concept and representative of the rationalistic ideal of culture, based on Aristotle's testimonies; or finally, on the basis of Plato's dialogues, as a dissatisfied, problematic enquirer, or a religious missionary invested by the god of Delphi with a spiritual mission towards the whole people, or even as a metaphysician. But in every case these images reflected the particular sensibility and turn of mind of each interpreter, and were therefore the products of a double distortion, caused by the

definire bene la parte rispettiva di Socrate e di Platone'', p. 37. This "classic" solution of the problem of the sources is adopted by L. Stefanini, *Platone*, 2 vols., Padova, 1949 ed., I, p. 7, and to a greater or lesser degree by G. Calogero, *Socrate*, in *Enciclopedia Italiana*, 1936, vol. XXXI, 1950 ed., p. 1025; Martinetti, *cit.*, p. 411 f.; R. Mondolfo, *Sócrates*, Buenos Aires, 1955, p. 27 f. On the other hand, A. Tovar, *Vida de Sócrates*, Madrid, 1953, while looking for agreement between Plato and Xenophon, p. 37, refuses to make any use of Aristotle, pp. 41-42.

I must admit that I would not now write what I wrote previously in *Giorn. Crit. d. Filos It.*, 4, 1954, and in other articles and reviews, concerning the reliance to be placed on Aristotle as an external indicator of the distinction between Socrates and Plato.

14. The opinion of A. Banfi, *Socrate*, Milano, 1944, p. 159, was suggested by Maier, *cit.*, I, p. 156, who was the first to point out that the problem of the historical Socrates was identical with the historical problem of socratism, cf. Montuori, in *Giorn. Crit. d. Filos. It.*, n. 3, 1956, pp. 431-435, esp. p. 432; Maier set himself the task of finding in the thinking and interests of Socrates the points of origin of and the links with each of the varieties of Socratic philosophy, since the different representations of Socrates and the different philosophical intuitions of the Socratics have to be considered as having a common origin in the work of the master. Also inspired by Maier are W. Jaeger, *Socrate*, in *Paideia*, 1944, Ital. trans., Firenze, 1954, p. 17 ff.; De Magalhães-Vilhena, *Le problème de Socrate*, *cit.*, p. 13, according to whom although "la personnalité réelle de Sòcrate nous échappe, la critique a encore à faire avec le socratisme". "Ainsi le problème du Socrate historique devient dans toute son ampleur le problème historique su socratisme"; and Mondolfo, *Sócrates*, *cit.*, who claims that Socratic philosophy, identified with the seriousness and profundity of religious experience, was the central source on which the numerous schools of the Socratics drew over a long period of history, each school interpreting a different aspect of Socrates' activities and doctrine.

15. This is basically what Humbert, *Socrate et les petits socratiques*, *cit.*, in line with Maier, De Magalhães-Vilhena and Mondolfo, now proposes to do.

31

transposition into the terms of modern culture of images in the sources which had already been distorted by an original transposition from the historical to the literary plane[16]. Not without good cause, therefore, did first Dupréel[17] and then Gigon[18] recall the attention of historians to the emphatically literary and inventive nature of the sources, coming to the conclusion that the historical Socrates is irretrievable and that it is therefore futile to continue to search for him[19]. The Socrates that we know, wrote Gigon, is nothing other than the "Zentraler Gegenstand einer philosophischen Dichtung"[20] and Socratic literature "nicht geschichtliche Biographie, sondern Dichtung"[21]; accordingly, in Gigon's view, the disparate images

16. On Plato's transposition, see the excellent study by A. Diès, *Autour de Platon*, 2 vols., Paris, 1927, II, pp. 400-409. On the nature of Plato's literary and doctrinal transposition, see De Magalães-Vilhena, *Socrate et la légende platonicienne*, cit., p. 12 ff.; 179-180; for the way in which modern reconstructions of Socrates' life and work are based on this transposition, see the same author's *Le problème*, cit., p. 105; 355; 362.

It will be made clear in the following pages that, at least where Plato is concerned, we are not dealing with mere literary transposition but rather with a conscious and deliberate remodelling of Socrates' personality.

17. E. Dupréel, *La légende socratique et les sources de Platon*, Bruxelles, 1922. According to Dupréel, the work, the life and even the death of Socrates are nothing but a literary invention created out of the Athenian nationalism of Plato and the so-called Socratics, who attempted to use the image and the work of their supposed master to hide their own sterility and the fact that they appropriated the doctrines of foreign sophists such as Protagoras, Gorgias, Prodicus and Hippias. For a full discussion of Dupréel's paradoxical theory, see Diès, *cit.*, I, pp. 182-209.

18. O. Gigon, *Sokrates, Sein Bild in Dichtung und Geschichte*, Bern, 1947, 1979[2] who sees the contrasting images of Socrates produced by the Socratics as simply aspects of the "Sokratesdichtung" intended to create the ideal of the "sage", p. 16. For the ideal of the sage in Greek philosophy, see Gigon's *Les grands problèmes de la philosophie antique*, Paris, 1961, p. 292 ff. Together with Dupréel and Gigon, H. Kuhn, *Sokrates*, Berlin, 1934, p. 129, maintains that it is impossible to achieve a historically sound reconstruction of Socrates' life and work; and L. Robin, *Fins de la culture grecque*, in *Critique*, III, n. 15-16, 1947, esp. p. 208 ff., reaching the end of his life's work, emphasized his agnosticism concerning the problem of Socrates, at the same time as Gigon was expressing his similar view.

19. Gigon, *Sokrates*, *cit.*, p. 15.

20. Gigon, *cit.*, p. 16

21. Gigon, *cit.*, p. 14

of Socrates presented by the Socratics merely consitute different aspects of the "Sokratesdichtung"[22]. In the final analysis, he points out, all we know is that a man called Socrates lived in Athens, that this Socrates took part in a few military campaigns, and that he was later accused, tried and condemned to death: to seek to know more is a waste of effort[23].

Clearly, Gigon's sceptical conclusion threatened not only to destroy the justification for continuing to debate the Socratic problem, but also to erase the name of Socrates from the history of philosophy and ultimately from the history of human civilization. But precisely this danger has provoked in recent years a vigorous revival of Socratic studies which have been no less radical than Gigon's dissent.

3. — Historians, philosophers and philologists were prompted by Gigon's provocative thesis into searching the sources for elements of indisputable historical reliability which would refute the sceptical conclusions of the Swiss scholar and permit, for the purpose of a reconstruction of Socrates, the re-adoption of the very sources which Gigon had ruled out once and for all as mythopoetic creations[24].

22. Gigon, *cit.*, p. 15.

23. Gigon, *cit.*, p. 64: "Mehr wissen zu wollen, ist unfruchtbaress Bemühen".

24. Among the attempts made to do this, the first to be noted, in chronological order, is that of E. De Strycker, *Les témoignages historiques sur Socrate*, in *Annuaire de l'Institut de Philologie et d'Histoire orientale et slave*, Tome X, Bruxelles, 1950, pp. 199-230, according to whom there exists evidence in the form of three accounts by contemporaries, inserted in non-Socratic texts, p. 200, such as Xenophon, *Anabasis*, III, 5-7; Xenophon, *Hellenica*, I, VII, 14-15; Plato, *Letter VII*, which support, among others, the Platonic texts concerning the mantic manifestations and the Delphic oracle, p 240; Socrates' devotion to the sanctuary of Delphi, p. 205, and the oracle given to Chaerephon, p. 206; "the outstanding courage as a citizen", p. 207, shown by Socrates in the trial of the generals of the Arginusae (this serving to confirm an entire narrative section of the *Apology*, 32bc pp. 210-4); Socrates' refusal to take part in the arrest of Leon of Salamis, pp. 217-18. Consequently De Strycker accepts all the other biographical data in the *Apology*, p. 224, as well as Alcibiades' account in the *Symposium*, p 226. Moreover, De Strycker believes that the evidence of Aristotle is enough to permit the reconstruction of Socrates' philosophy, p. 222, and thus to give Socrates his proper place in the history of philosophy, p. 223.

But the most important contribution of all is that made by A. Capizzi, *La*

One of the first testimonies to be redeemed by this search for

testimonianza platonica. Contributo alla ricerca di una determinazione dell'elemento socratico nei dialoghi, in *Rassegna di Filosofia,* VI, ff. III, IV, 1957, pp. 205-221, 310-337.
Capizzi attacks the problem of separating what is really Plato's from what is Socrates' in Plato's dialogues by examining the formal differences betweent two types of passage: that containing ideas expressed by the philosophers appearing in Plato's dialogues which correspond to those found in non-dramatized accounts by other authors concerning the philosophers imitated by Plato's characters, and that which contains ideas not found in the other sources, p. 221. Taking as his example the introductory formulas used in the discussion in the *Parmenides,* Capizzi distinguishes: a simple formula, "che presenta la tesi come sostenuta una volta e in una data occasione", p. 312; a paraphrastic formula, "che presenta la tesi come une parafrasi o un riassunto di dottrine contenute negli scritti di un filosofo", *ibid,*; and an iterative formula, "che presenta la tesi come abitualmente e notoriamente sostenuta dal filosofo stesso", ibid. Since these introductory formulas also occur in the exposition of the theories of the other philosophical characters, such as Protagoras, Gorgias, Hippias and Thrasymachus, p. 316 ff., they may be used as formal criteria for distinguishing Socratic from Platonic thought in all of the dialogues. While the paraphrastic formula cannot be used in the case of Socrates, since no writings by him exist, everything that the character "Socrates" expounds by means of the simple formula must be considered to be the inference of the author. On the other hand, any doctrine, method, study or trait attributed to the character "Socrates" by himself or by another character by means of the iterative fomula may be accepted as being that of the historical Socrates: p. 323.
By using this formal method, we find that only three actual doctrines can be considered to be those of Socrates: (1) that which states that an injustice is a misfortune for the one who perpetrates it, *Crito,* 49ab; (2) that which states that learning is remembering, *Phaedo,* 72e; (3) that which states that the most well--founded *lógos* is true, that the things which are in closest agreement with it are true, and that there exist the concepts of the beautiful, the good and the large, *Phaedo,* 100ab, p. 324.
Capizzi's formal method thus confirms Burnet's opinion of the Socratic nature of the doctrine of anamnesis and his acceptance of the autobiographical account in the *Phaedo* of Socrates' youthful interest in physics and, in particular, his adherence to Anaxagoras' doctrine of the *lógos,* p. 324; at the same time, however, the formal method provides more evidence for the Platonic nature of the doctrine of the Ideas, which Burnet believes to be Socratic because of the way in which it follows on from the autobiographical account. Capizzi notes, p. 325, that the transition from the doctrine of the *lógos* to that of the Ideas occurs in *Phaedo,* 100b, "mediante una brusca contrapposizione tra la formula iterativa, che conclude la prima, e la formula semplice, che introduce la seconda", this being a sign that Plato passed at this point from an exposition of Socrates' thought

34

reliable documentary evidence concerning Socrates, was the story

to the deduction of his own ideas, *ibid*. The following may also be accepted as elements of Socrates' thought:

1) the profession of philosophy, *Gorgias*, 481d, 482a; *Phaedo*, 59a, 60e; *Theaetetus*, 164c; understood as the search for truth, *Gorgias*, 482e, 492c; and for the best *lógos*, Crito, 46b;

2) the assertion that nothing is known, *Apology*, 29b; *Ion*, 532d; *Charmides*, 165b; *Hippias Major*, 286d; *Hippias Minor*, 372a, 376c; *Euthydemus*, 296e, 295a; *Gorgias*, 506a, 509a; *Republic*, I, 337e, 338b; *Phaedrus*, 234e, 235a; and that everything is to be doubted, *Hippias Major*, 340bc; *Meno*, 79e, 80a; *Theaetetus*, 149a;

3) figurative expressions such as that speaking of the profession of midwifery, *Theaetetus*, 149a; and the experience in matters of love in the *Symposium*, 117d, 212b;

4) the lack of interest in the natural sciences, *Apology*, 19c, 19d; and the lack of masters, *Laches*, 186c, and pupils, *Apology*, 33a, 20d; *Phaedrus*, 230d;

5) the practice of public questioning, *Apology*, 21be, 33c; *Laches*, 187e; *Hippias Minor*, 369d; until the opponent is caught out in a contradiction, *Gorgias*, 482d; *Republic*, 337e;

6) discussions consisting of short arguments, *Alcibiades*, 106b; *Protagoras*, 334c, 335b;

7) complete disregard of the identity of the interlocutor putting forward a *lógos* that proves to be unacceptable, *Gorgias*, 458a; and of the number of people supporting it, *Gorgias*, 474a;

8) the exhortation to virtue, *Apology*, 30ab; *Crito*, 53c;

9) the certainty of receiving signs from the gods, *Apology*, 31cd, 40ac; *Euthyphro*, 3b; *Alcibiades*, 124c; *Euthydemus*, 272e; *Phaedrus*, 242b;

10) incredulity regarding the myths, *Euthyphro*, 6a; *Phaedrus*, 230a;

11) irony, *Menexenus*, 235c; *Symposium*, 216e, 218a, 221d; *Republic*, 337a.

Capizzi's detailed and penetrating investigation shows that the dialogues most useful for the study of Socrates' thought are, first of all, the *Apology*, and then, in decreasing order of value, *Gorgias*, *Phaedrus*, *Crito*, *Euthydemus*, *Phaedo*, *Republic I*, *Theaetetus*, *Euthyphro*, *Alcibiades*, *Laches*, *Hippias Major*, *Meno*, *Symposium*, *Ion*, *Menexenus*, *Charmides*, and *Protagoras*. Thus Capizzi refutes the theory of Gigon, who refuses to accept any evidence from Plato concerning Socrates' thought; at the same time, the traditional division of Plato's works into the Socratic dialogues of his youth and the later speculative dialogues would appear to be meaningless, since the proportion of useful evidence is roughly the same in both the *Apology* and the *Theaetetus*.

Capizzi's is certainly the most penetrating and original of recent investigations into the highly complex problem of the Socratic sources, although I feel that it does not entirely rule out the possibility that the Socrates who is made to speak in the same way as the other philosophers is a reflection, not so much of the historical Socrates, as of the consistency of the imagination of Plato, who,

of the Delphic pronouncement about Socrates' wisdom[25], the essential historicity of which was authoritatively confirmed by students of Greek religion and specialists of the Apollonian oracle at Delphi[26]. This seemed to indicate that Plato's portrait of

treating shadows as solid objects, is careful to make his Socrates speak in exactly the same way as his historical characters. This criticism is not intended to detract from the merit of Capizzi's study, but rather to point out the necessity for the historical verification of the results of the formal investigation. As the present study will show, almost all of these results match up well with the results of historical investigation.

25. As already mentioned in the previous note, De Strycker, *Les témoignages, cit.*, reassesses the historicity of the Delphic pronouncement regarding the wisdom of Socrates, p. 206, as does J. Patočka, *Remarques sur le problème de Socrate*, in *R. Philos*, no. 4-6, 1949, pp. 186-213; A. Delatte, *La figure de Socrate dans l'Apologie de Platon*, in *Bulletin de l'Ac. Belge, cl. Lettres*, 1950, pp. 213-26, who, while maintaining that "la thèse de l'historicité intégrale" of the *Apology* is "bien moins assurée que l'autre", p. 214, believes that Socrates' consciousness of knowing that he did not know gained him the recognition of the god of Delphi, and that this makes it possible to outline the religious aspect of Socrates' personality, p. 215; C.J. De Vogel, *Une nouvelle interprétation du Problème socratique*, in *Mnemosyne*, 1951, pp. 30-39, who, reacting strongly against Gigon's destructive argument, confirms the documentary validity of the traditional historical sources; De Magalhães-Vilhena, *Le problème, cit.*, p. 466, who indirectly accepts the truth of the oracle given to Chaerephon, which formed the division between the earlier and later stages of Socrates' spiritual development.

In general, however, all, or almost all, the studies of Socrates published in the last twenty years insist on the historical truth of the oracle given to Chaerephon; see, *inter alios*, R. Mondolfo, Sócrates, *cit.*, p. 13; J. Chevalier, *Histoire de la pensée*, 1, *La pensée antique*, Paris, 1955, p. 162; M. Sauvage, *Socrate et la conscience de l'homme*, Editions du Seuil, 1956, p. 35; G. Galli, *Socrate ed alcuni dialoghi platonici*, Torino, 1958, p. 85; A.H. Chroust, *Socrates, cit.*, p. 31; more recently, G. Calogero, *Il Messaggio di Socrate*, in *La Cultura*, IV, 1966, pp. 289-301, p. 289 f.; J. Humbert, *Socrate, cit.*, p. 29 ff., who all confirm the essentially Socratic nature of the *Apology* and, therefore, the accuracy of Plato's portrayal of Socrates.

26. The responsibility of the confirmation of the historicity of the oracle given to Chaerephon concerning the wisdom of Socrates, must be attributed to those students of Greek religion who, over the last twenty years, have dealt specifically with the Delphic religion and the Apollonian oracle, for example H. Eibel, *Delphi und Sokrates*, Salzburg, 1949, p. 1-3 and *passim*; J. Defradas, *Les Thèmes de la propagande delphique*, Paris, 1954, p. 276; M. Delcourt, *l'Oracle de Delphe*, Paris, 1955, p. 273; R. Crahay, *La littérature oraculaire chez Hérodote*, Paris, 1956, p. 37 f.; Parke & Wormel, *The Delphic Oracle*, 2 vols.,

Socrates in the *Apology* was historically faithful, since the response of the oracle not only confers upon Socrates' enquiry among his fellow-men the conscious sense of a religious mission in the service of the god of Delphi, but also shapes and defines the nature of Socrates' personality[27]. And the picture that Plato draws in the *Apology*, which is generally thought of as a vivid and faithful representation of that personality, would therefore constitute, at least in its most salient and distinctive features, the most important document concerning the figure and the work of Socrates[28]. Plato's portrait of Socrates in the *Apology*, which is consistently reproduced in dramatic form in the early dialogues, was then re-adopted as the ideal model against which to set the other numerous and divergent sources in order to measure their reliability[29]. Thus Plato was credited afresh with having furnished us with a historically faithful portrait of the personality of Socrates, while the *Apology* came to be regarded once more as the most important documentary source concerning the figure and the work of Socrates, capable, therefore, of leading us out of the nebulous realms of myth on to firm historical terrain.

Oxford, 1956, I, p. 431; A. Schroeder, *Apollo en Dionysius*, Amsterdam, n.d., pp. 88-89; not because they share the *communis opinio*, but because they, more than any others, will have felt obliged to go more deeply into a question which interests the historian of philosophy no less than the historian of Greek religion.

At the same time, Capizzi's remark, *La testimonianza platonica*, *cit.*, p. 327, is important; according to this, "l'introduzione relativa all'oracolo da [*Apologia*] 20e a 21b ci sembra per la sua forma semplice une cornice mitica e ironica di Platone".

27. The reader is referred to the authors listed in n. 25 above, especially to Mondolfo; I have not mentioned any of the older studies on Socrates which have recently been reprinted.

28. G. Galli, *l'Apologia di Socrate*, in *Socrate*, *cit.*, maintains, for example, that Plato's *Apology*, taken as a whole, has "il valore di un documento storico", p. 83. It is hardly necessary to add that Galli appears not to have felt the force of Gigon's arguments and that he does not appear to have paid much attention to them.

29. As well as Mondolfo, *cit.*, we may mention Calogero, who has recently emphasized his confidence in the *Apology* as a faithful document; see *Socrate*, in *Nuova Antologia*, *cit.*, p. 294 ff., and also *Il Messaggio di Socrate* in *La Cultura*, *cit.*, consequently, Calogero develops an interpretation of Socrates as the "difensore dell'assolutezza della volontà di dialogo", *Socrate*, *cit.*, p. 300, and believes that this view is shared by "anche tutte le altre fonti", *cit.*, p. 294.

Thus it seemed that the possibility of a historical reconstruction of Socrates' personality had been definitively re-established and that the Socratic problem had been redeemed from the dangerous attempt to eliminate it as a problem of historical knowledge.

Indeed, anyone who troubled to make even a cursory inspection of the innumerable studies which have appeared in these last twenty years would come to the conclusion that, in the end, the sceptical thesis of Gigon represents nothing more today than a brief digression in the history of Socratic historiography: a salutary digression, certainly, prompting as it did a radical questioning of all the data which had been presumed valid for the purposes of the enquiry, but one which could now be ignored, following the new crop of results which Gigon's scepticism had in fact provoked.

It would be a simplistic conclusion, however, which failed to observe that, despite the contribution of a large number of learned and penetrating studies, Gigon's fundamental objection is still far from being overcome, namely that the so-called Socratic sources are not historical sources properly speaking, but, rather, Socratic literature, "Sokratesdichtung", and that the protagonist of the "Sokratesdichtung" is not the historical Socrates, "le Socrate tel qu'il fut", but the central character of a philosophical poem: the Socrates, in other words, created by Plato, Xenophon or Aristotle according to their particular sensibilities and contingent historical situation.

The search for new historical elements failed, then, to add anything substantial to what little we knew before about the existence of an Athenian citizen called Socrates who was condemned to death in 399[30]; and the subsequent investigation of the sources merely resulted in critics asserting the validity of one, or other, or all, of the sources and again offering us a representation of Socrates based on the presumed reliability of that source or group of sources[31].

---

30. With the exception, naturally, of Capizzi's formal investigation, whose importance has been stressed in the lengthy résumé in n. 24.

31. De Magalhães-Vilhena, *Socrate, cit.*, p. 223, says in conclusion: "si le Socrate platonicien n'est pas le Socrate de l'histoire, il est du moins le portrait le plus compréhensif et le plus convaincant qui reste entre nos mains. Plato seul

4. — Are we then to renounce any attempt at an interpretation of Socrates? Must we regard as final the Socratic judgement of Joël that about Socrates all we know is that we know nothing? Or could there not be another solution to this tormenting yet fascinating problem? Gigon is undoubtedly right; indeed, anyone who wishes to make a fresh attempt at resolving the Socratic problem is bound to take Gigon's sceptical position as his point of departure in the hope that he will be able to overcome his scepticism[32]. But to start from Gigon means starting from a position where the only known historical acts are that a man called Socrates lived in Athens and that this Socrates was condemned to death in 399. Now if this is all we know, what critical approach are we to adopt towards the so-called Socratic sources?

In my view there is only one feasible approach, and that is to direct the enquiry towards the task of collecting and co-ordinating those elements (in so far as they exist) which explain the reason for the death of Socrates, i.e. those elements in the doctrine and teaching of Socrates, which made him appear ungodly and a corrupter to the Athens of 399, given the values, traditions and laws of that time, and which could therefore have provoked his accusation, trial and condemnation[33]. In other

fait figure de nous le restituer dans toute la perpétuelle et troublante complexité de sa vie intellectuelle et pratique. Nul mieux que lui n'a fixé pour nous l'homme tel qu'il fut au-delà du héros dramatique auquel la postérité s'est attachée. Chercher à connaître le Socrate historique c'est en somme interpréter ce mythe qu'est le Socrate platonicien, fausse image, à coup sûr, parce qu'image, mais toutefois image de la vérité''.

32. Calogero, *Socrate, cit.*, p. 292, rightly observes that "da un punto di vista metodologico convenga tener conto il più possibile dello scetticismo di Gigon e partire, provvisoriamente almeno, dalla sua posizione, anche senza condividerne, per così dire, lo spirito di sfiducia''. Aware of the complexity of the problems arising out of the crisis in the historiography of Socrates caused by Gigon's work, Capizzi, in *Il problema socratico, cit.*, p. 205, accepts as "validi, dal 1947 in poi, quegli studi che hanno tentato di battere Gigon nel suo stesso campo, riesaminandone gli argomenti: perché solo liberandosi in modo esauriente di quegli argomenti, sarà possibile in un futuro prossimo o lontano tornare alla speranza di ricostruire in qualche modo la personalitá speculativa del fondatore della filosofia ateniese''.

33. The text of the accusation, transcribed by Favorinus, is given by Diogenes Laertius, II, V, 40, as follows: "Hanc accusationem detulit et jurejurando confirmavit Meletus, Meleti filius, Pittheensis adversus Socratem Sophronisci filium

words an interpretation of Socrates should set out to explain the tragic connection between Socrates dialogues and his death by hemlock in the prison of the Eleven always endeavouring to draw cause and effect together as tightly as possible.

Such a line of enquiry would permit us, firstly, to surprise the true Socrates behind the screen of literary idealization provided by the sources, since the very process of literary idealization must have left at least some traces of the concrete Socratic reality from which it derived; and secondly, it would give us an insight into the spirit, intention and ultimate purpose of those dialogues which Socrates was constantly engaged in and which caused Anytus, Meletus and Lycon to accuse him and the jury of the heliasts to condemn him.

The question, though, is wether all this is possible. I believe it is, provided that we can resist the temptation of attributing to Socrates anything which falls wide of this simple line of enquiry,

Alopecensem; jura violat Socrates, quos, ex majorum instituto suscepit civitas, deos esse negans, alia vero nova demonia inducens; contra jus et fas juvenes corrumpit. Poena, illi mors" (trans, Cobet). The reliability of this text has been questioned for many years and has frequently been denied, cf. M. Schanz, *Dialoge Platos mit deutschem Commentar*, III, *Apologie*, Leipzig, 1893, *Einleitung*, p. 15; E. Derenne, *Les procès d'impiété intentés aux philosophes à Athène au Ve et au IVe siècle avant J-C.*, Liège; Paris, 1930, p. 141 ff. The merely literal differences between Favorinus' text in Diogenes and that recorded by Xenophon and Plato are not enough to cast doubt on Favorinus' account. Xenophon, *Memorabilia*, I. 1, only reproduces the text of the accusation "approximately", with substitutions and omissions which are noteworthy but do not damage the authenticity of the text; in Plato, *Apology* 24b, Socrates recites the text of the sworn accusation from memory, and the inverted order of the counts of the indictment may be ascribed to the defence procedure adopted by Socrates-Plato, cf. J. Burnet, *Plato's Euthyphro, Apology of Socrates and Crito*, ed. with notes by J. Burnet, Oxford, 1924 & 1957, *Apology*, p. 102, comm. 24b 8; and Maier, *Socrate, cit.*, II, 40; 176, n. 4, who, in line with Meyer and Menzel but in opposition to Schanz, takes as "assodata la credibilità del racconto di Favorino". Gigon, *Sokrates, cit.*, p. 89 ff., has again subjected the text of the accusation to a radical and destructive criticism, but his arguments may be countered by the fact that the counts of the indictment were precisely anticipated in the satire of Aristophanes, as pointed out in my *Socrates between the first and second clouds,*, while the present study is intended to demonstrate the way in which Socrates' activities justified each count of the indictment, and to confirm both the reliability of Favorinus' text in Diogenes Laertius, *cit.*, and the nature of Socrates' teaching.

and that we renounce the allure of speculative conjecture. Indeed, it should not be assumed that historical research must always reach a definite conclusion, if, in order to do so, it exchanges truth with the hypothesis which explains everything, as happens in certain presumptive procedures.

5. — If we approach the so-called Socratic sources afresh with the investigative criterion explained above, we are provided with the first and clearest proof of the validity of this criterion by the least expected of the sources, namely, Aristophanes' satire[34]. The caricature of Socrates drawn in *Clouds* has been the subject of a long debate, and two opposing theses have been put forward. The first inclines towards a radical devaluation of Aristophanes' satire as a source, maintaining that the Socrates of *Clouds* is nothing but a symbol, a comical example of a philosopher both naturalistic and sophistic who really has nothing to do with the Socrates of history[35]; the second thesis, on the other hand, seeks

34. Aristophanes' comedy, *Clouds*, its different editions, its nature and its documentary value as a source for Socrates, are studied in greater depth in my *Socrates between the first and second clouds*, to which the reader is referred, and from which I have drawn my observations regarding Aristophanes as a source.

35. The theory, suggested by Plato, *Ap.*, 19c ff., that there was no connection at all between Aristophanes' Socrates and the real son of Sophroniscus, was first put forward in modern times by G.E. Lessing, *Hamburgische Dramaturgie*, 1767-1769, XCI Stück, March 1768, Leipzig, n.d., p. 381 ff., and introduced into the historiography of Socrates by J.W. Süvern, *Ueber Aristophanes Wolken*, Berlin 1826, according to whom the philosopher portrayed in *Clouds* was not a real person but a symbol, p. 19 & p. 26, and Aristophanes' satire was not aimed at Socrates but at the school of sophists and rhetoricians flourishing in Socrates' Athens, p. 30 ff.; 55 ff. Zeller, *Socrates and the Socratic Schools*, *cit.*, p. 217, strongly opposed Süvern's theory, but still ruled out Aristophanes as a source for Socrates, p. 98. Similarly, G. Grote, *History of Greece*, London, 1849, VI, p. 659, considered that the Socrates of *Clouds* "is not even a caricature, but a totally different person"; however, Labriola, *Socrate*, *cit.*, recognizes *Clouds* as historical evidence of the influence of Socrates, even in those times, and of his reputation in Athenian society; Schanz, *Platonis Apologia*, *cit.*, p 45, denies that any features of the real Socrates, even in caricature, are to be seen in Aristophanes' Socrates. According to Schanz, Aristophanes showed his audience the nature of the new science, the rhetoric and the wisdom of the sophists by concentrating all the cultural trends of the time in the character of Socrates. Consequently, the Socrates of *Clouds* should be thought of as a type, rather than as

41

to re-establish the documentary value of *Clouds*, arguing that in it Aristophanes portrayed Socrates as a physiologist and a master of the natural sciences, as he was (so it is claimed) in the early part of his life, about which Aristophanes, unlike Plato and Xenophon[36], was in a position to know a good deal. However,

an individual, p. 50. A similar view is taken by R. Pöhlmann, *Sokratische Studien*, in *Münc. AKSB*, 1906, p. 49 ff., esp. p. 70 ff; U. von Wilamowitz-Möllendorf, *Platon*, I, 2nd ed., Berlin, 1920, pp. 99-100; G. Gentile, in *La Critica*, 1909, p. 289, and more recently in *Storia della Filosofia, Dalle origini a Platone*, Firenze, 1964, p. 96; Maier, *Socrate, cit.*, I, p. 169, according to whom Aristophanes intended to attack, not the real Socrates, but the leading figure of the enlightenment, "l'illuminista alla più alta potenza", the "spiritus rector" of all the contemporary disorder, so that he was perfectly able to represent Socrates on the stage as "maestro a un tempo di filosofia della natura e di sofistica", W. Jaeger, *Paideia*, 1934, Ital. trans., Firenze, I, p. 625, who believes that Aristophanes' Socrates personifies the whole of the decadent culture of his age, shown for the first time in *Clouds* in the form of a spiritual physiognomy of an entire epoch; and that Aristophanes gave his Socrates all the features of the class of people with which he was evidently identified, namely the sophists, rhetoricians and natural philosophers or "meteorologists" as they were then called: Banfi, *Socrate, cit.*, p. 125; G. Bastide, *Le moment historique de Socrate*, Paris, 1939, p. 78, according to whom "le grossissement caricatural équivaut à une déformation derrière laquelle l'originale nous échappe"; G. Cornford. *The Philosophy of Socrates*, in *The Cambridge Ancient History*, IV, 1933, pp. 302-303 (Cornford did not even mention Aristophanes in his discussion of Socrates in *Before & After Socrates*, 1932, Cambridge, 1950); V. Ehrenberg, *The people of Aristophanes*, 2nd ed., Oxford, 1951, pp. 273-78. Without attempting to provide a complete list of relevant works, I might also mention P. Decharme, *La critique des traditions religieuses chez les Grècques, des origines au temps de Plutarque*, Paris, 1904, p. 126; M. Croiset, *Histoire de la Littérature Grecque*, 3rd ed., Paris, 1935, III, p. 239; H. van Daele, *Notice*, in *Les Nuées* in *Aristophane*, I, 3rd ed., Paris, B.L., 1948, pp. 148-150; K. Hildebrandt, *Platon*, Berlin, 1933; and, from the last twenty years, Nilsson, *Greek piety*, Oxford, 1948, p. 74; J. Zafiropoulo, *Diogène d'Apollonie*, Paris, 1956, p. 23; Galli, *Socrate, cit.*, p. 18; R. Cantarella, Aristofane, *Le Commedie*, III, Milano, 1954, *Premessa a Nuvole*, p. 23, to whom the Socrates in *Clouds* appears to be "una maschera, un buffo manichino"; E. Paci, *Storia del pensiero presocratico*, *ERI*, 1957, p. 240, for whom Aristophanes' Socrates is "un simbolo [...] il filosofo che rappresenta tutti gli altri"; H. Erbse, *Sokrates im Schatten der Aristophanischen Wolken*, in *Hermes*, 82, 1954, p. 386, who echoes the judgement of Lessing, *cit.*, a century after it was pronounced, holding the character in *Clouds* to be a poetic image completely unconnected with the historical figure of the son of Sophroniscus.

36. This theory was proposed more than a century ago by A. Boeck, *De*

there are serious objections to be made to both of these very different interpretations of the figure of Socrates in *Clouds*: the first thesis effectively excluded Aristophanes altogether as a Socratic witness, thereby depriving the enquiry of the only source which, even in its satirical distortion of the figure of Socrates, reflected the judgement of a large section of the Athenian public about the personality and work of Socrates, prior to all the idealizing and legendmaking which followed the condemnation of 399[37]; the second thesis, on the other hand, by attempting to rehabilitate Aristophanes' satire as a testimony of a naturalistic phase in the teaching of Socrates, resulted in the introduction into the history

Socratis rerum physicarum studio, Berolino, 1838, reprinted in *Kleine Schriften*, IV, Berlin, 1874, pp. 430-436; and again by C.A. Brandies, *Handbuch der Gesch. der griechische romischen Philos.*, Berlin, 1835-60, II, p. 34 ff., *Die Entwicklung d. griech. Philos.*, I, Berlin, 1862, p. 236; E. Alberti, *Sokrates*, Göttingen, 1869; A. Fouilée, *La Philosophie de Socrate*, I, Paris, 1874; taken up again and expanded by A. Chiapelli, *Il Naturalismo di Socrate e le prime Nubi di Aristofane*, Rend, dell'Accademia dei Lincei, Roma, 1886, pp. 284-302, and *Nuove Ricerche sul Naturalismo di Socrate*, in Archiv für Geschichte der Philosophie, IV, 1891, pp. 369-413; then by Zuccante, *Socrate, cit.*, and C. Pascal, *Dioniso*, Catania, 1911; it became the standard theory in the historiography of Socrates thanks to Burnet, *Plato's Phaedo, op. cit.*, p. XXXIV ff., *Greek philosophy, op. cit.*, p. 124 ff., *Early Greek Philosophy*, 1892, 2nd ed., London, 1908, p. 192 ff., 358, 415, *Plato's Apology, op. cit.*, p. 91; and to Taylor, *Varia Socratica, op. cit.*, esp. pp. 129-177, *Socrates, op. cit.*, p. 60 ff.; these writers were followed more or less closely by Derenne, *Les procès d'impiété..., op. cit.*, pp. 73, esp. 92-93; Jaeger, *Paideia, op. cit.*; much less closely by Tovar, *Vida de Sócrates, op. cit.*, p. 121, and finally by Mondolfo, *Sócrates, op. cit.*, p. 12 ff, and J. Chevalier, *Histoire de la Pensée*, I, Paris, 1955, p. 151.

In addition, the views of V. de Magalhães-Vilhena, *Socrate et la recherche scientifique*, in *Le Problème de Socrate*, Paris, 1952, p. 16 ff., appear to me to be very similar to those of the authors who suppose that there was an initial naturalistic phase in Socrates' activity.

37. Zeller, *Socrates and the Socratic Schools, cit.*, p. 217, had already noted that the essential features of the portrait of Socrates in *Clouds* have an objective basis in an opinion prevalent among the Athenians and whole-heartedly shared by Aristophanes; similarly, J. Bruns, *Das Literarische Porträt der Griechen im 5 und 4 Jahrhundert v. Chr.*, 1896, Berlin, 1961, p. 181 f., esp. p. 196 ff., believes that Aristophanes represented Socrates according to the idea that the majority of citizenz had of him, but which, in the opinion of Ehrenberg, *The people of Aristophanes, op. cit.*, p. 276, was not shared by Aristophanes, who "will have known better".

of Socratic historiography of an image of Socrates which was un-familiar to his own contemporaries, and which turns out to be in-consistent as soon as it is examined in the light of certain historical facts which are hard to dispute.

We have argued in *The Trial of Anaxagoras* that, in 433-31, Anaxagoras was condemned not for ἀσέβεια, as is generally believed, but simply because he had concerned himself with the science of nature, μετάρσια. If this is so, it is hard to see how Socrates could have openly practised the same science, not merely before, but after the ψήφισμα of Diopeithes which had provided the legal basis for bringing the charge of μετάρια against the Clazomenian[38].

The truth is that a decade before *Clouds* was performed Socrates, who had been the friend and teacher of Alcibiades from as early as 434-33, was the same who met Plato twenty years later[39]. And in reality the Socrates of *Clouds* is conceived not as

38. On the trial of Anaxagoras, its legal framework and the grounds for it, and the repercussions of the conviction of the Clazomenian on the problem of Socrates, which have some bearing on the point under discussion, see *The trial of Anaxagoras* in this volume.

39. See Plato *Symp.* 219e, according to which Socrates was friendly with Alcibiades in the years immediately before the events of Potidaea; in other words, according to the note by J. Hatzfeld, *Alcibiade*, Paris, 1953, not before about 434-433, when Alcibiades, having reached the age of majority, 18 years, and having undergone the δοκιμασία, G. Glotz, *La Cité grecque*, Paris, 1953, p. 255 f., ceased to be under the guardianship of Pericles, Hatzfeld, *cit.*, p. 30, and had his own house and slaves, and freely entertained his friends, *ibid,*. p. 33. And while the *Charmides*, 153a, depicts Socrates, on his return from Potidaea, 432 B.C., questioning his friends περὶ φιλοσοφίας, 153d, thus resum-ing a practice temporarily abandoned, the *Protagoras*, set at a time not long before the campaign of Potidaea, portrays Socrates at the height of his spiritual mission among men and already in pursuit of the handsome Alcibiades.

Plato's evidence as to the relationship between Socrates and Alcibiades seems entirely trustworthy to me, since if Plato was trying to assign the earliest possible date to the end of the relationship, he would have found it difficult to give an earlier date to the beginning of it than the one which he did give, namely the time immediately after the end of Pericles' guardianship of Alcibiades, *Symposium*, or even before this, when Alcibiades was still a young lad, *Protagoras*. If Alcibiades, at some time before the outbreak of the Archidamian war, sought and received the friendship of Socrates, then Alcibiades must have seen Socrates, not as a natural scientist, but as a teacher of ἀνθρωπίνη σοφία, *Apology*, 20d,

a comic character or type, much less as a "meteorosophist" having disciples engaged in the study of Nature[40], but rather as a master in the art of speaking in the assemblies and the law-courts[41], a master in the art of politics in fact, who taught Critias and Alcibiades, the latter even being suggested by the name of the horse-loving youth of *Clouds*[42]. The Socrates of *Clouds* was a sophist[43], in other words, who repudiated the native gods and cor-

which Socrates identified with political virtue, and, in general, of that human and political wisdom which later attracted to him the young Plato, who was no less eager than Pericles' ward to devote himself to a political career, Plato, *Letter VII*, 342c. The most valuable evidence for the activity of Socrates at the time of *Clouds*, however, is provided by Aristophanes himself, in *Clouds*, v. 101, where he calls the Socratics καλοὶ τε κἀγαθοί, obviously meaning that, as early as 423, the aim of Socrates' teaching was to turn his associates into men who were καλοὶ κἀγαθοί; this aim, expounded by Socrates as part of a religious mission in the service of God, must have been well known to the Athenian public at large, if Aristophanes could use it as the butt of his humour in the theatre. The fact that Euripides' *Medea*, vv. 380 ff., showed signs of the philosophical and moral influence of Socrates' discussions as early as 431, has been noted by B. Snell, *Die Entdeckung des Geistes*, 1946, Ital. trans. *La cultura greca e le origini del pensiero europeo*, Torino, 1951, p. 165. On Socrates' relationship with Euripides, see the essay by L. Rossetti in *Aspetti della letteratura socratica antica*, Chieti, 1977, p. 111 ff., which considers Snell's conjecture, p. 117.

40. I am taking account of the fact that Capizzi's formal investigation, *La testimonianza platonica*, *cit.*, p. 326, confirms that it was the historical Socrates who stated he was not concerned with the natural sciences, *Apology* 19c-d. See in this volume *Socrates between the first and second Clouds*.

41. *Clouds*, vv. 245-46, 434, 445 & *passim*, to which should be added the evidence, valuable in this case, of Xenophon, *Mem.*, I, II, 48.

42. Süvern, *Ueber Aristophanes Wolken*, *cit.*, p. 33, was the first to suggest that Pheidippides in *Clouds* was intended to resemble Alcibiades. This suggestion was firmly rejected by M. Croiset, *Aristophane et les partis à Athènes*, Paris, 1906, p. 150, n.1, but adopted in a cautious way by Hatzfeld, *Alcibiades*, *cit.*, pp. 34-35, who denies that the resemblance had any effect on the public at the Dionysia, but does not deny its existence. In my opinion, it cannot be a coincidence that Aristophanes gave to the horse-loving youth in *Clouds* a name suggestive of Alcibiades mother, Hatzfeld, *cit.*, p. 18, nn. 5 & 6, whose extravagant passion for horses must have been well known in 423, cf. Thucydides, VI, 12, 2.

43. Socrates is always called a sophist in the comedies, not only by Aristophanes, *Clouds*, v. 112 ff, 636 ff., 658 ff., 111, 1308-9, but also by Ameipsias, in *Connus*, which was performed in competition with *Clouds* in 423, and especially by Eupolis, fr. 351 & 355, Kock,I, on which see Maier, *Socrate, cit.*, I, 164.

rupted the youth, just like the Socrates who was later to be accused by Anytus, Meletus and Lycon and condemned to death by the heliasts.

When, in fact, in the conversation between Socrates and Strepsiades, the strange teacher speaks to his slow-witted pupil about the divinity of the Clouds, Aristophanes puts into Socrates' mouth the following sacrilegious assertion: "There is no Zeus", οὐδ᾽ ἔστι Ζεύς[44], adding that "ethereal vortex", αἰθέριος δῖνος[45], has taken his place; whence Strepsiades' confusion and the fearful acknowledgement: "Zeus doesn't exist" ὁ Ζεὺς οὐκ ὤν[46]. This timorous admission soon grows however into a resolute assertion, following the stringent demonstrations produced by Socrates; so much so, indeed, that Strepsiades laughs at his son Pheidippides for cursing in the name of "Olympian Zeus"[47], and repeats his conviction that Zeus does not exist[48] and that Δῖνος reigns in his place[49], declaring that it is Socrates who says these things and that Chaerephon repeats them[50]. But when, at the end, Strepsiades, disillusioned and repentant at having entrusted himself and his son to Socrates, sets fire to the "thinking-house"[51], he shouts that Socrates and his disciples deserve to be similarly punished for a thousand reasons, but above all because they have offended against the gods[52].

It is clear from all this that twenty-four years before the accusation against Socrates was placed in the hands of the archon, signed and sworn by Meletus, Aristophanes had formulated in precise terms a denunciation which corresponded perfectly on all counts with the later judicial indictment[53].

44. *Clouds* v. 367.
45. *Clouds* v. 380.
46. *Clouds* v. 381.
47. *Clouds* v. 817.
48. *Clouds* v. 827.
49. *Clouds* v. 828.
50. *Clouds* vv. 830-31.
51. *Clouds* v. 1476.
52. *Clouds* v. 1509.
53. On the text of the legal accusation recorded by Diogenes Laertius, II, V, 40, and its reliability, see note 33 above.

"Socrates does not believe in the deities which the State worships", said the indictment[54];

"there is no Zeus", says the Socrates of *Clouds*[55];

"introduces new divinities"[56];

"Δῖνος reigns in his place"[57];

"corrupts the young"[58];

"youth-corrupting", is called the discourse learnt at Socrates' school[59].

Once stripped, then, of all the comic distortions and obvious contrivances of the character, the satire stands as a clear denunciation of impiety and corruption and a fearful death sentence which ominously foreshadows the verdict of the heliasts. The value of *Clouds* as a historical document lies, in my view, precisely in this denunciation.

Aristophanes' comedy presents us with a problem, then, which is quite different from that of deciding what sort of man Socrates must have been for Aristophanes to feel entitled to present him as the head of an established school and engaged in the study of nature. Rather, we should ask ourselves what provoked the accusation of ἀσέβεια which we already find so precisely formulated in Aristophanes' comedy and which contemporary judgement continued to associate with Socrates' activities for another twenty-five years at least, until the charge was given formal expression in Meletus' judicial indictment and the heliasts' sentence. For if all we know for certain about Socrates is that he was accused, tried and condemned for ἀσέβεια[60], any interpretation of him which does not wish to remain a mere hypothesis will

54. Favorinus, in Diogenes Laertius, *cit.* For the meaning of the verb νομίζειν, found in the text of the accusation, see *The trial of Anaxagoras* in this volume.

55. *Clouds* v. 367.

56. Favorinus, in Diogenes Laertius, *cit.*

57. *Clouds* v. 380.

58. Favorinus, in Diogenes Laertius, *cit.*

59. *Clouds* v. 928.

60. As said in note 33, even the reason for the conviction and the counts of the indictment are contested by Gigon, *Sokrates, cit.*, p. 89 ff., but I have already indicated in advance the arguments which lead me to accept Favorinus' text as genuine, and which will be set out in the present study.

have to succeed in explaining above all why Socrates was accused and what legitimated his condemnation.

Meanwhile it is already a positive result to find that the Socrates of *Clouds* coincides perfectly with the Socrates of history.

6. — If we now turn from Aristophanes to Plato, we find ourselves in front of not one, but a host of Socratic images, including that of the *Apology*, which presents the exact opposite of the image depicted in *Clouds*[61].

61. The many different depictions of Socrates in Plato have all been pointed out by the critics, each of whom has emphasized one particular image as being the most authentic expression of Socrates' real character. Thus, together with an unlearned, aporematic Socrates, *Apology*, 20e, 21b-d, 23b, 33a, 41b-d-e; *Charmides*, 165b-e; *Euthyphro*, 5b; *Protagoras*, 348e, 361c; *Gorgias*, 506a; *Symposium* 117d, 216d; *Alcibiades I*, 109e; *Meno*, 70e, 80a-c, 80d, 83b, 98b; *Theaetetus*, 149a, 150c-d, 187d, 210e; *Statesman*, 334b, 337e, 450e, 473e, 491e; *Republic*, 337b, brought out especially in the work of M. Hiestand, *Das sokratische Nichtwissen in Platons ersten Dialogen*, Zurich, 1923; H. Kuhn, *Sokrates*, Berlin, 1934; A.J. Festugière, *Socrate*, Paris, 1934, et al., we also find the figure of Socrates the religious missionary, depicted in *Apology*, 20a ff., 29d-30d, 33b, and pointed out and emphasized by Grote, *History of Greece, op. cit.*, vol. VIII, p. 588 f.; E. Curtius, *Griechische Geschichte*, Berlin, 1887, III, 102; Boutroux, *Socrate, op. cit.*, p. 62; Labriola, *Socrate, op. cit.*, p. 28 ff., 62-62, esp. 150; Zuccante, *Socrate, op. cit.*, p. 118; Maier, *Socrate, op. cit.*, vol. I, p. 136 ff.; L. Robin, *La pensée grecque et les origines de l'esprit scientifique*, Paris, 1923, p. 193; Gernet et Boulanger, *Le Génie grec dans la religion*, Paris, 1932, p. 384 ff.; Mondolfo, *Sócrates*, in *Moralistas Griecos, op. cit.*, p. 61 ff., and *Sócrates, op. cit.*, p. 29; Jaeger, *Paideia, op. cit.*, vol. II, p. 61; Tovar, *Vida de Sócrates, op. cit.*, p. 162; R. Guardini, *La mort de Socrate*, 1947, Paris, 1959; Bergson, *Les deux sources de la morale et de la religion, op. cit.*, I, p. 60; Chevalier, *Histoire de la Pensée*, I, *La Pensée antique, op. cit.*, p. 170 ff.; finally, there is the figure of Socrates the metaphysician, as depicted by Burnet, in *Plato's Phaedo, op. cit.*, in *Greek Philosophy, op. cit.*, and in *Hastings' Encyclopedia of Religion and Ethics*, vol. XI, Edinburgh & New York, and by Taylor, *Socrates, op. cit.*, and *Socrates*, in *Encyclopedia Britannica*, London, 1936, accepted by Martinetti, *Socrate, op. cit.*, p. 445, and recently taken up again by E. Turolla, *Platone: I Dialoghi, L'Apologia, Le Epistole*, 3 vols, Milano, 1953.

Between the image of an ignorant Socrates in the early dialogues of Plato and that of a learned Socrates who professes a theory of innate Ideas, *Phaedo*, and a maieutic system for bringing them to light, *Meno*; who discusses with well-informed certainty the life of the soul before birth, *Phaedrus*, and is sure of the

Aristophanes presented Socrates to us as a sophist[62] who had an organized school[63] and who taught, for money[64], the art of speaking in the assemblies and in the law-courts[65] to initiated disciples[66] whom he corrupted morally[67], inciting them to repudiate the native gods[68]; Plato, on the other hand, portrays Socrates in the *Apology* as a man specially favoured by the god of Delphi[69] and invested with a spiritual mission towards the whole people[70]; a man who has no disciples[71] and nothing to teach, since he knows nothing[72]; a man who does not have a school of his own, but simply goes about the squares and palaestrae of Athens talking to anyone who cares to listen[73]; a man who accepts no money[74] and has in fact been reduced to great poverty[75] by this mission of his in the service of Apollo and the City[76].

immortality of the soul, *Phaedo*; who has a thorough knowledge of the essence of all virtues and, as an ideal legislator, founds the "just city", *Republic*; and who knows more of love, poetry, and the soul then any other man, *Symposium*, *Phaedrus*, *Phaedo*, we find an inspired Socrates, *Meno*, 81a-d; *Symposium*, 201d; *Menexenus*, 236a; *Phaedrus*, 235c, 244a; *Phaedo*, 70c, 97bc, 107d, who forms the counterpart of the ironic Socrates, *Ion*, 530b ff.; *Hippias Minor*, 368b; *Hipparchus*, 228b ff.; *Protagoras*, 328e, 329a-b; *Euthydemus*, 71c; *Hippias Major*, 300d, 301e, 304c-d; *Euthyphro*, 5a; *Republic*, I, 336e, 337a; *Cratylus*, 384b-c, etc. On the nature of Socratic irony and the question of which instances of it are attributable to Socrates an which to Plato, see Stefanini, *Platone, op. cit.*, I, p. 20, n.l.

62. *Clouds*, v. 112 ff.; v. 636 ff.; v. 658 ff.; v. 111; v. 1308-1309. Cf. Montuori, *Socrate, cit.*, p. 16 ff., 35 ff., 51 ff.

63. *Clouds*, vv. 95, 133 ff.

64. *Clouds*, vv. 98, 249, 669, 856 ff., 1146-1147.

65. *Clouds*, vv. 11 ff., 239 ff., 430 ff., 748-783 ff., 874 ff., 1149, 1229, 1339.

66. *Clouds*, vv. 140, 143 ff., 250 ff.

67. *Clouds*, vv. 830, 1321-1453.

68. *Clouds*, vv. 367, 381, 423, 813-30, 1241, 1470.

69. *Apology*, 21a ff.

70. *Apology*, 22a, 23b, 33c.

71. *Apology*, 33a.

72. *Apology*, 19e, 21d, 22d, 23b, 33b.

73. *Apology*, 23c, 33a-b.

74. *Apology*, 19e, 31b, 33b.

75. *Apology*, 23c, 37b, 38b.

76. *Apology*, 23c, 29c, 30a, 31a-b.

We are faced, then, with two completely contradictory and ir-reconcilable figures: the first drawn from the square and street-corners of Athens[77] and kept at the level of the popular audiences at the Dionysian festivals; the second, clearly idealized beyond all human measure. But whereas the first figure has either been dismissed as a poetic fiction or been seen as an image whose documentary value is strictly limited to an early phase of Socrates' activity, the second has been welcomed and celebrated as the most historically faithful representation of Socrates' perso-nality[78]. The Platonic portrait has been granted this special status

77. It has already been pointed out that Zeller, *Socrates and the Socratic Schools*, cit., p. 287, observed that the essential features of the portrayal of Socrates in *Clouds*, far from being mere literary inventions, were founded on the objective basis of an opinion widespread in Athens and whole-heartedly shared by Aristophanes; similarly, Bruns, *Das literarische Porträt*, cit., p. 181 ff., esp. p. 196 ff., believes that Aristophanes represented Socrates according to the view of him held by the great majority of the citizens, a view which was evidently quite different from that expressed by Socrates' disciples, according to Derenne. *Les Procès d'impiété intentés aux philosophes à Athènes au V et au IVe siècle avant J.C.*, cit., p. 79. M. Croiset, *Aristophane et les partis à Athènes*, Paris, 1906, p. 22, writes: "Il n'est pas un seul de ses lecteurs qui ne sente, à chaque page de ses oeuvres, ce qu'il a dû à la rue, à l'agora, au port, aux rencontres et aux réu-nions. Tout ce qu'il y a de réalité dans son théâtre vient de là, et sa fantaisie même s'en inspire largement".

78. Zeller, *Socrates and the Socratic Schools*, cit., p. 102 and, even earlier, F. Schleiermacher, *The worth of Socrates as a Philosopher*, in *Platon*, ed. by Smith, London, 1879, p. 9, maintained that Plato's account was authentic only in the *Apology* and in Alcibiades' speech; thus, defining the aim of his investigation as the establishment of areas of agreement between the views of Xenophon, Plato and Aristotle, *op. cit.*, p. 105, he measured the agreement among these different views according to their closeness to Plato's historical writings. Zuccante, *Socrate*, *cit.*, pp. 17 ff., 31-32, 37, and Stefanini, *Platone*, *cit.*, I, pp. 7-8, note, followed the example of Zeller. On the other hand, Grote, *History of Greece*, *cit.*, VIII, p. 511-684, emphasized the superiority of Xenophon's account, as Hegel had, *Lezioni sulla storia della Filosofia*, *cit.*, II, p. 72, but saw the *Apology*, *Crito*, and *Phaedo* as the Platonic texts containing the greatest amount of authentically Socratic material. A similar view was taken by Labriola, *Socrate*, *op. cit.*, p. 24, and Boutroux, *Socrate*, *cit.*, p. 18, who found an unusual proof of the historical truth of the *Apology* in the prediction made by Socrates to his judges, *Apol.*, 39cd; the prediction turned out to be false, "che sarebbe stata cer-tamente omessa, in un'apologia immaginata dallo stesso Platone". On this sub-ject, cf. Maier, *Socrate*, *cit.*, I, p. 109, and Jaeger, *Paideia*, *op. cit.*, II, p. 24.
    In accordance with Joël, *Der echte und der Xenophontische Socrates*, *op. cit.*,

because it has seemed to critics that Plato could not have invented
the story of the oracle given to Chaerephon without discrediting
himself in the eyes of his contemporaries[79], and that the veracity

who broke with tradition in calling the attention of historians to Aristotle's ac-
count of Socrates, p. 210 ff., Gomperz, *Greek thinkers*, *op. cit.*, based his inter-
pretation of Socrates on the "curt but thoroughly trustworthy statements of
Aristotle", *op. cit.*, II, p. 64, but still used the *Apology* to fill out the details of
Socrates' personality, *op. cit.*, II, pp. 100-101, 109. On the other hand, A.E.
Taylor, *On the alleged distinction in Aristotle between* Σωκράτης *and* ὁ
Σωκράτης in *Varia Socratica*, Oxford, 1910, taking up the challenge of
Gomperz's appeal to the authority of Aristotle, proposed to establish "the direct
opposite of such a view", p. 40, and consequently, like Burnet, trusted Plato's
account of Socrates unreservedly; indeed, both of these Scottish scholars saw the
Apology as so typically and authentically Socratic that they went on to attribute
much of the thinking expressed in Plato's dialogues to Socrates, even denying
that Plato was responsible for the doctrines of the Ideas of the immortality of
the soul. Cf. Burnet, *Plato's Phaedo, Introduction*, *op. cit.*, XII ff. and XLV,
and especially *Plato's Apology cit.*, *cit.*, p. 64, in which we read: "the *Apology*
will provide the most secure foundation for our reconstruction of the historical
Socrates"; Taylor, *Socrates*, *op. cit.*, pp. 18, 19; Turolla agrees with both
writers, Platone, *I Dialoghi, l'Ap. e le Epistole*, *cit.*, vol. I, *Introd. all'Apologia*,
p. 736 ff. As for other, more recent historians and critics, I would mention the
following, albeit without any pretence of comprehensive coverage: F. Kiesow, *Il
Processo di Socrate*, in *Rivista di Fil. Neo-Scolastica*, 3, 1918, p. 261; *Sul
δαιμόνιον di Socrate*, n. 2, 3, & 4, p. 34-40; 52-57, who believes the *Apology* to
be "un meraviglioso documento"; M. Croiset, Platon, *Oeuvres Complètes*,
Paris, 6th ed., 1953, I, *Apologia de Socrate, Notice*, p. 138, who sees Plato's text
as "une témoignage de la plus haute valeur", a view accepted by G.C. Field,
Plato and his contemporaries, 1930, London, 1948, p. 154; K. Hildebrandt,
Platon, Berlin, 1933, p. 65, to whom it appears that "für die Kenntnis des
'historischen' Sokrates ist gerade die *Apologie* die wichtigste Quelle"; Stefanini,
Platone, *cit.*, 24-25; Martinetti, *Socrate*, *cit.*, p. 412; Jaeger, *Paideia*, *cit.*, II, p.
57, *Aristotle*, Eng. trans., Oxford, 1934, p. 15; Tovar, *Vida de Sócrates*, *cit.*, p.
28; Galli, *L'Apologia di Socrate*, in *Socrate*, *cit.*, p. 83; Cornford, *Before and
after Socrates*, *cit.*, p. 35; Delatte, *La figure de Socrate dans l'Apologia*, *cit.*, pp.
213 ff.; Mondolfo, *Sócrates*, *cit.*, p. 17; Calogero, *Socrate*, in *Nuova Antologia*,
cit., p. 300, who points out that the figure of Socrates in the *Apology* corresponds perfectly to "la maggioranza, se non addirittura la totalità delle dottrine e degli atteggiamenti che gli attribuiscono gli altri documenti della
tradizione".

79. Gomperz, *cit.*, II, p. 105; "No-one could credit Plato with the unprincipl-
ed folly of attempting to pass of an invention of his own for evidence given at
a recent trial, with the object of influencing present and future opinion upon an
event of great importance". According to Taylor, *Socrates*, *cit.*, p. 55, it would

of this story is sufficient to guarantee the historical fidelity of the *Apology*'s portrayal of Socrates[80]. The validity of all or nearly all the modern reconstructions of Socrates thus hangs on the tenuous assumption that Plato's story of the Delphic oracle's pronouncement regarding the wisdom of Socrates was factual. Not enough, clearly, to guarantee the credibility of those interpretations of Socrates based on the Platonic source; especially since there are many reasons for believing that the story of the Delphic oracle itself belongs to the Socratic legend[81] or, rather, constitutes the

have been "insane to tell such a story, and to offer to produce witnesses to its truth, as Socrates does, unless the thing had really happened". According to Stefanini, *Platone, cit.*, p. 24, "L'autore [dell'*Apologia*] avrebbe gettato il discredito sulla propria opera e sul maestro se avesse alterata radicalmente la difesa pronunciata pochi anni prima dinanzi ai giudici popolari, molti dei quali erano ancora presenti e non immemori del clamoroso processo". Among the motives for the trial, Stefanini includes "il responso dell'oracolo di Delfi", which corresponds "certamente alla verità storica". Recently, Calogero, *Il Messaggio di Socrate, cit.*, p. 289, also confirms that the "risposta dell'oracolo delfico alla domanda di Cherefonte [...] non può verosimilmente essere stata inventata dalla leggenda socratica".

80. Typical of this are the opinions, described in the previous note, of Stefanini, *Platone, cit.*, I, p. 24 ff., and Calogero, *Il Messaggio di Socrate, cit.*, p. 289 ff.

81. The authenticity of the reply to Chaerephon was denied in ancient times by Colotes, cf, Plutarch, *Adv. Colotem*, 6, 116e, and by Athenaeus, *Deipnosophistai*, v. 218e. Tertullian, *Apologeticus*, 46, makes use of the oracle to demonstrate the stupidity of the pagans: "O Apollinem inconsideratum! Sapientiae testimonium reddidit ei viro qui negabat deos esse". Cf. W. Nestle, *Sokrates und Delphi*, 1910, in *Griechische Studien, Untersuchungen zur Religion, Dichtung und Philosophie der Griechen*, Stuttgart, 1948, p. 173, n.l.

In modern times, the account of the Delphic oracle has been rejected as a historical document by M. Schanz, *Sokrates als vermeintlich Dichter* etc., in *Hermes*, XXIX, 1894, pp. 597-603, esp. p. 599 ff.; Robin. *Les Mémorables de Xénophon, cit.*, p. 30, n.l, who, with some reserves, shares Schanz's view, but later rejects it in *La pensée grecque, cit.*, p. 182; K. Joël, *Geschichte der Antiken Philosophie*, Tübingen, 1921, p. 769; and, naturally, Gigon, *Sokrates, cit.*, p. 95 ff. The suggestion that there is no documentary value in the account of the oracle given to Chaerephon is supported by Capizzi's formal investigation, *La testimonianza platonic, cit.*, p. 227, which concludes that this account, *Apology*, 20e-21b, is "una cornice mitica e ironica di Platone". A much larger, thoroughly examined and quotated discussion on the oracle given to Chaerephon about the Socrate's wisdom, can be found in my *Socrates Physiology of a Myth*. Amsterdam 1981, Cf. III. pp. 57-143.

corner-stone on which the whole cumbersome edifice of Socratic legend rests. The story of the oracle given to Chaerephon is in glaring contradiction with the Delphic oracular tradition[82] and with the Apollonian religion and its concepts of limit and measure and the subsequent inflexible law of *hybris*[83]; so badly documented by

82. With the exception of the oracle which the Pythia is said to have given to Anacharsis concerning the wisdom of Myson, Diogenes Laertius, I, IX, 106 ff., and I, I, 30, which is evidently based on an ancient model, Parke and Wormell, *The Delphic Oracle, op. cit.*, I, p. 385, II, pp. 99-100, there is no record, in all the copious oracular literature which has come down to us, of any statement by the Delphic oracle of the same type as that supposedly received by Chaerephon.

83. There is a vast body of literature concerning the Apollonian religion, which has been dealt with both as the object of a particular study and as an indispensable part of any history of Greek religion. On the area which interests us here, I shall mention only Del Grande, *Hybris*, Napoli, 1947; Nilsson, *Greek piety*, Oxford, 1948, who, contrary to Del Grande's view of *hybris* as a religious concept, maintains that *hybris* was "una concezione di saggezza comune", p. 59, being related, R. Pettazzoni, La *Religione nella Grecia antica fino ad Alessandro*, Torino, 1921, 1953, p. 95, to those golden rules of the practical morality which saw human wisdom as being a matter of moderation and the avoidance of excess, and which may be attributed to the Seven Sages of history and legend. Cf. M. Losacco, *Introduzione alla Storia della Filosofia greca*, Bari, 1929, p. 217 ff. But see, in particular, Parke and Wormell, *The Delphic oracle*, I, *op. cit.*; Amandry, *La mantique Apollonienne à Delphes, op. cit.*; Defradas, *Les Thèmes de la propaganda Delphique, op. cit.*; Delcourt, *L'Oracle de Delphes, op. cit.*, who makes clear the contradiction between the oracle given to Chaerephon and the moral teaching of the Seven Sages, accepted and professed at Delphi: "Ce qui est très étrange", writes Delcourt, p. 81, "c'est que celle-ci [the pronouncement of the Delphic oracle] ait donné à Socrate le prix de la sagesse. C'est un des principes de la morale des Sept Sages qu'aucun homme ne doit se croire ni le plus heureux, ni le plus pieux, ni le plus instruit. Toute prétention de cet ordre est immédiatement suivie d'un rappel à la modestie". This being so, it is hard to understand why Delcourt, after recognizing that "l'oracle à Chérèphon [...] comporte plusieurs difficultés", p. 81, and that in answer to questions like that put to the oracle by Chaerephon concerning the wisdom of Socrates "la pythie répondait ou était censée répondre en déboutant le présomptueux", p. 273, still concludes that "l'authenticité [of the oracle's reply] ne paraît pas douteuse", *ibid.* In fact, Delcourt does not come to grips with the problem of the authenticity of the Pythia's pronouncement, believing that the reliability of Plato's *Apology* is a sufficient guarantee: "L'oracle à Chérèphon, dont l'*Apologia* de Platon garantit cependant l'authenticité", p. 81. Thus historians of philosophy continue to believe that the oracle given to Chaerephon proves the authenticity of the *Apology*, Stefanini, *cit.*, and Calogero, *cit.*, *inter al.*, while

Plato himself, who never mentions it again[84], even in the *Seventh Letter* when he is probably talking about Socrates in factual historical terms[85]; is an event of which Socrates' own friends ap-

historians of religion believe that the authenticity of the *Apology* proves that of the oracle's pronouncement, so that scholars in both of these fields take for granted what still remains to be proved.

84. It is, to say the least, strange that Plato never mentioned the oracle's reply in any of his dialogues, even in Alcibiades' speech in the *Symposium*, or in the *Gorgias*, the two works most specifically designed as polemics in defence of the memory of the master against the accusations of Polycrates, cf. Chroust, *Socrates, op. cit.*, pp. 69, 98, 202 and *passim*, and for the *Gorgias* in particular, Humbert, *Le Pamphlet de Polycrates et le Gorgias de Platon, cit.*

85. Throughout the long history of the dispute over Plato's *Letters*, whose authenticity was accepted by almost all the ancient biographers, totally rejected by the hypercritical scholars of the first part of the last century, and gradually re-established with increasing confidence by a long series of works, cf. Stefanini, *Platone, cit.*, I, p. XXVIII, note, *Letter VII* has always had the greatest degree of acceptance. Its authenticity was strongly supported by G. Pasquali, *Le Lettere di Platone*, Firenze 1938, esp. p. 21, but equally strongly rejected by A. Maddalena, Platone, *Lettere*, Bari, 1948, p. 77, who, confirming that "le lettere platoniche hanno suscitato e suscitano sospetti [...] per discordanze di pensiero o d'ingegno o di stile o d'animo che si notano o si credono di notare tra esse e i dialoghi platonici", p. 88, subjects *Letter VII* to a detailed and penetrating analysis, and concludes that "la lettera è falsa, perché altro è lo stile, altro il pensiero, altro l'animo di Platone", p. 346. Recently, E. Edelstein, *Plato's Seventh Letter*, Leiden, 1966, has declared himself to be in agreement with Maddalena, and with the whole critical tradition which denies the authenticity of *Letter VII*; however, he does not deny the importance of *Letter VII* as a source for the life and doctrine of Plato.

Not wishing to reopen the debate over the authenticity and reliability of *Letter VII*, I shall simply remark, for the purpose of the present enquiry, that there are references to Socrates in *Letter VII* that correspond exactly to passages in the *Apology*, 32c, concerning the episode of Leon of Salamis and the resistance to the Thirty, and in the *Gorgias*, 521d, concerning Socrates' teaching of political virtue, the latter being confirmed by Xenophon, *Memorabilia*, I, II, 17, 47; while the assessment of Socrates, 324 f., as "the best man then living" is an almost exact repetition of that found in the *Phaedo*, 118a. If *Letter VII* is by Plato, it is hard to see why Plato, in speaking of his unjustly condemned friend, 325c, should not have thought it appropriate to inform the Dionists of the favour shown to Socrates by the Delphic priesthood, if the incident had really occurred, since by doing this he could have given the best possible proof of his opinion of the justice of his friend's case and the injustice done by certain leading figures of the restored democracy. If the *Letter* is not by Plato, then, in my opinion, the author of the forgery, while drawing some elements of Socrates' life from the

pear to have been inexplicably ignorant, as they were not called to give evidence about it, despite its great importance for his destiny[86]; it is interpreted by Plato himself, incidentally, in terms of Pythagorean wisdom, according to which only the God is wise and human wisdom is worthless[87], and in terms of the ancient

Apology, did not wish to repeat a Platonic falsehood which, to his eyes, would have seemed too obvious. Therefore, the fact that *Letter VII* contains no mention of the Delphic reply concerning Socrates' wisdom may prove, *ex silentio*, not that the document is unreliable, but that the Platonic account of the oracle's pronouncement is unreliable. If this is the case, it could be taken, conversely, as partial proof of the authenticity of *Letter VII*.

86. Out of all the acquaintances of Socrates present in court, and listed by Plato in the *Apology*, 33e-34a, not one was called by Socrates to testify to the reply given by the Pythia to Chaerephon. Evidently, no-one knew about it, and therefore Socrates revealed the Delphic pronouncement to the public only in the course of his defence in court. This would explain the lack of references to the oracle given to Chaerephon in the later dialogues, which, although written after the *Apology*, deal with earlier events in the life of Socrates. But it does not explain why the "passionate" Chaerephon, on his return from Delphi, did not tell anyone about the extraordinary preference for the Master shown by Apollo, apart from secretly informing his brother of it, *Apology*, 21a. And who was this brother? Plato does not name him at all, either here or in any of his other writings. He is only named in Xenophon, *Memorabilia*, I, II, 48, as being one of Socrates' associates, but also (which should be noted) as being involved in litigation against his brother Chaerephon, which caused Socrates to give Chaerephon a short lecture on love and concord, *Memorabilia*, II, III, 1-15.

87. Cf. *Apology*, 23a: "God only is wise", while "the wisdom of men is worth little or nothing", transl. B. Jowett. Cf. also *Phaedrus*, 278b, *Lysis*, 218a, *Symposium*, 202e.

Whether the first use of the word φιλόσοφος, in the sense of a lover of knowledge, is to be attributed to Heraclitus (Diels-Kranz) or to Pythagoras (Diog. Leart., I, 12, "neminem esse sapientem praeter deum", transl. Cobet), and whether, consequently, it was Heraclitus or Pythagoras who made the distinction between σοφία and φιλόσοφία, and, finally, whether Plato derived this distinction, celebrated as being characteristic of Socrates, from "the obscure one" of Ephesus or from "the inspired one" of Samos, is a question that has been debated from antiquity until today, cf. Mondolfo, in Zeller & Mondolfo, *La filosofia dei Greci*, I, IV, *Eraclito*, Firenze, 1961, pp. 329 ff., note. Although Mondolfo's conclusion, *ibid.*, presents us with a dilemma: "resta il problema se l'introduzione della parola 'filosofo' sia da attribuire a Pitagora o a Eraclito", I believe that it is possible to respond to this by saying that both Pythagoras and Heraclitus could have drawn on a common fund of popular wisdom, which, in the legend of the tripod, related to that of the Seven Sages, Diog. Laert. I, I, 28, had already implied that only the god of Delphi was worthy of being called wise.

legend of the tripod, returned to the god of Delphi because he alone was wise[88]. This story, in short, is not an "unsolved problem"[89], but simply a non-problem: a Platonic invention, in other words, not a historical fact. It is certainly no coincidence that the oracle, which proclaimed Socrates to be the wisest man on Earth, was given to Chaerephon, whom Aristophanes had already satirized in *Clouds*, including him in the same charge made against Socrates, and in the same death, for having offended against the gods[90].

The story of the oracle given to Chaerephon is, then, a Platonic invention, on which Plato founded the legend which he built

But if the distinction between σοφία and φιλοσοφία was derived by Plato from Pythagoras or from Heraclitus, it appears to me that it is impossible to accept the view of K. Praechter, *Die Philos. des Altertums*, in Ueberwegs, *Grundriss der Gesch. der Philos.*, I, Basel & Stuttgart, 14th ed., 1957, p. 2, who believes that the reference in Diogenes, Diog. Laert., I, I, 12, *cit.*, is an incorrect attribution to Pythagoras of the Socratic-Platonic interpretation of the difference between σοφία and φιλοσοφία. From the close links between the Socratics and the Theban Pythagoreans, and the decisive influence of Pythagoreanism on the formation of Socratic-Platonic thought, it appears that the opposite is true, in other words that the Socratics took this doctrine from the Pythagoreans. Moreover, the Delphic precept, γνῶθι σαυτόν, also derived from the ancient popular wisdom, was interpreted by Socrates, in the same way as the Pythagoreans, as an exhortation to know the divine that is in us, the order and harmony that govern the soul.

88. For the poem of Callimachus about Thebes, which told the legend of the return of the tripod (destined according to prophecy to go to the wisest of all) to the god of Delphi, see Diog. Laert. I, I, 28.

The ancient legend of the tripod was evidently the model for the account of the oracle given to Chaerephon, *Apology*, 21a ff., which describes how Socrates, having been declared by the Pythia to be the wisest of all, investigates mankind and concludes that only God is wise and that human wisdom is worthless.

89. J.B. Bury, *History of Greece*, 1900, 3rd ed., Oxford, 1952, p. 580.

90. It is interesting to note the differences between Aristophanes' and Plato's portrayals of Chaerephon, who is described by Aristophanes as "half dead", *Clouds*, v. 504, pale and sickly, shut up in his house and only emerging in the evening, whence his nickname "the bat", *Birds*, vv. 1296, 1564; whereas Plato presents him as passionate and determined, *Apology*, 21a, prepared to face voluntary exile rather than submit to the odious tyranny of the Thirty. Perhaps this was an artificial remodelling of Chaerephon's character by Plato, to make it appear more likely that Chaerephon would have dared, ἐτόλμησε, to ask the Pythia if anyone was wiser than Socrates?

around the historical figure of Socrates; and undoubted falsification, in short, of the human and philosophical personality of the Socrates who was accused of ἀσέβεια. This act of falsification introduces a new and unexpected element into the fabric of the legend: we can no longer talk of Plato's portrait of Socrates as being the result of a transposition from the historical to the literary plane; rather, it is a conscious and deliberate fiction, by means of which Plato sought to transfigure the real personality of Sophroniscus' son.

7. — But why should Plato have done this? Why, in other words, should he have decided to present us with a literary, fictious Socrates instead of the real Socrates he knew, admired and loved?[91] For a very simple reason in my view, namely that the charge brought against Socrates of having corrupted the youth implicated the young men who had associated with him, and the court's subsequent judgement could be taken to imply that these men were no less corrupt that Critias[92] and Alcibiades[93]. And if

91. De Magalhães-Vilhena, *Socrate et la légende platonicienne, op. cit.*, p. 182, asks why Plato would have invented an entirely fictitious Socrates, if it was the real Socrates that he admired, and gives the answer that Plato is telling the truth "au moins lorsqu'il exprime son admiration pour Socrate", *ibid.* I do not agree with this, because the Socrates for whom Plato, in his writings, expresses his admiration, is precisely the literary, fictitious Socrates created by him; whereas the Socrates whom he knew and loved had been accused, tried and condemned. In other words, Plato's enthusiasm does not make the legend any less fictitious; nor can the admiration of the disciple for his master be taken as a criterion for evaluating, and discriminating between, the real and the fictitious Socrates; not to mention the extreme elasticity of such a criterion, which can, and does, lead to the conclusion that the Socrates of the legend is "tel quel" the Socrates of history; cf. *op. cit.*, p. 221-223.
92. On Critias, the very detailed discussion by Grote, *History of Greece, cit.*, VIII, 314-383, is still useful; for his relationship with Socrates, Grote, *op. cit.*, VII, p. 48 ff. Polycrates's *Kategoria*, Humbert, *Le Pamphlet de Polycratès et le Gorgias de Platon*, in *R. Philol.*, V, 1931, pp. 20-77, is commented on in Xenophon, *Memorabilia*, I, II, 12; on the connections with Polycrates' pamphlet, Chroust, *Socrates, cit.*, p. 44 ff. For Socrates' responsibility for the conduct of Critias, according to the popular view, see, in addition to Xenophon, *loc. cit.*, Aeschines, *adv. Timarch.* 173, who reminds the Athenians that they put Socrates to death because he was the teacher of Critias.
Fragments by Critias, edited by Battegazzore, are to be found in *Sofisti*, IV,

it was Plato's intention, once safe with his friends at Euclides' house in Megara[94], to take up and continue those activities of Socrates which the condemnation had tragically interrupted, and to launch the Socratic community's programme with the *Apology*[95]; then he was perfectly well aware that he was proposing to carry on his Master's work at a moment in the civil history of Athens when trials against freedom of thought were still fresh in the memory, and when the impulse to revive them could be aroused by any doctrine which appeared dangerous to popular religious and political fanaticism[96].

If Socrates had already been indicted and condemned for his activities, Plato, who was preparing to carry on his teaching, could hardly have expected a better fate if he had revealed in his

edited by M. Untersteiner and A. Battegazzore, Firenze, 1962, together with extensive notes providing further references and clarification; on Critias, see M. Untersteiner, *I Sofisti*, Torino, 1949, p. 376 ff.

93. On Alcibiades, his character, his friendship with Socrates and his attitude towards the Athenian democracy, see Grote, *cit.*, VII, esp. p. 41 ff., and also the exhaustive study by J. Hatzfeld, *Alcibiades*, Paris, 1951.

94. The flight of Plato and the Socratics to Megara after the condemnation of Socrates is reported by Diogenes Laertius, II, X, 106, and III, 6, on the basis of evidence supplied by Hermodorus, a disciple of Plato; there appears to be no reason to doubt the truth of this account. Still on the basis of Hermodorus' evidence, Diogenes, *loc. cit.*, declares that fear of the "cruelty of the tyrants" (= the democrats who had condemned Socrates) caused "Plato and the other philosophers" to seek refuge with Eucleides. It is futile, therefore, to argue that "dopo la morte di Socrate, Platone fugge non le rappresaglie della città che aveva ucciso il Giusto, ma la città deserta da colui che le aveva dato un'anima e una speranza di salvezza", Stefanini, *Platone, cit.*, I, p. 22. The truth of the matter is that the Socratics were itching to be off, Maier, *Socrate, cit.*, I, p. 10; none of them had distinguished himself by services rendered to the City, Gomperz, *cit.*, II, p. 114, and the fact that they took refuge in Megara, which was ruled by an oligarchic regime, is also indicative of the Socratics feelings about the restored democracy.

95. "L'Apologia", writes Maier, *Socrate, cit.*, I, p. 110, "era [...] un manifesto che si gettava in Atene dal di fuori, da Mègara."

96. Before Socrates, in fact, Anaxagoras, Diagoras and Protagoras had been condemned, and, after him, Stilpo, Aristotle, Theophrastus and Theodorus were tried. On the trials of the philosophers in Attica and the motives underlying them, see P. Decharme, *La critique des traditions religieuses chez les grecs des origines aux temps de Plutarque*, Paris, 1904, chs, VI, and VII; E. Derenne, *Les procès d'impété intentés aux philosophes à Athènes au Ve et au IVe siècle avant J.C.*, Liège, 1930.

writings not only the method and tone of Socrates' dialogues but also their innermost spirit: that dangerously subversive spirit which characterized the moral, religious and political aspects of Socrates' conversation; that spirit, in fact, which caused Anytus, Meletus and Lycon to accuse Socrates and the jury of the heliasts to condemn him.

This means that in order to survive and to realize its programme, the Socratic-Platonic community had to transfigure, at least in its writings, those unpopular aspects of Socrates' dialogues which might remind the Athenians of the reasons for his death. The only way, then, for Plato to secure his Master's inheritance was to resort to a conscious remodelling of Socrates' personality, virtually to the point of divesting it of all its historical reality.

I believe that it was in this particular historical and psychological context that the Platonic "Sokratesdichtung" was born; not, therefore, in Dupréel and Gigon's sense[97], but as the product on the literary plane of a conscious and deliberate falsification of Socrates' human and philosophical personality, a fiction which Plato sustained throughout the entire course of his long career as a writer, from the *Apology* onwards. In writing the *Apology*, Plato had no intention of recording Socrates' unsuccessful selfdefence; rather, he sought carefully to obscure the tragic consistency between Socrates' life and his death by hemlock, and in this way to vindicate the community of Socrates' disciples from the same charge of corruption on which their Master had been tried and condemned. The invention of the Delphic judgement therefore came to be at the basis of the "Sokratesdichtung", while Plato's idealization of Socrates' personality — which the oracle's reply characterized as an eminently religious personality — was to become the model that later inspired the ideal of the θεωρητιχὸς βίος[98] which, by transforming the human natures of philosophers into absorbed, contemplative spirits, created a distorted image of the most ancient philosophy of all which we are not yet altogether rid of.

97. See above, p. 32, n. 17 ff.
98. See Jaeger, *Über Ursprung und Kreislauf des philososphischen Lebensideals*, Berlin, 1928.

8. — What has been said about Plato applies, broadly speaking, to Xenophon too. However, there is the difference that whereas Plato placed Socrates outside history and above humanity, Xenophon seeks to defend Socrates at the level of his real historical and human situation. Unfortunately, the disciple's devotion is not matched by his talent, and his attempt to defend his Master actually has the effect of dragging Socrates down to the level of his own mediocrity. Yet precisely this mediocrity makes the first two books of the *Memorabilia* valuable: although designed to rebut the κατηγορία Σωκράτους of Polycrates[99], they are actually more useful to us for highlighting the accusations which Polycrates repeated some years after the trial of 399[100] than for the banal defence which Xenophon attempts.

99. C.G. Cobet, *Novae Lectiones*, Lugd. Bat. 1858, p. 662 ff., was the first to identify the κατήγορος of the first two books of the *Memorabilia* as the rhetorician and sophist Polycrates, cf. K. Kiesow, *Chi è ó κατήγορος nel II Cap, del I lib. dei Memorabili di Senofonte*, in *Boll. di Fil. Classica* XXIV, pp. 129-133, the author of a κατηγορία Σωκράτους which can be dated with a high degree of probability to 393-392, and which was followed by a swift response from Xenophon, between 392 and 390; cf. P. Treves, *Per la cronologia di Senofonte*, extract from *Mélanges Desrousseaux*, Paris, 1937, esp. p. 462 f., and the long article on *Polykrates*, in Pauly-Wissowa, *RE*, 42, 1736-1752 *s.v.* See also Chroust, *Socrates, cit.*, p. 69 ff. Another essential source for the reconstruction of Polycrates' κατηγορία is the *Apologia Socratis* of Libanius, cf. H. Markowski, *De Libanio Socratis Defensore*, Breslau, 1910, whose areas of agreement with Xenophon were precisely pointed out by R. Förster, *Libanii Opera*, V, Leipzig, 1909, and by Markowski, *cit.*, pp. 20-30, and, more recently, by Chroust, *cit.*, who has also emphasized elements which correspond with Plato. A reconstruction of the κατηγορία, in addition to that made by Markowski, has been made by Humbert, *Polycrates, l'accusation de Socrate et le Gorgias de Platon, cit.* The most detailed and far-reaching study of Polycrates' κατηγορία, placing it in the context of the vast body of literature on Socrates, is that of Chroust, *cit.*, p. 69, who has shown how Polycrates' pamphlet caused the apologetic literature to be written, and how this literature corresponds to the κατηγορία, although, working on this assumption, Chroust, p. 319, n. 1409, he is led to believe that it is not improbable that Plato's *Apology* is also part of the literature provoked by the renewed accusation of Polycrates, and should therefore be dated to the years following 393-392, in accordance with R. Hackforth, *The Composition of Plato's Apology*, Cambridge, 1939, p. 8 ff.

100. On the date of the composition of the κατηγορία see the authors and works above.

One source which will definitely have to be rejected, however, is Aristotle, whose references to Socrates have no positive contribution to make to the line of enquiry being pursued here. The scattered testimonies[101] of the so-called minor Socratics have little more to offer, although the nature of the disciples may tell us something about the character of their master's teaching.

9. — We now come to the heart of our problem. Do there really exist among the Socratic sources, particularly in Plato, testimonies which will enable us, despite the literary transfiguration and the conscious alteration of Socrates' personality, to identify those elements in the thought and activity of Socrates which led first Aristophanes and then Anytus, Meletus and Lycon and later Polycrates to accuse him of impiety and corruption of the youth and which, eventually, caused the jury of the heliasts to condemn him to death? In other words, if we overturn the traditional notion of the "just man condemned" and re-examine the literature about Socrates in relation to his tragic fate in the prison of the Eleven, will we be able to uncover those elements which explain the tragic consistency between Socrates' life and his death by hemlock? If so, the way will be open for a critical interpretation of that persistent conversing and discussing which made Socrates seem impious and a corrupter of the youth to the Athens of 399, given its values, traditions and laws, thus provoking and legitimating his indictment, trail and condemnation.

Our aim, therefore, is to find out not who the philosopher Socrates was and what his position in history is, but rather why he was condemned, for we know nothing else about him, and the reasons for his condemnation must themselves tell us at least something about his way of being and thinking.

10. — If, with this aim in mind, we re-read the *Apology* (which reveals Plato's literary and inventive nature more than any other of his writings, contrary to the general opinion of the critics), we already find there a hint of a Socratic conception of the divine

---

101. The remaining works of the minor Socratics are described as "pitoyables débris" by Humbert, *Socrate, cit.*, p. 5 & p. 9.

which conflicts sharply with popular religion, which had its *Gospels* in the myths and fables of the poets.

In the account which Socrates gives to his judges of the oracle given to Chaerephon[102] Socrates himself interprets the Pythia's reply as meaning that he had been declared wiser than other men not because he really knew anything, for only the god is wise, but because he merely knew that he did not know anything[103]. According to Socrates, then, the oracle rewarded not his wisdom, but his honest ignorance[104]. This way of interpreting the oracle's reply to Chaerephon would seem (and has seemed) to be a humble profession of ignorance, a sincere testimony of Socrates' obedience to the precepts of Apollo[105], were it not for the fact that it insinuates a dangerously sceptical attitude, not only towards that wisdom of which only god is wise, but also towards the very existence of the divine. For knowing nothing implies not knowing whether the god exist or not[106], as well as absolute ignorance about that wisdom of which only god is said to be wise. Thus conceived, Socrates' ignorance, which he himself defines as the only human wisdom[107], creates an irreducible distinction between the gods already fully realized but quite unattainable, and the

102. Plato, *Apology*, 21a.

103. *Apology*, 23ab. It should be noted that Capizzi's enquiry, *La testimonianza platonica*, *cit.*, p. 326, leads us to believe that "l'affermazione di non sapere" is truly Socratic.

104. On the unlearned Socrates, see n. 61.

105. The view that Socrates professed a particular devotion to Apollo of Delphi is held by E. Curtius, *Griechische Geschichte*, 3 vols., Berlin, 1887-1889, vol. III, p. 97; Pettazzoni, *La religione greca*, *cit.*, p. 218; Gernet and Boulanger, *Le génie grec dans la religion*, Paris, 1932, p. 385; Kranz, *Die Kultur der Griechen*, Leipzig, 1943, p. 338; Tovar, *Vida de Sócrates*, *cit.*, p. 160; Guardini, *La Mort de Socrate*, *cit.*, p. 241 & 243 ff., the major proponent of this view; Parke and Wormell, *The Delphic oracle*, *cit.*, II, p. 404; Nestle, *Sokrates und Delphi*, 1910, in *Griech. Stud.*, *cit.*, p. 180 f.; De Strycker, *les Témoignages historiques sur Socrate*, *cit.*, p. 206; *et al.*

106. It is hardly necessary to point out that Socrates' agnosticism is identical with that of Protagoras, as expressed in his well-known proposition on the gods, Diog. Laert., IX, 51, in *Sofisti, Testimonianze e Frammenti*, I, ed. by M. Untersteiner, 1949, Firenze, 1961, *Protagora*, 64, p. 79. On the accusation and condemnation of Protagoras for the opening sentence of his book on the gods, Decharme, *cit.*, p. 120, p. 162; Derenne, *cit.*, p. 45 ff.

107. *Apology*, 20d.

wisdom of men. The latter, being an awareness of one's own ignorance[108], is destined to take form of a constant, restless searching after wisdom[109], φιλο-σοφία in fact, but always strictly confined to the sphere of human things[110].

Socrates accentuated, then, the distinction between heaven and earth, between god and man, between the actuality of divine wisdom and the problematic nature of human knowledge, in line with the Pythagorean tradition and, more generally, the free thinking which had been going on around the borders of the empire and which Anaxogoras had first brought to Athens[111]. Accordingly, he did not conceal his distaste for the fantastic tales of the poets about gods and heroes [112], rejecting totally not only the popular religious tradition but also the venerated wisdom of the poets[113]. The poets had made the gods in their own image, attributing to them all their own passions, and had consequently reduced them to the level of their own humanity[114]. Socrates did not deny the poets' right to invent stories about the gods, but he did deny the truth of those stories, and therefore the validity of that poetic religious tradition which not only underlay popular belief and devotional practice, but had also moulded the spiritual character of the Athenian people. For, if the truth of this poetic theology was denied, those fundamental concepts which had become an inseparable part of the Greek soul collapsed as a result: concepts such as that of fate, the vengeance of the gods, necessity, divine justice and its executive powers[115]. The rejection

108. *Apology*, 21d; 22de.
109. *Apology*, 23b.
110. *Apology*, 20d; *Phaedrus*, 230ac; Xenophon, *Memorabilia* I, I, 16.
111. On this subject, see Decharme, *cit.*, chs, II, V, VI; Pettazzoni, *cit.*, ch. VI; Del Grande, *Hybris*, Napoli, 1947, ch. VIII; and the chapter entitled *Dalla sofia alla filosofia*, in A. Capizzi, *Protagora*, 2nd d., Firenze, 1955, p. 394 ff.
112. *Euthyphro*, 6a-c; *Phaedrus*, 229d-223ca; *Republic*, II, 307d ff.; cf. Decharme, *cit.*, p. 127; Jaeger, *Paideia*, *cit.*, II, 363 ff. Disbelief in the myths is an attitude of mind and, according to Capizzi's formal analysis, *La testimonianza platonica*, *cit.*, p. 327, is characteristic of the historical Socrates.
113. *Apology*, 22d; *Ion*, 533e ff.; *Republic*, II, 379a ff; III, 386a ff.
114. Xenophanes, *Fragments* 11-12, in Senofane, *Testimonianze e frammenti*, edited by M. Untersteiner, Firenze, 1965, p. 129.
115. Cf. Mondolfo, *Nota sulla filosofia presocratica*, in Zeller & Mondolfo, *La filosofia dei Greci*, 2nd, ed., 1950, II, pp. 27-93, esp. p. 52 ff.

of the religious tradition therefore involved the rejection of divinity itself, the object of that tradition, and consequently the rejection of the view of life and the world connected with that particular way of conceiving of the gods.

In other words traditional religion was not the religion of Socrates, any more than the stories of the poets were for Socrates the revelation of truth. We may therefore conclude, without going outside the line of enquiry which we are pursuing here, that Socrates' attitude both towards the religious tradition and towards the wisdom of the poets is one of radical criticism or even total dissent — an attitude capable, in any case, of provoking the first charge made against him at his trial: Socrates does not believe in the gods which the state honours[116].

---

116. Although Socrates paid due honour to the gods of the City, this does not prove that he believed in these gods; nor is anything proved by the solemn νομίζειν in the *Apology*, 35d, since the original meaning of νομίζειν was to respect the gods, to consider them worthy of esteem, and therefore to render them their due honours, Liddell-Scott, *s.v.*; Snell, *La cultura greca e le origini del pensiero europeo*, p. 52; J. Burnet, *Plato's Apology*, note to 24c. And since the idea expressed by the verb was related to that of performing a civic duty, because the cult of the gods of the polis was protected by the laws of the State, νομίζειν the gods of the City meant no more and no less than to behave in accordance with the laws of the State, νόμο πόλεως, Xenophon, *Memorabilia*, I, III, 1; IV, III, 16 f.; IV, IV, 2 ff.; cf. Maier, *Socrate, cit.*, II, p. 154 and n. 2, according to whom it would be difficult to confuse the civic duty of keeping to the forms of worship with the spontaneity of a religious faith. "The word *nomízei*", writes M. Nilsson, *Greek piety*, Oxford, 1948, p. 82, "is hard to render correctly; it means to make a custom of something, especially something ordained by law; it could at a pinch mean that Sokrates alleged there are other gods than those recognized by the State, but to render it 'believe in' is to import a shade of meaning which does not belong". Cf. also Eckermann, Menzel, Frese, Taylor, in Derenne, *Les procès, cit.*, p. 277. But it has already been observed — see *The trial of Anaxagoras* in this volume, esp. n. 85 ff. — that Diopeithes' ψήφισμα of 433-31, which provided the legal basis for the trial of Anaxagoras by introducing an offence previously unknown in Athens, namely that of disbelief in the gods, gave the verb νομίζειν a new meaning which, if it did not supersede the former meaning, at least became accepted in addition to it. Consequently, even when Diopeithes' decree was rescinded by the amnesty of Eucleides, the second meaning survived, so that Plato was able to play on the double meaning of the verb, *Apology*, 18c, 26c, thereby leading astray not only the judges, before whom Socrates could show that he had not investigated the celestial phenomena and subterranean secrets, *Apology*, 18b, and could therefore reject the accusa-

11. — Socrates' attitude towards the civil and political institutions of Athens, and even towards the Athenian democratic system in general, is no different. But whereas Plato drew a discreet veil over Socrates' rejection of the official Olympian religion, so that we only catch the briefest glimpse here and there of that good-natured irony with which Socrates treated the myths and stories of the poets which sustained the naive beliefs of the people[117], he does not conceal Socrates' strong aversion to the democracy, which Socrates attacks as much for its ideals as for its leading representatives[118]. Indeed, the *Protagoras* and the *Gorgias*, as well as the *Alcibiades* and the *Apology* itself express forthright and radical criticisms of the systems implemented by the democracy. "When they have to deliberate on something connected with the administration of the State", it says in the *Protagoras*[119], "the man who rises to advise them on this may equally well be a smith, a shoemaker, a merchant, a sea captain, a rich man, a poor man, of good family or of none". In other words, it is the political incompetence of the people as judge and sovereign which Socrates condemns; for, just as one would not entrust one's shoe to anyone who was not a shoemaker, it is hard to see why one should entrust political affairs to anyone and

tion of disbelief in the gods, *Apol.*, 26c, based on his supposed naturalistic enquiries, cf. my essay in this volume: *Socrates, between the first and second clouds*; but also modern translators, from Marsilio Ficino who translates *Apology*, 18c, as "non credere deos esse", to Stallbaum,*ad loc.*, "ne deos quidem esse credere", and M. Croiset, *ad loc.*, "ne croient pas aux dieux", while Burnet translates, *ad loc.*, "do not worship the gods", and then in 26c, "to think", suggesting that Plato tried to confound Meletus in this way.

In any case, the double meaning of the verb was present in the νομίζειν in 35d, at least as far as the judges in the trial of 399 were concerned, and it is certain that the word was solemnly pronounced with this in mind, even though Socrates' beliefs were quite different from those of his judges.

117. Cf. esp. *Euthyphro*, 6a-c.

118. Cf. *Apology*, 17ab, 18a, 22d, 34c, 38dc; *Hippias Major*, 304ab; *Alcibiades I*, 106b, 113d, 119b-120b; *Protagoras*, 319d, 329b, 335a; *Gorgias*, 423a, 433b, 447e-453a, 454b, 459e, 502e-503a; *Menexenus*, 235e; *Meno*, 96d; *Phaedrus*, 228b, 230c, 238c, 267b. These passages will be referred to in the course of the present section.

119. *Protagoras*, 319d. Transl. W.R.M. Lamb, London, 1924 (1980 ed.)

everyone indiscriminately, whether they are competent in the art of politics or not[120].

But who is competent in political affairs? Certainly not Pericles, Cimon, Miltiades or Themistocles, since these celebrated politicians left the State in worse condition than they had found it[121]. Good politicians do not exist[122]; "I am of the few Athenian if not the only one, says Socrates, who conceives the true art of politics, and the only one who practizes this art nowadays.[123]. This emphatic assertion put into Socrates' mouth in the *Gorgias*, the dialogue which replies to Polycrates' accusation[124] that Socrates had been the teacher of Critias and Alcibiades[125], two of

120. For the condemnation of the political incompetence of the common artisans, required by the democratic system to make judgements on matters in which they were less skilled than they were in their own crafts, see, in addition to the quoted passage in the *Protagoras*, *Apology*, 22d; *Alcibiades I*, 113d; *Gorgias*, 459d, 516a ff.

121. *Gorgias*, 515c-526cb; *Alcibiades I*, 105e.

122. *Gorgias*, 517a.

123. *Gorgias*, 521d.

124. See J. Humbert, *Le pamphlet de Polycrates et le Gorgias de Platon*, *cit.*, and Chroust, *Socrates*, *cit.*, esp. p. 69, 98, 202, and notes 291, 597 and 1228, which has already been quoted several times, and also P. Treves, i.v. Polykrates in P.W. RE. 40, 1736-1752.

125. Xenophon, *Mem.* 1, 2, 124: "But his accuser [Polykrates] argued thus. Among the associates of Socrates were Critias and Alcibiades; and none wrought so many evils to the state. For Critias in the days of the oligarchy bore the palm for greed and violence: Alcibiades, for his part, exceeded all in licentiousness and violence under the democracy" (transl. E.C. Marchant); there is an Italian translation of this passage by A. Battegazzore, *Crizia*, in *Sofisti, Testimonianze e frammenti*, IV, edited by A. Battegazzore and M. Untersteiner, Firenze, 1962, 14(88) A.4. Battegazzore's dissent, "Io non posso seguire i sostenitori della sostanziale storicità del testo senofonteo", note *ad loc.*, concerns the reason for Critias' regulation preventing Socrates from teaching, rather than the earlier relationship between the two men; although there is no documentary evidence for this relationship, it may be assumed "che un ben profondo legame di interessi politici reazionari, improntati al più assoluto realismo, dovesse essere alla base della loro conversazione", *loc. cit.* Cf. *The trial of Anaxagoras*, in the present volume, and the remainder of the present study. Xenophon's account of the accusation made by Polycrates corresponds exactly to what Libanius writes in *Apologia Socratis*, 136 ff., 148-150, cf. n. 3 in Aeschines, *Contra Timarchum*, I, 173, and is accepted by Markowski, *De Libanio Socratis defensore*, *cit.*, by Humbert, *Le pamphlet*, *cit.*, and by Chroust, *cit.*, p. 74 ff., as one of the main arguments in Polycrates' κατηγορία.

the enemies of the Athenian democracy, shows that Plato saw Socrates' activities as being specifically concerned with the practice or teaching of politics, as the sources unanimously testify[126], and also bestows a precise meaning and intention on all of Socrates' dialogues.

It has already been pointed out, in fact, how those dialogues on the subject of justice and the other virtues were nothing other than discussions about the political virtues, and how that particular human wisdom which Socrates claimed to possess was nothing other than political wisdom[127].

126. Not only do Plato and Xenophon agree that Socrates was "un maestro di politica", Jaeger, *Paideia, cit.*, II, p. 77, but Aristophanes too, in *Clouds*, had already presented Socrates as a sophist, vv. 112 ff.; 636 ff.; 658 ff.; 1111, 1308-9; as a master of the art of speaking, vv. 240, 1105; and as an expert in the use of a *Lógos* especially suitable for winning arguments in the courts and political assemblies, vv. 244 ff., 434, 445 and *passim*; cf. *Socrates between the first and second Clouds, cit.*, Aristophanes' account should be examined in the light of the fact that Critias, not unmindful of the Master's lessons, forbade Socrates to teach the art of speaking, λόγων τέχνην μὴ διδάσκειν, Xenophon, *Memorabilia*, I, II, 31, 34, and I, II, 48, and in general the whole of ch. I, II, in which Xenophon explicitly recognizes the political nature of Socrates' teaching, cf. esp. I, II, 16, 17, 18, 47 and 48; II, IV, 11, 37; IV, VI, 14. In Plato's *Apology*, 36c, Socrates' activity — his work of teaching true *aretè* — is brought to bear on the "polis stessa e la sua missione riceve così un'impronta politica", Jaeger, *Paideia*, II, *cit.*, p. 157; Jaeger has also pointed out the political significance of such Dialogues as the *Crito, Laches, Charmides, Euthyphro, op. cit.*, p. 157-8, to which may be added the *Gorgias*, 121d, in which Socrates is recognized as a master of the art of politics, the *Alcibiades I*, 105d-e, in which Socrates presents himself to Alcibiades, who is preparing to speak in the Assembly, as the only person capable of teaching him the art of politics, and the *Protagoras*, 319a, in which the investigations into the individual virtues are included in the concept of the art of politics, πολιτικὴ τέχνη, Jaeger, *cit.*, II, p. 159. The political nature of Socratic teaching was particularly emphasized by Polycrates, in Xenophon, *Memorabilia*, I, II, 9; 12, and by Libanius, *Apologia Socratis*, esp. 136 ff., 148-150.

Among modern historians, Jaeger, *Paideia*, II, *cit.*, p. 77 ff. & 154 ff., following Maier, *Socrate, cit.*, I, 145, has clearly shown the way in which Socrates' political instruction was intended to guide young men towards *Kalokagathia*, and the degree to which Socrates' concept of politics was responsible for his accusation and condemnation and for the spiritual development of Plato, *op. cit.*, 120 ff.

127. Maier, *Socrate, cit.*, I, p 145, for whom "il gruppo di idee, che a Socrate era stato accessbile e familiare, e in cui l'opera di lui era stata a suo posto, è la

67

However, I believe it has not yet been pointed out how Socrates' enquiry did not confine itself to the innocent, ironical confutation of the conventional ways of understanding those concepts which were so common in everyday speech as to be considered in no need of clarification, such as the concepts of piety[128], friendship[129], strength[130], wisdom[131] etc.; for Socrates extended his enquiry, with greater critical zeal and more passionate dialectical vigour, to the study of men. He does not investigate what men know τί ἐστιν, but what they are τίς ἐστιν[132]; not, in other words, a category of knowledge, but a way of being, because what really interests Socrates and constitutes the true object of his enquiry is not conceptual essence, but, rather, the degree of self-awareness which man possesses[133]. This is borne out by the fact that it is the pious Euthypro whom Socrates questions about piety τὸ εὐσεβὲς καὶ τὸ ἀσεβές[134], and the handsome Hippias ὁ καλὸς whom he asks what beauty is τὶ ἐστὶ τὸ καλόν[135], just as it is Charmides, the wise one σώφρωσύνην,

sfera della φρόνησις e delle altre virtù" which reaches its culmination in the wisdom which is meant to be applied in the governing of the state and of the family, and Jaeger, *Paideia, cit.*, II, pp. 158-159, who has pointed out that the investigations into the individual virtues find their common ground in the *Protagoras*, which "caratterizza la direzione di tutte queste ricerche col comprenderle sotto il concetto di arte politica".

128. The object of the enquiry in the *Euthyphro*.

129. The object of the enquiry in the *Lysis*.

130. The object of the enquiry in the *Laches*.

131. The object of the enquiry in the *Charmides*.

132. On this point, see *Apology*, 24d, τί ἐστιν; τίς ἄνθρωπος; *Crito*, 47d; *Alcibiades*, 109cd; *Laches*, 185a, 185e; *Lysis*, 204d; *Protagoras*, 311d; *Gorgias*, 447d. But the most important passage, which clarifies all the others, is in *Apology*, 41b, where Socrates, turning to his judges after his condemnation, tells them: "Above all, I shall then be able to continue my search into true and false knowledge, as in this world, so also in the next; and I shall find out who is wise, and who pretends to be wise, and is not", transl. B. Jowett.

133. *Alcibiades I*, 133bc; *Charmides*, 164de. Bréhier, *Histoire de la Philosophie*, I, I, *cit.*, p. 93, makes the point well when he says, "l'enseignement de Socrate consiste en effet à examiner et à éprouver non point les concepts, mais les hommes eux-mêmes et à les amener à se rendre compte de ce qu'ils sont".

134. *Euthyphro*, 5c-d.

135. *Hippias Major*, 287d.

whom he asks what wisdom is τὶ εἶναι σωφροσύη[136]. The negative
conclusion of this enquiry reveals not that the specific essence of
piety, beauty or wisdom is indefinable, but that neither pious
Euthyphro, nor handsome Hippias, nor wise Charmides know
themselves, since they do not know what piety or beauty or
wisdom is. It follows that the knowledge that Socrates exhorts us
to seek, and in which the eternal value of his message consists, is
not a conceptual knowledge constitute beforehand the human
behaviour, but precisely self-knowledge, which nevertheless is
never actual knowledge but always and only an untiring eagerness
and persistent search[137] for knowledge of the self[138], of the divine
in human nature[139], and of the order and harmony which govern
the soul[140]. For Socrates it is in this eternal search for the self, in
this constant self-questioning, in this ceaseless endeavour to
clarify one's moral experience, σωφροσύνη consists equated in
the *Charmides* with self-knowledge τὸ γιγνώσκειν ἑαυτόν[141]. A
man is wise, therefore, if he knows himself or, rather, if he is
aware of the inescapable moral obligation to know himself; and
to the extent that he possesses such wisdom he is good, just and
pious[142].

Hence the constant appeal to self-knowledge, γνῶθι σαυτόν,
which concludes the Socratic enquiry, and the purifying and
spiritually elevating quality wich the ἔλεγχος acquires[143]. The
confutation of false wisdom, by compelling men to recognize
their own ignorance, which is ignorance of themselves and of
their human condition, and by making them aware of the need to

136. *Charmides*, 159a. See also *Laches*, 190e and *Lysis*, 223b.
137. Symposium, 203b ff.
138. *Charmides*, 164e; *Laches*, 149 d; *Lovers*, 138a; *Alcibiades I*, 133d; *Protagoras*, 343b.
139. *Alcibiades I*, 133c. Whatever may be said about the authenticity of
Alcibiades I, I still believe that it contains so much genuinely Socratic material
that Plato's portrayal of Socrates would be the poorer if this work had to be
removed from the Platonic corpus.
140. *Charmides*, 161b; 165a ff.
141. *Charmides*, 164d.
142. *Charmides*, 164e-165a ff., esp. 169e; Xenophon, *Memorabilia*, IV, II,
26, although Xenophon gives the concept a utilitarian significance which in
Plato, and certainly in Socrates, it did not have.
143. Mondolfo, *Sócrates, op. cit.*, p. 32 ff.

undertake their own personal search for truth. This at last opens men's eyes to the possibility of a new spiritual dimension, a higher ideal of moral life.

While, however, the ἔλεγχος, in its good-humoured, ironic confutation of false wisdom implied the negation and rejection of a certain human state or way of being, it opened the mind up to doubt and enabled it to glimpse a new conception of mankind, a new human ideal conceived at a different spiritual level, the ἔλεγχος it also implied the rejection of custom, tradition, the laws, and, therefore, the civil, political and religious institutions which had been establishing themselves in the sphere of human experience and which were a projection of the society's perception of itself.

12. — This extension of the ἔλεγχος from the individual conscience to human society confirms the political nature and intention of Socrates' teaching. His exhortation to the individual to take moral care of himself[144] extended to the city as a whole, since the moral regeneration of the individual through the purifying process of the ἔλεγχος, immediately posed the need, the imperiousness of which was expressed through the radical nature of the criticism, for a moral reform of the forms and institutions of civil, political and religious life.

Consequently, we would disagree with Bréhier[145] when he says that "contrairement à la critique des sophistes, celle de Socrate ne porte ni sur les lois, ni sur les usages réligieux". Firstly, as we have seen, Socrates' intuition of man demanded the moral regeneration of the individual and, then, the regeneration of private, social and political relationships — hence his criticism of the politicians and civil institutions of Athens, and therefore of its laws too, which derived from a particular way of perceiving man and human relationships; secondly, this view of man bestowed a new and different meaning on the traditional idea of the divine — hence Socrates' criticism of the old religious myths and popular beliefs, and consequently of the forms and practices of divine worship too. For, whereas men had conceived the gods in

144. *Apology*, 29d-e, 303; *Alcibiades I*, 129b ff. See n. 147 below.
145. Bréhier, *Histoire de la Philosophie*, *op. cit.*, I, p. 95.

their own image and had brought them down to the level of their own wretchedness, even ascribing to them all the vices and crimes of men, such as theft, adultery and mutual deception[146], Socrates raised man to the dignity of the god by transferring the divine, τὸ θεῖον, into the intimacy of the individual soul, ψυχή[147]. Thus the limit which the rigorous Apollonian measure had imposed on human aspirations was extended, even to the point of bringing the whole of the divine sphere within the compass of the human, whilst γνῶθι σαυτόν, which in its primitive Delphic meaning was intended merely as a reminder of that limit, took on for Socrates the meaning that it already had in the Orphic-Pythagorean doctrines of an appeal to men to discover the divine which is within them, the divine nature of the soul, the dignity and nobility of human nature[148].

The internalization of the divine in the human soul legitimated the second count of the judicial accusation; for if Socrates did not believe in the gods of the City, his daemonic mythification of religious feeling[149] entitled Anytus, Meletus and Lycon, like Aristophanes before them[150], to accuse him of introducing new

146. Xenophon, *fr.* 11, 12, *loc. cit.*
147. *Alcibiades I*, 133b-c; "And if the soul is ever to know herself, must she look at the soul; and especially at that part of the soul where resides her virtue, which is wisdom, and at any other which is like this? [...] And so we know of any part of our souls more divine than that with which wisdom and knowledge to do? [...] Then this is part of the soul which resembles God; and he who looks at this and at the whole class of things divine, at God and at wisdom, will be most likely to know himself", transl. B. Jowett.
148. The Orphic-Pythagorean significance of the Delphic precept has been pointed out by Delatte, *Etudes sur la littérature pythagoricienne*, Paris, 1915, p. 69; Pettazzoni, *La religione greca fino ad Alessandro, op. cit.*, p. 107; P.M. Schuhl, *Essai sur la formation de la pensée grecque*, Paris, 2nd ed., 1949, p. 251; Jaeger, *Paideia, op. cit.*, I, p. 313 ff.; II, p. 61; Mondolfo, *Sócrates, op. cit.*, p. 31; Mondolfo, *La comprensione del soggetto umano nell'antichità classica*, Firenze, 1958, p. 469.
149. The Socratic δαιμόνιον has been discussed at length, and the most diverse theories have been advanced at different times; to mention them all here would take too long and would not serve any useful purpose. In my view, the daemon can only be a mythical personification of Socrates' experience of the divine.
150. *Clouds*, v. 381.
151. *Alcibiades I*, 128c-129a; 130e, 134c; *Gorgias*, 515bc; 521a.

divinities different from those which were recognized and honoured by the State.

13. — It becomes apparent at this point that politics and morality were one and the same for Socrates, and that the true essence of politics or, rather, of political virtue, consisted in urging others to strive to improve themselves morally[151]. This identification of politics with a moral duty to improve others explains Socrates' condemnation of men such as Pericles, Cimon, Miltiades and Themistocles[152], who, whilst they had made the City great and powerful[153], had done nothing to make its citizens better[154], showing therefore themselves actually not good politicians[155]. Indeed, these celebrated politicians failed in their duty not only towards the citizens of Athens but also towards their own sons, whom they failed to turn into good men[156], let alone good politicians[157]. For political virtue, understood as the virtue of making others better, is a virtue which can neither be taught nor learnt[158], which has neither masters nor pupils[159], with the exception of Socrates himself, who alone, as Plato tells us, had a proper understanding of politics[160] — who alone, in other words, understood and practised the virtue of impressing upon

---

152. *Gorgias*, 515a ff.; *Alcibiades I*, 118d.
153. *Gorgias*, 518e-519a.
154. *Gorgias*, 515e.
155. *Gorgias*, 515c.
156. *Protagoras*, 319e ff.; *Alcibiades I*, 118de; *Laches*, 179d; *Meno*, 93a-94c; *Theages*, 126d.
157. *Gorgias*, 517a.
158. That political virtue cannot be taught is the aporematic conclusion reached in the *Protagoras*, where the fact that politics is identified with knowledge makes it appear as though politics can be taught, but the identification of knowledge with the virtues of justice, temperance and fortitude turns knowledge into knowledge of the self, which therefore cannot be taught, but can only be the object of investigation *in interiore homine*. In the *Meno*, political virtue is definitely stated to be unteachable because it is not the object of knowledge as such, but rather, as said in the *Protagoras*, the object of the knowledge and consciousness of one's self, which, since it is the consciousness of the divine within man, is a consciousness only available to a few, as if by divine favour.
159. *Meno*, 96bc.
160. *Gorgias*, 531d.

others the vital need to renew themselves morally through ceaseless self-questioning[160b].

Socrates' ethical and political ideal, is presented by Plato, then, as a moral duty, endowed with all the intensity of a religious mission[161], to urge young men destined for political life[162] to strive to improve themselves morally through the cathartic virtue of the ἔλεγχος. Consequently, only those who have felt the tarantula's bite[163], those, in other words, who have carried out this task of moral purification through ceaseless self-questioning can properly regard themselves as good and virtuous, καλοὶ κἀγαθοί[164], and therefore as good politicians, fit to direct the fortunes of the State and to govern over others who, having failed to carry out this moral exercise, ought to regard themselves as κακοί.

This distinction between ἀγαθοὶ and κακοί, the good men and the bad men, which is at the same time a distinction between the competent and the incompetent[165] in the exercise of political virtue, emerges clearly from Socrates' constant and apparently innocent references to shoemakers and blacksmiths, cowherds and sailors, which not by mere clause Critias disapproved and forbade[166]. For whilst Socrates recognized the artisans' com-

---

160b. *Alcibiades I*, 117d; 124b.

161. *Apology*, 23bc, 30a.

162. For Socrates' amorous interest in the young men destined for a political career, see the *Menexus, Charmides, Alcibiades I, Symposium*, 216d-222ab.

163. *Symposium*, 217e-218a.

164. That *Kalokagathia* was the aim of Socrates' political teaching had already been pointed out by Aristophanes, *Clouds*, v. 102, and was made clear by Xenophon, *Mem.*, I, II, 14, 18, 29, 48 and then by Plato in the *Apology, Charmides, Alcibiades I, Protagoras*, and *Gorgias*, to which may be added the *Symposium*, 209ab, and in general the whole of Alcibiades' speech.

165. The distinction between the competent and the incompetent is expressed in the eternal question τίς ἐστιν ὁ τεχνικός, with which Socrates attempts to discover and define the specific quality of each person, the ability of the artisan as well as the virtue of the politician. Cf. *Apology*, 24de, *Alcibiades I*, 106cd; *Laches*, 185ac; *Lysis*, 204a; *Protagoras*, 312d; 318b ff.; 319b ff.; *Gorgias*, 447a, 459bc, 515a; *Ion*, 533e, 534c, 535d, 537a-538bc.

166. Xenophon, *Memorabilia*, I, II, 37; Alcibiades, in his speech in the *Symposium*, 221e, says that blacksmiths, shoemakers and tanners were the subject of Socrates' conversation. It is perhaps not out of place to suggest that a tanner was Cleon, the demagogue violently detested by Aristophanes, and one of the most important leaders of the Athenian democrats. See my *The trial of Anaxagoras* in this vol.

petence in their own specific crafts[167], he did not accept that artisans, peasants and sailors possessed equal competence in political affairs[168], in which they were also called upon to take part, whether directly, in the exercise of the City's judicature, or indirectly, in the exercise of the right to vote in the assemblies. But by asserting that artisans, peasants and sailors lacked political competence, meaning competence in the virtuous art of making others better[169], and that they had no right to make decisions about public affairs and hold public office, Socrates was virtually denying that the people had any right to exercise power, which amounted to a rejection of the very principle of democracy or of any honest democratic system[169b].

The distinction between ἀγαθοί and κακοί then, ended up creating a moral and social distinction in the *Polis* between those who governed and those who were governed, or rather between men fit to govern the City ἀγαθοί and men destined to be governed κακοί. This distinction that Socrates instilled in Athenian society in his dialogues revealed the contradiction that separated Socrates' ethical and political ideal from that deep-rooted need for *isonomia*[170] which, from the time of Solon[171], had been at the

167. *Apology*, 22d; see above, n. 165.
168. *Protagoras*, 319bc; *Gorgias*, 459bc; *Memorabilia*, I, II, 9, where Polycrates accuses Socrates of condemning the selection of the city's leaders by drawing lots because of the incompetence of those chosen, *Memorabilia*, IV, IV, 9.
169. *Gorgias*, 515a ff., in which Socrates asks Callicles if, when in power, he will occupy himelf entirely with improving the citizens, since everything that is done should be done for the best, 499c.
169b. It is worth pointing out that Plato, both in the *Republic*, II, 369b-374e; IV, 419a-444a, etc., and in the *Laws*, 1, IV, 1, VIII; 1, XI, 919-920, excludes the artisans from the government of the State. For Plato's disdain for the manual trades, cf. A. Bartolotti, *Le arti nel pensiero di Platone*, ed. RCSF, 1970, IV, pp. 355-386.
170. On the concept of *isonomia*, cf. Herodotus, II, 80, in which Otanes, in his discourse on the best form of government, praises government by the people as that which has the fairest of all names: isonomia, or equality as the principle of justice. *Isonomia* has been wel defined by Nilsson, *Greek Piety*, *cit.*, p. 53: "the catchword isonomia meant not only equality before the law, but also an equal share in the good things the State apportions to its citiznes, whether material or immaterial".
171. On the work of Solon as a legislator: "E leggi in modo uguale al plebeo

basis of public and private law in the Athenian republic, as the animating principle of the trend towards social equality which was the goal of democracy and the incentive for all its battles. Socrates, however, completely overturned the democratic ideal of *isonomia*, replacing it instead with the oligarchical and aristocratic ideal of *eunomia* which had its models in Megara and Thebes, as well, of course, as in Sparta — models which Socrates and the Socratics were in complete sympathy with[172].

It is therefore no coincidence that just as the Athenian democracy was nearing exhaustion in the struggle with the Spartan oligarchy and its Theban and Megarian allies, the Socratics clamorously took sides with the enemies of Athens[173], thus demonstrating in practical terms how much closer the political teaching of Socrates was to the aristocratic ideal of Theognis of Megara than to the democratic ideal of Solon the Athenian.

14. — Socrates' aristocratic ideal of political virtue opposed to the desolating spectacle provided by the Athenian democracy at the time of the Peloponnesian war — that decadent democracy of

e al nobile applicando, a ciascuno retta giustizia prescrissi'', in G. Fassò, *La Democrazia in Grecia*, Bologna, 2nd ed., 1967, p. 38, see, in particular, G. De Sanctis, *Atthis, Storia della Republica ateniese dalle origini all'età di Pericle*, facsim. ed., Roma, 1964, chs. VI-VII, pp. 193-259.

172. Admiration and respect for cities with oligarchic governments, and especially for Sparta, are clearly expressed in Plato's dialogues, *Alcibiades I*, 120e-124a; *Crito*, 52e, 53b; *Laches*, 183ab; *Protagoras*, 342bd; 343b; *Gorgias*, 515e; *Letter VII*, 329a, and especially the *Republic*, VIII, 544c, and *Laws*, 691e ff., in which the Lacedaemonian model is often plainly visible; while the *Spartan Constitution* attributed to Xenophon, provides a retrospective view of the perfect city. For Xenophon, see esp. *Mem.*, II, 5, 14-16; IV, 4, 15; *Symp.*, 8, 35-39.

173. Critias the tyrant "apertamente parteggiò per gli Spartani", Battegazzore, *Crizia, cit.*, 14(88)A 1; as did Alcibiades, cf. Hatzfeld, *Alcibiade*, Paris, 1951, ch, VI ff., and Xenophon, "banished by the Athenians for siding with Sparta", Diog. Laert., II, VI, 51, trans. R.D. Hicks; not to mention the relationship which Socrates maintained with the Megarians and Thebans even during the Peloponnesian war, and which were responsible for the legend of Eucleides' entering Athens by night, dressed in a woman's clothes, Gell., *noct. att.*, VII, 10; a legend which, in the view of Grote, *History of Greece, cit.*, VIII, p. 555, n. 2, is "an absurdity". As a factual account, indeed, it may be absurd; but it is none the less an indication of the opinion of the ancient scholars concerning Socrates' relationships with friends in cities at war with Athens.

Hyperbolus and Cleon which Aristophanes derided so mercilessly[174] — explains how and why it was that Socrates aroused such enthusiastic fervour in the young men who associated with him[175], and hence why he was condemned by the democracy when it was restored. And above all, it becomes easier to understand why, at a time when there were celebrated men of learning already teaching in Athens, so many men who took a keen and active interest in politics sought the friendship of Socrates — men such as the Theban Pythagoreans, Simmias, Cebes and Echecrates of Phlius, who were already disciples of Philolaus; the Eleatics of Megara, such as Euclides, Terpsion and Aristippus the Cyrenian; men such as Critias and Alcibiades, Theages, Adeinantos and Plato, all of whom shared the latter's desire to take up political life at the earliest opportunity[176]; and finally, statesmen and soldiers such as Pericles and Nicias, Xenophon and Meno. The reason for these men's interest in Socrates must have been that they saw in Sophroniscus' son a master of political virtue[177b], the only man, in other words, who had a proper understanding of politics, as Plato tells us[177].

174. Cf. esp. Aristophanes' *Acharnians, Knights, Wasps, Peace*; on their significance as political criticism, M. Croiset, *Aristophane et les partis à Athènes*, esp. p. 95 ff., and G. Murray, *Aristophanes*, 1933, Oxford, 1965, p. 39 ff.

175. Gigon, *Sokrates, cit.*, p. 14, does not deny the enthusiasm of the young men who associated with Socrates, although he states that he is unaware of the reasons for this enthusiasm.

176. Plato, *Letter VII*, 323e.

176b. Cf. Xenophon, *Mem.*, I, 2, 47, where it is clearly stated that Critias and Alcibiades really joined Socrates' circle for political reasons, as Plato disclosed later, *Letter VII*, 232e, cit.

177. It is inconceivable that men such as those named here would have associated with Socrates in order to hear the trite discussions of virtue which Xenophon describes, or the harmless elenctic exercises imagined by Plato, unless the examination of men was performed, as has been shown, with the clear intention of political criticism; it is even less conceivable that Socrates would have carried out his teaching in the squares and palaestrae of Athens, speaking to whoever wished to hear him, whether they were rich or poor, noble or common, foreigners or citizens, *Apology*, 33ab. In fact, Plato does not conceal Socrates' amorous interest in the young men destined for a political career; nor does he remain silent about Socrates' distaste for those who, skilled in their own professions, attempted to involve themselves in politics as well. Moreover, the obvious political aims of Socrates' discussions, which criticized both individuals and the

It also explains why we do not find disciples of Socrates among those men who were notable for their services to the State. Indeed Polycrates[178] was not unjustified in repeating the accusation which had already been made against Socrates in court, namely that he had turned his friends into subverters of the established

institutions of democracy, as well as the whole traditional conception of God and the world, appear to have been such, as has been stated, that Socrates would have found it impossible to teach in public places. If he had done so, if, in other words, he had denied the existence of the state gods and criticized democracy before anyone who wished to hear him, then the teacher of Critias and Alcibiades would have been unlikely to have reached the age of seventy before being accused, tried and condemned. In fact, all the evidence leads us to believe that Socrates' teaching was of an esoteric nature, including a mystic initiation of a Pythagorean type, as may be inferred from Aristophanes, *Clouds*, v. 354 ff.; cf. T. Gelzer, *Aristophanes und sein Sokrates*, *Mus. Helv.*, 13, 1956, p. 67 ff.; while the φροντιστήριον of *Clouds* may well be identified with the house in which Socrates, at his most prosperous, cf. Winspear & Silverberg, *Who was Socrates?*, New York, 1939, p. 63 (which is in contrast with p. 52 ff.), entertained his friends, including the Pythagorenas from Phleius and Thebes and the Eleatics from Megara, who, as the story goes, entered Athens secretly during the Peloponnesian war. This would explain, more convincingly than Plato does in *Phaedo*, 265de, the frustrating lack of writings by Socrates. The fact that none of Socrates' writings have survived is due not only to the elenctic nature of his dialogues and his aim of political criticism, but also to the fact that Socrates' doctrine, based on principles inspired by Pythagoras, had to be imparted orally and memorized. This practice was characteristic of the Pythagoreans, Diog. Laert., VII, I, 15, and, through Socrates, reappears in Plato, *Letter VII*, 341c, and in Aristotle, Clement of Alexandria, *Stromata*, V, 681, who were also convinced that true knowledge had to be passed on orally to the few, while for the uninitiated masses popularizing writings were more suitable.

This does not, of course, rule out the possibility that Socrates also frequented the squares and palaestrae of Athens, and stopped to talk to anyone who asked him questions and wished to hear him; but the accusation of teaching for money, which was made against Socrates throughout his long teaching career and even more often after his death. *Clouds*, 98, 245f., 669, 856 ff., 1146-1147; *Apol.*, 19e, 31b, 33b, is indirect proof of both the acroamatic nature of Socrates' teaching and the existence of a φροντιοτήριον, or private meeting-place, where the master and a few privileged disciples could gather, the prohibition of the Thirty, λόγων τέχνη μὴ διδάσκειν, Xenophon, *Mem.*, I, 2, 31, would make no sense if Socrates did not have a regular teaching practice. Cf. Xenophon, *Mem.*, I, 1, 17. It is likely that the philosopher hidden away in a corner, surrounded by a group of boys, in *Gorgias*, 485d, was meant to symbolize Socrates.

178. Polycrates, in Xenophon, *Memorabilia*, I, II, 12 = Libanius, *Apologia Socratis*, 136 ff., 148-150.

order. Critias and Alcibiades had actually done violence to the city, the first by becoming a tyrant, the second by taking up arms against his own country; and even Xenophon's behaviour[179] had provided more grounds for accusing his Master than he was able to demolish with his apologetic writings.

If we judge Socrates' teaching by the behaviour of his disciples then, it is difficult to deny that his accusers were perfectly right. To permit Socrates to continue that teaching, which had had such disastrous consequences just when the Athenian democracy was engaged in mortal combat with the Spartan oligarchy, was to expect to be able to restore the democracy in Athens while Socrates was undermining its foundations and his disciples were assailing it from every side. Socrates' disciples, in fact, constituted a greater threat than Socrates himself[170], as the facts had proved. The accusation made against Socrates of corrupting the young implicated also, therefore, the young men who had associated with him, and the court's subsequent judgement could be taken to imply that these men were no less corrupt than Critias and Alcibiades. Plato and Xenophon do not, in fact, find a single valid argument of defence against this accusation of corrupting the youth, which had already been formulated twenty-four years before the judicial indictment[181]. Plato, indeed, says nothing about the most disturbing of the accusations made against Socrates, namely that he had subverted the family order by inciting the young to disobey their parents. Accusation which Aristophanes had already formulated in crude terms[182], Polycrates was to repeat it[183], and a slight indication in Plato's *Apology* seems to suggest that it was probably also made in court[184].

179. Gomperz, *Greek thinkers*, op. cit., II, p. 114.

180. On this point, it may be noted that Socrates predicted to his judges, *Apology*, 39cd, that after his death his young friends would become even harsher critics.

181. See above, p. 000

182. *Clouds*, v. 132 ff.

183. Polycrates, in Xenophon, *Memorabilia*, I, II, 49 = Libanius, *Apologia Socratis*, 102 ff.

184. *Apology*, 33d.

Socrates certainly did not teach the young to beat their fathers and mothers, as Pheidippides does in *Clouds*; nor did he discredit parents in the eyes of their children by teaching the young to abuse them, as his accuser claims. But it is equally certain that the institution of the family and the ideals which it had always traditionally upheld were subjected to the same radical criticism with which, as we have seen, Socrates undermined the foundations of the civil, religious and political institutions of Athens.

Plato's *Republic* shows even more clearly than the conduct of Critias, Alcibiades and Xenophon, or the satirical attack on Socratic education in Aristophanes' *Clouds*, the full extent of the spiritual gap which existed between the Socratics and the generation of Marathon mourned by Aristophanes[185], and the total irreconcilability of the new ethical-political ideals inspired by Socrates' teaching and the democratic, polytheistic ideals of ancient Athens[185].

15. — It has been said that the condemnation of Socrates was "un assassinio giudiziario", "una colossale ingiustizia", that the judges represented "un fascio di volgari interessi politici"[186] and therefore that "wer es billigt, hat kein Rechtsgefühl"[187]. I have come to the conclusion, however, that Socrates' judges were perfectly right[188], and I do not believe that this opinion places me

185. *Clouds*, v. 961 ff., esp. 986 ff.
185b. See Plato, *Republic*, 473c-478a; *Letter VII*, 325b.
186. Martinetti, *Socrate, cit.*, p. 443.
187. Hildebrandt, *Platon, cit.*, p. 72.
188. The motivs for the accusation and the legality of the sentence have been the objects of much controversy among those who have studied Socrates. On the one hand there is the radical theory of P. Forschhammer, *Die Athener und Sokrates. Die Gesetzlichen und der Revolutionär*, Berlin, 1837, which had already been upheld a century before by S.F. Dresig, *De Socrate iuste damnato*, Lipsia, 1738, and was taken up by G. Sorel, *Le procès de Socrate*, Paris, 1889, and H. Röch, *Der unverfälschte Sokrates, Der Atheist und 'Sophist' und das Wesen aller Philosophie und Religion*, Innsbruck, 1903, who accepts the judgement of Forschhammer, *cit.*, p. 74: "Das niemals von einem gesetzlicheren Gericht ein gesetlicheres Urteil gesprochen, als dasjenige, wodurch Sokrates zuerst des Verbrechen des Unglaubens an die Staatsgötter und der Verderbung der Jugend schuldig erkannt und darauf zum Tode verurteilt wurde". In Röch, *cit.*, 129; on the other hand there is the firmly stated opinion of Grote, *History*

among those who lack all sense of justice. For, whilst the myth of the just man condemned accords perfectly with the Platonic transfiguration of Socrates' personality, it conflicts with the few definite facts which we possess about Socrates; yet these facts are the only proper starting-points for an enquiry which seeks to arrive at a historically sound reconstruction of Socrates, free from myth. Faithful to its stated method, therefore, this essay has focussed attention on those elements in Socrates' dialogues which subverted the customs, traditions and laws of Athens — elements which made Socrates appear impious and corrupt to his contemporaries, thus provoking and legitimating his accusation, trial and condemnation, and which provide the historian with sufficient material for a precise delineation of Socrates' human and philosophical personality.

of Greece, op. cit., VII, p. 671, who sees the condemnation of Socrates as one of the many crimes for which religious and political intolerance is to be blamed, and which arouse in men feelings of indignation and reproach, "the force of which", writes Grote, "I have no desire to enfeeble", an opinion shared by Labriola, *Socrate, op. cit.*, p. 4, who sees in Socrates the "vittima innocente" of an excessive conservative tendency in Athenian democracy, and by M. Croiset, *Histoire de la Littérature Grecque*, 2nd ed., Paris, 1935, II, P. 237, for whom the moral greatness of Socrates lacked only the consecration of a "condemnation injuste", which his enemies provided for him in making him the "victime d'une violente réaction religieuse étroitement associée avec le recent triomphe de la démocratie", *cit.*, p. 238. To Martinetti, *Socrate, op. cit.*, p. 444, the condemnation of Socrates appears, as it did to R. Pöhlmann, *Sokrates und sein Volk*, München und Leipzig, 1899, pp. 111-112, to be "una delle innumerevoli manifestazioni di quella violenza bestiale, con cui lo strato inferiore della spiritualità umana dappertutto recalcitra e resiste al pieno svolgimento del contenuto spirituale interiore della cultura, della ragione e della moralità. La tragedia che qui si svolge, si ripete attraverso tutta la storia dell'umanità fino ad oggi sotto sempre nuove forme, ma sempre con lo stesso risultato: l'oppressione dell'individualità intellettuale e moralmente libera e del pensiero autonomo per opera dello spirito elementare, in breve l'oppressione del puro elemento spirituale dell'alta cultura per opera del peso bruto del volgare, che la psiche collettiva getta nella bilancia". Between these two opposing schools of thought we find the views expressed by Hegel, *Vorlesungen über die Gesch. d. Philos. It. transl. II.*, Firenze, 1932, p. 82 ff., Zeller, *Socrates and the Socrates Schools*, *cit.*, p. 221, and Maier, *Socrate, cit.*, II, p. 174, who examine the accusation and condemnation in the context of the law as it existed in Athens in 399 B.C., recognizing the good faith of the judges and the legality of the sentence, which was reached for religious, moral and political reasons. On the trials of the philosophers in Attica, see *The trial of Anaxagoras* in the present volume.

We have seen how Socrates' attitude to the religion of the State sharply accentuated the rift which had been apparent for some time between freedom of thought and traditional religion. We have seen too that, because it encompassed the sphere of the divine, Socrates' new conception of man negated the old religion of the State and undermined the foundations of Greek thought and Greek spirituality; furthermore, by urging men to change their view of themselves and, therefore, of god and of the world, it implied the necessity for a radical change in the mentality, customs and laws of Athens, and, hence, a change in the institutions of civil life which had been developing in the sphere of human experience and which reflected the society's perception of itself.

It was the dangerously subversive character of Socrates' dialogues which made him seem an irreligious corrupter of the youth, thus legitimating the accusation and condemnation even from the point of view of the law in Athens in 399 B.C. Certainly, it is easier to explain the accusation and condemnation of Socrates on political grounds than on religious grounds, and not because they were determined by petty factional interests, as is generally believed[189].

The truth is that ἀσέβεια[190], impiety, was above all a civil

189. Maier, Socrate, *op. cit.*, II, p. 180, had already pointed out that, if anything was certain, "è che l'avversione politica non ebbe alcuna parte nel processo", although "non può dubitarsi che le opinioni politiche di Socrate fossero ad Anito poco simpatiche", *op. cit*, n. 3.

190. ἀσέβεια was defined by pseudo-Aristotle, *De virtut. et vit.*, 7, 1251a 31, as "wrong-doing towards gods, deified spirits, the departed, one's parents, and one's country". See Caillemer, in Daremberg-Saglio, *s.v.*, who provides a detailed survey of the offences of impiety, cf. Decharme, *La critique, op. cit.*, p. 114 ff.; Derenne, *Le procès , op. cit.*, p. 9 ff. On the meaning which ἀσέβεια acquired in Diopeithes' decree, see *The trial of Anaxagoras*, in the present volume.

The political nature of the offences of *asébeia* has been clearly demonstrated by Pettazzoni, *La Religione, cit.*, p. 184, and G. Glotz, *Histoire Grecque*, Paris, 1931, II, p. 429: "Les athéniens ne recherchèrent jamais d'autres crimes contre les dieux que ceux qu'ils estimaient en même temps des crimes contre l'Etat"; cf. Nilsson, *Greek piety, op. cit.*, p. 79, and Maier, *Socrate, op. cit.*, II, p. 199, according to whom "lo stato si era posto sotto la protezione della divinità ed ogni offesa alla divinità, potendo divenire per esso esiziale, finiva con l'essere un'offesa ai fondamenti dell'ordine statale". On the political motive for the impiety

crime, an attack on the established order of the State perpetrated by means of offences against the gods, kith and kin, and country. In Greek consciousness, as we have seen, religious concepts were constantly exchanged or combined with ethical and political concepts, in such a way that the political constitution took on a sacred character; thus, every crime against the State assumed the form of a crime against religion, and conversely, every crime against religion became a crime against the State. The accusation of ἀσέβεια was therefore directed not only at Socrates' radical rejection of the native gods, but also at the implicit subversion of the family institution and order and at his implacable opposition to the Athenian democracy, which he condemned for the incompetence of the men elected to the supreme magistracy of the State. Hence the legitimacy of the accusation and the condemnation.

Hegel perceived correctly how "by placing truth under the jurisdiction of the inner conscience", Socrates came "into conflict with what the Athenian people considered just and true"[191]; this is how Hegel explains the reason for Socrates' greatness and for his special place in history, and, at the same time, the cause of his guilt. Bury[192] was right then, when, rejecting the myth of the just man condemned, he wrote that the intensity of the Socratic tragedy was that there was no man in Athens more just than Socrates and yet his accusers were perfectly right.

16. — In this essay we have sought to show:

- that the sceptical conclusion of Gigon, far from eliminating the Socratic problem, provides the starting-point for a more fruitful enquiry;

- that an|enquiry|directed|at understanding the reasons for the accusation and condemnation of Socrates confirms the truthfulness of the charges made during the trial, and therefore provides sufficient material for a critically valid interpretation of Socrates' personality;

trials, Snell, *La cultura greca*, *op. cit.*, p. 52, and Gernet & Boulanger, *Le génie grec dans la religion*, *op. cit.*, p. 346.

191. Hegel, *Vorlesungen über die Gesch. d. Philos. It. tr.*, *op. cit.*, II, p. 84.

192. J.B. Bury, *A history of Greece*, *op. cit.*, p. 580.

- that the philosophical personality of Socrates may be identified with his ethical and political teaching aimed at producing virtuous men fit to govern the State;

- that Socrates' ethical and political teaching celebrated the aristocratic ideal which had its models in the institutions of Megara, Thebes and Sparta, and therefore came into conflict with the democratic ideal and the civil, religious and political institutions which were founded on that ideal, whence the accusation of Anytus, Meletus and Lycon and the condemnation of the heliasts.

The emphasis on Socrates as a predominantly ethical and political personality clarifies the meaning and intention of Socrates' dialogues and explains why political criticism continued to be a common feature of all the various schools of thought which were inspired by those dialogues. The relationship between Socrates and the sophists on the one hand, and between Socrates, Plato and the Socratics on the other, thus appears to be closer and deeper whilst the figure and the work of Socrates are drawn out of the nebulous realms of myth and restored to their proper dimensions at the concrete level of history.

SOCRATES BETWEEN THE FIRST AND SECOND CLOUDS

δitταì δὴ φέρονται Νεφέλαι.
Arg. IV ad *Nubes*

1. — The *Clouds* was staged during the great City Dionysia of 423, the archon being Isarco[1], the producer Aristophanes himself[2]. Aristophanes' comedy gained only third place, after Cratinus' *Wine-flagon*, winner of the contest, and Ameipsia's *Cònnos*[3].

The defeat caused feelings of great bitterness in the poet, who, as early as the following year, in the Lenaean *Wasps*[4], reproached the audience[5] for not having understood his play[6] which, in his view, had never been surpassed[7]. Refusing to accept the defeat Aristophanes then planned to resubmit the *Clouds*[8] in a contest

---

1. Cf. *Argument VI*, ap. Aristophanes, *Clouds*.
Unless stated to the contrary, we will always quote from the edition of the *Clouds* in *Les Belles Lettres*: ARISTOPHANE, *Tome I, Les Acharniens, Les Cavaliers, Les Nuées*. Text established by V. COULON and translated by H. VAN DAELE, Paris, 1948[3].
2. Cf. C.F. RUSSO, *Aristofane autore di teatro*. Florence, 1962, 1984[2], p. 147 f.
3. Cf. *Argument VI*. For the reliability of these remarks, see RUSSO, op. cit., p. 147.
4. On the archon, olimpiad, contest, classification of the poets and title of the comedies staged in competition with the *Clouds*, cf. *Argument I*, ap. Aristophanes, *Wasps*, ed. Coulon-Van Daele, Tome II, Paris, 1958[4].
5. *Wasps*, 1. 1016.
6. *Wasps*, 1. 1045.
7. *Wasps*, 1. 1047.
8. Cf. *Clouds*, 11. 518, 520, 521, 535 which make sense only if referring to spectators, not to readers. Cf. Russo, cit., p. 166. For the hypothesis of J. VAN LEEUWEN, *Prolegomena ad ARISTOPHANIS, Nubes*, XI, Lugduni Batavorum, 1898, p. VII, according to which Aristophanes did not really intend to restage the *Clouds*, but merely to publish it again and to defend it from those

and, once again, in a Dionysiac festival[9].

However, for some reason, the task of revising the text, embarked upon with a further production in mind, was not completed and the *Clouds* was never again staged[10]. The text of the *Clouds*, revised but unfinished, is the one we know; however, the text which was produced on stage has not survived.

The precise nature of the corrections, changes and revisions which, according to the grammarian of Argument VII, were made to the text of the staged *Clouds* and, in particular, whether or not the text we know is substantially different from the staged version, is a matter for discussion. Such discussion, though conducted at length[11], has never been exhausted and, one might say,

who had not done it justice, see VAN DAELE, *Notice*, p. 154. ap. *Les Nuées*, cit.

9. See *Clouds*, 1. 609, where the poet greets "Athenians and their allies" who every year at the beginning of Spring, when the Dionysia took place, came to bring the tribute of their cities, cf. *The Acharnians*, 11. 643-44 and 11. 535 of the new *Parabasis* of *Clouds* in which Aristophanes will rebuke the public of the Dionysia, to whom, 1. 523, the *Clouds* had first been given.

10. ERATOSTHENES, scholium to *Clouds* 1. 552, lists, against Callimachus, the second *Clouds* amongst the comedies ἀδίδακτα, cf. R. CANTARELLA, *Premessa a Nuvole*, in ARISTOFANE, *Le Commedie*, III, Milan, 1954, p. 21; RUSSO, op. cit., p. 166.

DINDORF, *De Aristophanis Fabularum numero et nominibus* ap. ARISTO-PHANIS *Comoedias ex rec.* G. *DINDORFII*, Oxonii, 1835, T. II., p. 508. rightly accuses the unknown grammarian of Argument IV (= VI Coulon = I CANTARELLA), where he writes Αἱ δὲ δεύτεραι Νεφέλαι ἐπὶ 'Αμεινίυ ἄρχοντος, of having confused "*Vespas, quae aronte Aminia edita est, cum altera Nubium editione*". VAN DAELE, *Notice*, cit., p. 154, n. 1, has observed on this question: "*d'après cette assertion, la seconde représentation des Nuées aurait donc eu lieu aux Dionysia (mars); chose inadmissible, puisque la bataille d'Amphipolis, ou Cléon périt, fut livrée seulement dans le cours de l'été*". Cf. too the observations of W.G. TEUFFEL, *Praefation ad* ARISTOPHANIS *Nubes*, Lipsiae, 1863, p. 9 and of VAN LEEUWEN, in ARISTOPHANIS *Nubes* ed cit. *Argument IV* and n. 4, p. 5; note to 1. 553, p. 96 f. and the recent ones of K. DOVER, ARISTOPHANIS, *Clouds*, ed. w. *Introd.* and *Com.* Oxford, 1968. *Preface*, p. LXXX; *Aristophanic Comedy*, London, 1972, p. 103 f.

11. In modern times, the discussion after the remarks of DINDORF, *De Aristophanis fabularum*, cit., p. 507 ff., in concluding an already long controversy accentuated the extreme doubtfulness of the fragments of the first *Clouds* and the related difficulty in deciding about the variations made to the second *Clouds*,

could never be exhausted, since, with one of the terms of comparison removed from the judgement, the few uncertain elements in our possession mean that every conclusion is doomed to remain a hypothesis.

However, the discussion must again be conducted, given that it coincides with the one, with which we are more directly concerned, about the use of the *Clouds* as a Socratic source[12].

has been reopened by F.V. FRITZSCHE, *De Fabulis ab Aristophane retractatis*, Progr. Rostock, I 8, 1849-52, who with the double writing of the *Clouds* affirmed the substantial difference between the two texts, and by B. HEIDHUES, *Über die Wolken des Aristophanes*, Progr. Köln, 1897, who, — more radical than F. RITTER, *Über die Wolken des Aristophanes*, in *Philologus*, 1876, p. 447 ff., who conceded to our *Clouds* the innovation of only the scene of the *logoi*, in addition, of course, to the Parabasis of the chorus, — maintained that the first and second *Clouds* were identical in almost every respect except the Parabasis.

Recently the question has been taken up again by H. ERBSE, *Sokrates im Schatten der Aristophanischen Wolken*, Hermes, 82, 1954, p. 386 ff., who sides with the unitarian critics; by T. GELZER, *Aristophanes und sein Sokrates*, Museum Helveticum, 13, 1956, p. 65 ff. by RUSSO, op cit., p. 147 ff. and by DOVER, ARISTOPHANES, *Clouds*, cit., *Introd.*, p. LXXXI who relaunch the thesis of the dual writing of the *Clouds* and of the substantial difference between the two texts.

The problem of the duplicity of the *Clouds* regarding the representation of Socrates, despite the two comprehensive memoires of A. CHIAPPELLI, *Il Naturalismo di Socrate e le prime Nubi di Aristofane*, proceeding of the Accademia dei Lincei, Rome, 1886, pp. 284-302 and *Nuove Ricerche sul Naturalismo di Socrate* in Archiv für Geschichte der Philosophie, IV, 1891, pp. 369-413, and the discussion made of it by A.E. TAYLOR, *The Phrontisterion*, in *Varia Socratica*, Oxford, 1911, p. 129 ff., has been practically excluded from modern Socratic historiography.

12. The comparison between Plato the philosopher and Aristophanes the poet has, as we shall see, harmed the latter, whose satire, disproved moreover in all its points by Plato's *Apology*, has been excluded from the small number of Socratic sources, apart from H. RÖCK, *Der Unverfälschte Sokrates, der Atheist und "Sophist"*, Innsbruck, 1903. And even today, notwithstanding the changed historico-critical perspective in which we place the Socratic problem after the crisis instigated by O. GIGON, *Sokrates. Sein Bild in Dichtung u. Gesch.*, Bern, 1947, 1979[2], Aristophanes has not been taken into serious consideration as a Socratic witness. And so even today there are repetitions of the traditional interpretations of the figure of Socrates in the *Clouds* and of the ancient theses of a naturalist Socrates return, either of a Socrates as an exponent and symbol of all the sophist corruption complained of by Aristophanes, or of a figure or a comic type drawn on the boundary between fiction and reality; representations,

In our case, then, the discussion is couched in the following terms: did the failure of the *Clouds* and the revision, total or partial, of the staged version, involve, in addition to the change in the text, a change in Aristophanes' view of Socrates[13]? Clearly an answer to this question, if and insofar as it is possible, demands that the importance of the surviving variations between the *Clouds* performed on stage and unknown to us, and the *Clouds* which is unstaged and known to us, be ascertained as a preliminary measure. In other words: if there is a difference between the two texts, what exactly is the difference between the so-called first *Clouds* and the so-called second *Clouds*[14]?

2. — It has already been said that the text of the play which was a flop on stage has not survived. That this text, despite its failure and the revision embarked upon with a view to a second performance, was published, either by Aristophanes or others who came after him[15], is highly probable, but not yet proven;

in any case, into which further investigation would be of hardly any use for finding out about the historical Socrates and therefore scarsely quoted either in confirmation of the intellectual history of Socrates, to which the *Phaedo* refers, or when the question of the ancient accusors, to which the *Apology* refers, poses the question of Aristophanes' responsibility for the fate of Socrates. And yet eventually no serious research on Socrates can do without this precious source on Socrates, because nothing will ever be understood about Socrates nor will there ever be a solution to the problem created by the legend arisen around him unless we first try to understand the exact significance of the Aristophanic testimony.

13. The hypothesis, according to which the rewriting of the *Clouds* implies a revision of Aristophanes' judgement on Socrates, was first advanced by A. CHIAPPELLI, *Il naturalismo di Socrate e le prime Nubi di Aristofane*, cit., p. 289, who asks: "1) is there an essential diversity in the writing of the *Clouds* regarding the representation of Socrates? 2) Having established this diversity are we right to believe that it corresponded to a historical transformation of philosophical tendencies?" It is to these questions that, albeit with a different awareness of Socratic problems, this investigation finally proposes to respond.

14. The distinction between πρῶται Νεφέλαι and δεύτεραι Νεφέλαι dates back to the learned Alexandrians and is found in *Argument VI* ap. *Clouds* and, albeit less specifically, in *Argument IV*: Διτταὶ δὲ φέρονται Νεφέλαι. As far as our discussion is concerned however, we must not forget that *Argument VII* begins with this declaration: Τοῦτο ταὐτόν ἐστι τῷ προτέρῳ.

15. Like TH. KOCH, ARISTOPHANES, *Die Wolken*, Berlin, 1876³,

likewise, it is even less certain that in the Alexandrian library, alongside the text we know, there was the text recited in 423[16].

It is a fact that, if ever the learned Alexandrians had before their eyes a text which was different from the one we know, they never used it to adduce probative examples of the variations appearing in the second *Clouds*. Of that text no trace survives, nor is there any precise record of it among the ancient scholiasts to the second *Clouds*, who, though mentioning a second writing of the *Clouds*[17], never offer precise textual comparisons such as

Einleitung, p. 30 and like TEUFFEL, ARISTOPHANES, *Nubes*, Lipsiae, 1863, *Praefatio*, p. 8, CHIAPPELLI, cit., p. 297, believes that "Platone, quando scriveva l'*Apologia* non conoscesse le seconde *Nubi*", whereas "quando scriveva quel luogo del *Politico* (229b) conosceva certo le seconde *Nubi*", p. 398. The first *Clouds* would therefore have been published soon after the staging of the play in 423, whereas the second *Clouds* would have been put into circulation much later, in the last period of Plato's life, that is at the time of the great dialectic dialogues. According to CHIAPPELLI, in the first *Clouds* a caricature of Socrates as a metereo-sophist was presented, p. 298, whereas in the second *Clouds* the immorality of Socratic teaching would be attacked. And since Plato, speaking of Aristophanes, does not mention the second charge, Chiappelli concludes that at the time of the *Apology* Plato was not acquainted with the second *Clouds*. We will deal with this issue towards the end of this paper.

According to RUSSO, cit., p. 166-167, the first *Clouds* were published separately and in full prior to the publication of the second *Clouds*. Cf. also the perceptive observations on pp. 317-19 and p. 188, n. 5.

16. Nor in fact does proof lie in the statements, reported on n. 14, of *Arguments IV* and *VI*, since the very novelty of the Parabasis could make one suspect that the comedy presented other novelties not present in the staged version of 423. DINDORF, cit., pp. 508-9, RITTER, cit., p. 447 ff., VAN DAELE, cit., p. 155 et al., rule out, as we do, the possibility of the learned Alexandrians ever having had in their possession the text of the first *Clouds*.

On the other hand it is true that "se non si può dimostrare che gli Alessandrini conobbero le prime *Nubi*, ciò non prova che non l'abbiano conosciuto", CHIAPPELLI, cit., p. 289, n. 1. but the trouble is that if they did know the first *Clouds* they did nothing to make it known to us too, hence the legitimacy of our doubt.

17. RUSSO, cit., p. 188, n. 5, recalls that D. HOLWERDA, *De novo priorum Aristophanis Nubium iudicio*, Mnemosyne, 1958, pp. 32-41, reports "that in the manuscript Vaticano Barb. 126 of the 14th century, f. 43v, a scholiast refers to his metric comment of the first *Clouds*. The new document, comments Russo, therefore gives further indirect proof of different and integral editions of first and second *Clouds*". "Refers", then, but does not report even a passage of the commentated text. Now, this is just the point: that of these two different and in-

might permit the finding of a specific difference between the two texts[18].

As has been mentioned, substantial variations are indicated by the grammarian of Argument VII, if we accept that Argument VII was written by a single grammarian[19]. Such variations would concern, on the one hand, a series of minor corrections (διορθώσεις) which recur throughout the Comedy, and, on the other, certain parts that were completely rewritten (διασχευή), such as, in particular, the Parabasis of the Chorus (11.518-562), the contest of Right and Wrong (11.889-1104), and the final scene of the fire in the Phrontisterion (1.1483 ff.). But whether Argument VII has "a very clear mark of authenticity"[20] and, indeed, whether to illustrate the variations of the second *Clouds* the learned Alexandrian had at his disposal "a suitable means of comparison"[21], seem to us, to say the very least, highly dubious. Whether there was a complete rewriting of the Parabasis, dif-

tegral editions of the *Clouds* no-one has ever made use to point out the variants existing between the two texts.

18. The presumed fragments of the first *Clouds* have been collected by DINDORF, cit., who with RITTER, cit. VAN LEEUWEN, *Prolegomena ad Nubes* p. XXII ff., have unanimously shown that they were dealing with erroneous transcriptions or false attributions.

19. Cf. VAN DAELE, cit., p. 155.

19a. For the name of the two contestants in the Clouds 889-1112, see K.J. DOVER, *Aristophanes-Clouds, with Introd. and comm.* Oxford 1968, Introd. philos. LVIII, for whom "the best translation of the names is 'Right' and 'Wrong'.

20. CHIAPPELLI, cit., p. 289 and n. 2.

21. RUSSO, cit., p. 167, while on the one hand he states that the grammarian of *Argument VII* in order to point out the variants in the second *Clouds* must have had in his possession "una qualche pezza d'appoggio", p. 166 "un adeguato mezzo di collazione", on the other hand, then refuses its testimony, concluding that "per la estrema parte della commedia dove la scuola di Socrate viene incendiata da Strepsiade con l'aiuto dello schiavo Santia (11. 1483-1150) [...] lì il testo delle nostre *Nuvole* coincide senz'altro con quello di *Nuvole prime*". The dilemma is then: either it is right to believe that the alexandrian grammarians knew "directly or indirectly" (p. 167) the first *Clouds*, and therefore to accept all the radical novelties he records, or it is right to doubt the reliability of the grammarian of *Argument VII* and in that case it is no longer possible to be so categorical in saying that the learned Alexandrian possessed a suitable means of comparison and, in other words, that he knew the first *Clouds*.

ferent in content, character and meter from the staged version[22], with the courteous rebuke the poet addresses to the audience who had preferred, to the best[23] of his comedies, the excessive buffooneries of his rivals (1.560), the same cannot be said with equal certainty about the contest between the two Reasonings, identified as an innovation of the second *Clouds*, nor about the final scene of the fire in Socrates' school.

3. — In fact, both in content and tone, the Parabasis of the second *Clouds* rules out the possibility of the text known to us presenting innovations that might substantially change the structure and character of the first *Clouds*. In my view there is no doubt that, with the new Parabasis, Aristophanes, rather than present a comedy wholly or partially different from the one that flopped in 423, wants to defend and relaunch the best of his comedies which had undeservedly met with failure in the theatre:

Ὦ θεώμενοι, κατερῶ πρὸς ὑμᾶς ἐλευθέρως
τἀληθῆ, νὴ τὸν Διόνυσον τὸν ἐκθρέψαντά με.
Οὕτω νικήσαιμί τ᾽ἐγὼ καὶ νομιζοίμην σοφός,
ὡς ὑμᾶς ἡγούμενος εἶναι θεατὰς δεξιοὺς
καὶ ταύτην δοφώτατ᾽ ἔχειν τῶν ἐμῶν κωμῳδιῶν,
πρώτους ἠξίωσ᾽ ἀναγεῦσ᾽ ὑμᾶσ, ἣ παρέσχε μοι
ἔργον πλεῖστον· εἶτ᾽ ἀνεχώρουν ὑπ᾽ ἀνδρῶν φορτικῶν
ἡττηθεὶς οὐκ ἄξιος ὤν· ταῦτ᾽οὖν ὑμῖν μέμφομαι
τοῖς δοφοῖς, ὧν οὕνεκ᾽ ἐγὼ ταῦτ᾽ ἐπραγματευόμην[24]

---

22. Scholium to *Clouds*, 520. Cf. VAN LEEUWEN, *Aristophanis Nubes*, cit. note to 11. 518-562.

23. *Clouds*, 1. 522: σοφώτατ᾽ἔχειν is translated as *Optimam* by VAN LEEUWEN, a.l.; *La meilleure*, by VAN DAELE, a.l.; *The wisest and the best*, by Rogers, a.l.; *la migliore*, by Romagnoli, a.l.;*bellissima*, CANTARELLA, a.l.; *the cleverest*, MURRAY, cit. p. 8; *la più acuta*, RUSSO, cit., p. 29; *the best*, DOVER. cit. *Introduction*, p. LXXX.; *"my most brilliant comedy"*; *Aristophanic Com.* p. 103.

24. *Clouds*, 11. 518-529.

«Spectateurs, je vous dirai franchement la vérité, j'en atteste Dionysos qui m'a élève. Ainsi puisse-je être vainqueur et être réputé habile, s'il est vrai que, vous tenant pour des spectateurs judicieux et la présente pièce pour la meilleure de mes comédies, j'ai voulu, à vous les premiers, faire déguster à nouveau une œuvre

91

Aristophanes therefore speaks of "this [...] my most excellent conceited play", ταύτην (1.522), of this comédy, of "la meilleure de mes comědies" "my most brilliant comedy" ταύτην δοφώτατ' ἔχειν τῶν ἐμῶν κωμῳδιῶν, which, as is said soon after-wards, nevertheless met with an undeserved defeat in the Dionysiac contest of 423;

εἶτ᾽ἀνεχώρουν ὑπ᾽ἀνδρῶν φορτικῶν
ἡττηθεὶς οὐκ ἄξιος ὤν.[25]

This means that the unsuccessful 423 comedy and the comedy Aristophanes intends to restage and for which he has rewritten the first part of the Parabasis, "this play", are exactly the same comedy known to us and the audience of the 423 Dionysia.

If this were not the case, if, that is, with "my most brilliant comedy" reference was made only to the *Clouds* known to us and not also the *Clouds* recited in the theatre, the reproach addressed to the audience would not be justified, since the implicit distinction between "my most brilliant comedy" and that comedy which had already been staged unsuccessfully would imply a resigned acceptance of the defeat by the poet who would have recognized the opportunity totally or partially to rewrite the original text. On the contrary, the reproach for not having understood "straight-away" παραχρῆμα (*Wasps*, 1.1048) that comedy of which there does not exist "one more brilliant" ἀμείνων (*Wasps*, 1.1047) already staged before the public of the Lenaea *Wasps*, is more validly repeated here since it is addressed to that same audience in the Dionysia that the poet had thought worthy of being the first πρώτους (*Clouds*, 1.523) to enjoy in 423 "the most brilliant comedy" of all his comedies.

qui m'avait coûté tant de peine. Cependant, je me retirai de la lutte, battu par de grossiers rivaux, sans l'avoir mérité. Voilà ce que je vous reproche, à vous les habiles, pour lesquels, je m'étais donné ce mal.».

trans. VAN DAELE. Unless stated otherwise in the notes I shall always quote the translation, excellent in every respect, of VAN DAELE, and likewise I reproduce the Greek text established by COULON for the *BELLES LETTRES* edition on which the French translation is based.

25. *Clouds*, 11. 524-525, cit.

«Cependant je me retirai de la lutte, battu par de grossiers rivaux, sans l'avoir mérité.».

That the staged comedy and the one known to us are identical is again confirmed by the following line: 'Αλλ'οὐδ' ὡς ὑμῶν ποθ' εκὼν προδώσω τοὺς δεξιούς[26]. And how could the poet have betrayed those who showed good taste, that is those members of the audience who enjoyed the comedy during its first performance, whom the poet, while writing the new Parabasis, imagined meeting again in the theatre for the second production? By wholly or partially transforming that comedy that the discerning audience had enjoyed or, in other words, by presenting them with a comedy wholly or partially different from the one which they, as intelligent members of the audience, had enjoyed.

If, however, Aristophanes says he did not want to betray those members of his audience who enjoyed the *Clouds* the first time it was produced, that means that Aristophanes himself refuses to bring to the comedy he intends to restage, i.e. the *Clouds* known to us, changes such as to make it substantially new or different from the earlier version. And Aristophanes' refusal to draft a new comedy on the old unsuccessful one is again confirmed shortly after when he says:

οὐδ' ὑμᾶς ζητῶ 'ξαπατᾶν δὶς καὶ τρὶς ταῦτ' εἰσάγων,
ἀλλ' ἀεὶ καινὰς ἰδέας εἰσφέρων σοφίζομαι,[27].

Now, the originality of the *Clouds* had already been claimed the year after production, in the Parabasis of the *Wasps* (1.1044) and will again be asserted, as we shall see, exactly in the new Parabasis of our *Clouds*.

Holding the opposite view, Chiappelli[28] noted that 1.546 ff., in which the poet warns the audience that it is not his habit to deceive them by presenting the same thing two or three times, but always to contrive to find new inventions, all different from each

---

26. *Clouds*, 1. 527.
«Mais, même ainsi, jamais je ne trahirai volontairement ceux de vous qui sont judicieux».
27. *Clouds*, 11. 546-548.
«Et [je] ne cherche pas à vous tromper en représentant deux ou trois fois les mêmes sujets; mais toujours je vous apporte des fictions nouvelles».
28. CHIAPPELLI, *Il Naturalismo di Socrate*, cit., p. 291.

other and all brilliant, would substantiate the fact that "the *Clouds*, featuring this second Parabasis, carries a new idea which clearly distinguished it from the first version". But, it must be pointed out, while we are dealing with this matter, that the poet's warning does not refer specifically to the second version of the *Clouds*, but rather to all his comedies, including the so-called first *Clouds*, of which Aristophanes claims the singular originality. Proof of this, in the lines which follow immediately afterwards, lies in the mention of Cleon (1.549 f.), severely attacked in the *Knights* (424 B.C.), but saved after death (422 B.C.), whereas, says Aristophanes,

Οὗτοι δ᾽,ὡς ἅπαξ παρέδωκεν λαβὴν Ὑπέρβολος, ‖ τοῦτον
δείλαιον κολετρῶσ᾽ ἀεὶ καὶ τὴν μητέρα²⁹

What right would Aristophanes have had to make such a remark on his rivals if he had been the very first to plan to restage a few years later an unsuccessful play of his which, though partially or totally rewritten, still had the same Socrates as its protagonist?

Of that undeservedly failed comedy, however, Aristophanes, preparing a second edition, wants to emphasize in the new Parabasis those qualities which, as he complained in the *Wasps* (1.1048), the public had failed to grasp there and then.

And so, first and foremost, he emphasizes to the audience how this comedy points out the praised contrast between the Chaste and the Bugger³⁰ and, since this, the very first of his comedies,

---

29. *Clouds*, 11. 551-552.
«Mes rivaux, depuis qu'une fois leur a donné prise Hyperbolos, ne cessent de dauber sur ce malheureux ainsi que sur sa mère».
30. Aristophanes' first comedy, *The Banqueters*, Δαιταλῆς, centered on the contrast between the chaste and the bugger, was staged at the 427 city Dionysia, when Aristophanes, still very young (*Clouds*, 1. 530) was not yet old enough to ask for a Chorus in his own name. The comedy, produced by Callistratus, came second. Cf. VAN LEEUWEN, *Prolegomena ad Aristophanem*, Lug. Bat. 1908, p. 24 ff. The fragments in DINDORF, II, 526-37. A reconstruction of the themes in the comedy, in M. CROISET, *Aristophane et les partis à Athènes*, Paris, 1906, pp. 46-53. CHIAPPELLI well noted:
«Egli non cita i più recenti e maggiori trionfi degli *Acarnesi*, dei *Cavaliéri*, della *Pace*, del *Proagone* e delle *Vespe*, perché nella commedia di Δαιταλῆς si

had so great a success with the same audience at the Dionysia[31]

Νῦν οὖν Ἠλέκτραν κατ᾽ἐκείνην ἤδἢ κωμῳδία

— once again, this most brilliant of my comedies undeservedly unsuccessful at its first production[32] —

ζητοῦσ᾽ἦλθ᾽, ἤν που ᾽πιτύχη θεαταῖς οὕτω σοφοῖς·
γνώσεται γάρ, ἤνπερ ἴδη, τἀδελφοῦ τὸν βόστρυχον[33].

svolgeva un argomento affine a quello delle nuove *Nubi*, cioè il contrapposto dell'antica e della nuova educazione», *cit.*, p. 291.

Also Russo, *cit.*, p. 30. Murray, *Aristophanes*, Oxford, 1933, p. 85: «*The Clouds can be regarded as a development of the* Daitalês, *much as the* Knights *and the* Wasps *are developments of the* Babylonians».

We are not of a mind to suscribe to the conclusion of RUSSO, *cit.*, p. 31:

«I *Banchettanti*, insomma, non sono invocati pateticamente perché commedia dell'inizio, ma perché Aristofane con malizia vuol far passare la coincidenza degli'agoni come un segno di stima per gli spettatori di questi agoni».

31. *Clouds*, 1. 528: ἐνθάδε, right here, in this theatre of Dionysus, hence in front of the same audience. TEUFFEL, a.l.: "in scena"; STARKIE, a.l. "on this spot" in the theatre: VAN DAELE, a.l. "ici"; CANTARELLA "davanti a voi"; on the other hand VAN LEEUWEN, a.l.: "adverbium ἐνθάδε vertatur igitur *Athenis* (non: in hoc theatro)"; but see the correct remarks of RUSSO, *cit.*, p. 31. Also DOVER, a.l. takes it to mean "in the theatre".

32. In contrast, CHIAPPELLI, and others with him, believe that, where Aristophanes complains of the failure of the first *Clouds* (1. 527 ff.) «esprime la speranza che il pubblico accoglierà la nuova commedia (νῦν οὖν. v. 534) collo stesso favore col quale *accolse* i Δαιταλῆς della quale è sorella [...] Se, dunque — conclude. CHIAPPELLI, *cit.*, p. 291 — il poeta dice che questa parte, per la quale la nuova commedia si assomiglia ai Δαιταλῆς come Elettra a Oreste, gli procurerà un egual plauso, ciò vuol dire che questra parte, cioè appunto la scena dei due λόγοι, appartiene alle seconde *Nubi*.»

This is tantamount to saying that while Aristophanes was complaining to the public about the failure of the first *Clouds*, reproaching them for not having understood the best of his comedies, he then recognized the need to patch up the failed comedy in order to present it to the same public. Les us leave responsibility for such an inference to Chiappelli and whoever shares his view.

33. *Clouds*, 11. 534-526.

«Maintenant donc, pareille à l'antique Électre, cette comédie est venue voir si elle pourrait quelquefois rencontrer des spectateurs aussi éclairés; elle reconnaîtra, à première vue, la boucle de cheveux de son frère».

He then points out the propriety of the comedy[34], evidently in-sufficiently understood in 423, since for the first time ever it had done away with the phallic costume[35] of the comic actors

Ὡς δὲ σώφρων ἐστὶ φύσει σκέψασθ᾽ ἥτις πρῶτα μὲν
οὐδὲν ἦλθε ραψαμένη σκυτίον καθειμένον
ἐρυθρὸν ἐξ ἄκρου, παχύ, τοῖς παιδίοις ἵν᾽ ᾖ γέλως[36].

And finally he stresses how "this comedy" does not lapse into the exaggerated vulgarity of those coarse men, ἀνδρῶν φορτικῶν (1.524) at whose hands the comedy failed:

οὐδ᾽ ἔσκωψε τοὺς φαλακρούς, οὐδὲ κόρδαχ᾽ εἵλκυσεν,
οὐδὲ πρεσβύτης ὁ λέγων τἄπη τῇ βακτηρίᾳ
τύπτει τὸν παρόντ᾽ ἀρανίζων πονηρὰ σκώμματα,
οὐδ᾽ εἰσῇξε δᾷδας ἔχουσ᾽, οὐδ᾽ ἰοὺ ἰοὺ βοᾷ,[37]

---

34. *Clouds*, 1. 537. "Et voyez comme elle est de sa nature réservée".

35. The fact that on 1. 734 Strepsiades says he has in his hand τὸ πέος that is the male member, in this precise sense already used by Aristophanes in *The Acharnians*, 1. 158: τὸ πέος ἀποτεθρίακεν gives clear confirmation that the abolition of the phallic costume was already a novelty of the staged *Clouds*; a novelty stressed by Aristophanes in the new Parabasis and so the whole scene, 11. 723-805, extremely important for the characterization of Socratic teaching, coincides with the text of the first *Clouds*. CHIAPPELLI, *Il Naturalismo*, cit., pp. 290-91, following FRITZSCHE a.l. and TEUFFEL, a.l. believes in contrast that lines 537-38 of the new Parabasis introduce a novelty unknown to the staged *Clouds* and that the circumstances which on line 734 Strepsiades says he has τὸ πέος in his right hand would confirm that 1. 734 was not adapted to the novelty introduced by lines 537-38. But it must be pointed out in this context that Aristophanes is speaking of τὸ πέος the penis, and not of the σκυτίον, the piece of pendulous leather of the phallic costume. The latter having been abolished, Aristotle, when writing τὸ πέος was completely consistent with the novelty introduced in actors' costumes in 423 and pointed out in the new Parabasis. Indeed, we should add that in saying τὸ πέος, Aristophanes gave the scene a realistic feature that the phallic costume, obscene and ridiculous, could not have. Differently but not exactly explains, DOVER, a.l.

36. *Clouds*, 11. 537-539. "...tout d'abord, elle est venue sans avoir cousu sur elle un morceau de cuir pendant, rouge par le bout, épais, pour faire rire les gamins".

37. *Clouds*, 11. 540-543. "Elle ne raille pas les chauves, ni danse le cordax; on n'y voit pas de veillard, qui, tout en débitant les vers, frappe de son baton

This comedy, concludes Aristophanes,

ἀλλαὐτῇ καὶ τοῖς ἔπεσιν πιστεύουσ᾽ἐλήλυθεν.⁸

This is a conclusion which, if applied to a second version that would have made of our *Clouds* a comedy different from that staged, would implicitly have justified to the judges who had failed the comedy produced on stage. Except that, in the following line, Aristophanes comes out with this proud declaration:

Κἀγὼ μὲν τοιοῦτος ἀνὴρ ὢν πο[ι]ητὴς οὐ κομῶ³⁹,

which, as Van Daele[39b] points out, "équivaut à celle du grand Corneille à ses détracteurs: Je sais ce que je vaux" and which is certainly not that of a man resigned to a failure he knows he does not deserve. Indeed, far from recanting his favourite comedy, it is precisely that, the best of his comedies, which Aristophanes intends to offer once again, ἀναγεῦσαι,, for the delectation of the public of the Dionysia who had been unable to appreciate its true worth. Buth without modifying the text, without deliberately betraying those members of the audience who demonstrated good taste, without deceiving the public by presenting the same thing two or three times (1.546), but simply by helping the audience, with this new Parabasis, to grasp the qualities of a comedy which, as Aristophanes had said the year following the failure on stage, had never been surpassed (*Wasps*, 1.1047). And this fidelity of the poet to the comedy which had given him so much trouble (*Clouds*, 1.523-24), to the most brilliant of all his comedies, is such that he refused to change even those references to Cleon (1.584 ff.) and Hyperbolus (1.623) recurring in the epirrema of

celui qui est près de lui, pour faire passer de grossières plaisenteries; elle ne se précipite pas sur la scène avec des torches, ni crie 'iou iou' ".

38. *Clouds*, 1. 544, "C'est confiante en elle-même et dans ses vers qu'elle est venue".

39. *Clouds*, 1. 545. "Et moi, pour être un tel poète, je ne fais pas le fier à la longue chevelure", Ποιητής is read by BRUNCK, DINDORF, TEUFFEL, BERGK, VAN LEEUWEN, CANTARELLA; whereas Ποητής is read by COULON and DOVER.

39b. *Notice*, ap. *Clouds*, p. 157.

the Parabasis and proving to be completely irreconcilable with the circumstances recalled by the new Parabasis[40]. If there was anything to correct it was precisely those references to Cleon and Hyperbolus which instead remained, and not as evidence of the incomplete reworking of the original text, but rather as fresh proof of the punctilious faithfulness to a text which the poet did not intend to change or bring to the level of that section of the public who had not been able to appreciate the beauty of its verse and the originality of its ideas.

4. — If the remarks made about the new Parabasis have led us to conclude that our *Clouds* does not present any innovations that might differentiate it substantially from the staged *Clouds*, the confirmation or belying of this conclusion can reach us only from a discussion about the scene on stage of the contest of Right and Wrong; a scene that the Alexandrian grammarian of Argument VII records as an innovation of the second *Clouds*. In fact this scene, introduced and concluded peremptorily, so that it seems disjointed and almost suspended in its context[41], with the serious anomalies that this would cause in the recitative regime in use in the Athenian theatre[42], seems to support those critics who believe it to be superimposed on the first text, lacking furthermore "the final scenic and recitative refinement"[43] and hence the element of that διασκευή reported by the Alexandrian grammarians. Except that, the admission of the innovation of the scene of the two Reasonings consequently involves the admission of a radical revision of the primitive thematico-recitative structure of the comedy in order to make possible the insertion of that new scene. The novelty of this is believed to indicate that a change took place in

---

40. Cf. VAN DAELE, *Notice*, p. 156. Cleon had fallen at Amphipolis in 442, a year after the staging of the *Clouds*. In the epirrema of the *Parabasis* is recalled the election of Cleon to strategos, which took place in 424, one year before the *Clouds*; whereas in the new *Parabasis* 1. 550 Aristophanes mentions the death of Cleon. As far as Hyperbolus is concerned, the poet's attack is completely unexpected, after the charge addressed at his adversaries of always taking offence "with that wretched fellow and his mother", *Clouds*, 1. 552.
41. We will come back to this point shortly.
42. Cf. RUSSO, op. cit., p. 149 ff. and what will be said later about it.
43. RUSSO, cit., p. 165.

Aristophanes' view of Socrates following the change which occurred, between the two drafts of the *Clouds*, in the direction of Socratic thought[44].

Let us leave aside for the moment whether, in 419-18 B.C., the latest period in which the *Clouds* would have been rewritten, Socrates had become a different man from the one he was in 424-23 B.C.[45] so as to necessitate a radical transformation in the recited comedy. We will see, instead, whether our text gives grounds for believing that Aristophanes, despite his express refusal to modify that most brilliant of his comedies, had then in fact introduced to the recited *Clouds* so radical an innovation as the scene of the Reasonings.

It has often been observed that everywhere in the comedy where one speaks of the nature of the λόγος learnt at the school of Socrates are used the adjectives κρείττων and ἥττων, whereas for the contest of the Reasonings the metaphorical characters are called Δίκαιος and Ἄδικος.

The use of the latter terms, differing from those previously employed and replacing them[46], would, it has been argued, con-

---

44. Which, as has been said, is the thesis held by CHIAPPELLI, *Il naturalismo di Socrate*, cit., p. 291 ff. and *Nuove Ricerche*, cit., p. 371 ff.

45. Moved by the objections of ZELLER, CHIAPPELLI, *Nuove Ricerche*, cit., p. 378 is led to admit that "nulla ci costringe ad escludere che egli (Socrate) quand'Aristofane nel 423 lo definisce un vano speculatore, non si fosse già messo in un'altra via". The discussion at this point is taken up again by A.E. TAYLOR, *The Phrontisterion*, in *Varia Socratica*, Oxford, 1911, p. 129 ff. We will return to this towards the end of this paper.

46. CHIAPPELLI, *Il Naturalismo*, cit., p. 292, n. 2, believes that κρείττων and ἥττων λόγος had in the first *Clouds*, where Socrates is caricatured as a metereo-sophist, "un valore puramente eristico", whereas δίκαιος and ἄδικος λόγος in the second *Clouds* "avevano certo un valore morale". ZELLER, ap. CHIAPPELLI, *Nuove ricerche*, cit., p. 374, who while not believing Socrates is represented differently in the two versions of the *Clouds*, does admit the novelty of the scene of the λόγοι, precisely because of the different names of the discourses. And so E. MAIER, *Socrate*, Ital, trans. Florence, 1943, I, p. 163, n. 1, believes that in the place of the contest of the Discourses in the first *Clouds* there must have been a scene corresponding to Plato's Τὸν ἥττω λόγον κρείττω ποιῶν *Apol.*, 18b. J. BURNET, *Plato's Apology of Socrates*, Oxford, ed. 1957, comment on 18b8, p. 77 writes that "*κρείττων and ἥττων λόγος were personalized as the δίκαιος and the ἄδικος*". Similarly M. UNTERSTEINER, *Sofisti. Testimonianze e frammenti*, I, Firenze, 1962², p. 113, n. 2 and *I Sofisti*,

firm that the scene of the Reasonings was an innovation compared with the staged *Clouds*. Is this true? I would say not. And I would argue this for the simple reason that the speech that Strepsiades asks his son to learn at Socrates' school is precisely τὸν ἄδικον [...] λόγον (1.116) and he himself, when he is introduced to the φροντιστήριον, asks Socrates to teach him τόν ἀδικώτατον λόγον (1.657), since it is to learn this speech and nothing else, he says, that he came to his school[47]. And when,

Torino, 1948, p. 95. CANTARELLA, cit., note to 1. 889 ff. See now, DOVER, cit., *Introd.*, p. LVII.

47. It is wise to point out here that the discourse that Strepsiades wishes to learn at the school of Socrates is that which, running counter to laws and justice, 11. 888, 1040, 1400, is particularly useful for him in the judicial debate, 1. 434, in which he is preparing to engage. Now, in defining the λόγος learnt at the school of Socrates as an eminently judicial and forensic λόγος, Aristophanes certainly targeted his criticism far more at Protagoras than at Socrates. And this seems to me obvious given that for Aristophanes the learning of this discourse is possible only in the broader context of a certain παιδεία which, moving from a relativistic interpretation of the μέτρον ἄνθρωπος, supports against the univocality of the δίκη, a plurality of δίκαι that eristics realizes in turn as convenient and, in general, against the normativeness of the νόμος supports the relativity of the φύσις; such that Pheidippides, instructed by Socrates, will be able to believe himself to be the legislator: *"N'était-il pas un homme, celui qui le premier établit cette loi, un homme comme toi et moi, et n'est-ce pas par la parole qu'il persuadait les anciens? Serait-il donc moins permis à moi d'établir également pour l'avenir une loi nouvelle d'après laquelle les fils pourront battre les pères à leur tour?"*, 11. 1421-1424, trans. VAN DAELE. Here, obviously, Aristophanes presents the Protagorean teaching in a malevolently false light. Since if it is true that Protagoras made eloquence progress especially in its forensic aspect, T. GOMPERZ, *Griechische Denker. Eine Gesch. der antiken Philos.* It. ed. *Pensatori greci*, Florence 1950³, II, p. 302, it is equally true, as is noted by MAIER, *Sokrates. Sein Werk u. seine geschichtliche Stellung.* It.ed. *Socrate*, op. cit., I. pp. 238-239 "che le norme morali e giuridiche venivano da Protagora considerate non come creazione arbitraria di convenzione umana, ma come patrimonio originario della natura umana e come legislazione oggettiva, cui gli individui umani sono legati. Ed è altrettanto certo che per Protagora le vedute morali e giuridiche dominanti derivavano in complesso dall'accennata originaria coscienza etico-giuridica dell'uomo".

But I am so bold as to believe that the youthful comedy writer, in presenting Protagorean teaching, had clearly seen (and with him certainly some Athenian cultural circles) to what forms of moral, civil and religious degeneration Protagorean antilogic could lead. Therefore, what Aristophanes represents in the *Clouds* is not so much Protagoras' teaching as its possible exasperation and

unable himself to learn, he brings Pheidippides to the phrontisterion, he again recommends that his son learn τόν ἄδικον λόγον (1.885), the mode of speech that can twist justice πάντα τὰ δίκαια (1.888).

To this last injunction of Strepsiades Socrates replies that the young man will be taught by the two reasonings in person (1.886) and these could not of course be ἥττων and κρεῖττον λόγος but rather ἄδικος λόγος, which is exactly what Pheidippides was to learn, and, on the contrary, δίκαιος λόγος compared with which the other, which can twist justice, is called ἄδικος

Furthermore, on making a closer examination of those places in the comedy where, as has been said, mention is made of the nature of the -λόγος learnt at the school of Socrates, we will notice that the terms κρείττων and ἥττων, in their particular Aristophanic meaning, rather than true types of discourse personified in Δίκαιος and Ἄδικος λόγος, are a special eristic skill of the λόγος personnage to confound and surpass with verbal artifice and lack of moral scruple any other reasoning even though it might be logically and morally better.

The best proof of what has been said is given by the scene of the contest of Right and Wrong. Here, on line 893, Δίκαιος iden-

degeneration which in fact came about in those later Sophists who became the object of severe censure by Plato in the *Euthydemus* and in the *Sophist* and by Aristotle in the *Sophistici Elenchi*. And "questi sofisti, che si definiscono dalla eristica, sono," notes UNTERSTEINER, *Sofisti*, I, cit., p. XXII, "la conseguenza estrema della dialettica dialogica di Socrate". This means that at a given moment, as the *Symposium* could show, Plato and Aristophanes became travelling-companions. But ever since 423 Aristophanes had attacked Socrates' responsibility in the moral and cultural corruption caused by Sophistry; while, for his part, Plato distinguishes from, and clearly contrasts Socrates with the Sophists. It is probable that Aristophanes has exaggerated in the charge levelled at Socrates and that Plato, in turn, has exaggerated in the defence of his master by freeing him from any spiritual link with the Sophists; it is certain, in any case, that Socrates' points of contact with the Sophists are far more numerous and deep-rooted than Socratic historiography has hitherto recognized. It is precisely the caricature which Aristophanes makes of both parties, which urges to deepen the points of contact or, better, of the spiritual and cultural affinities between Socrates and the Sophists of his day. And we could add that Aristophanes also urges us to look closer into the connection, deep and indissoluble, existing between Greek sophistry and Ionian naturalism. This is an argument that will and should be taken up again sooner or later.

tifies Ἄδικος λόγος with ἥττων λόγος, and the latter, in reply, (11.894-95), jeers at the claim of Δίκαιος λόγος to be the strongest, which is tantamount to saying the jeers at the claim of Δίκαιος λόγος to be able to prevail by making use of ἥττων λόγος. Shortly afterwards, instead, Ἄδικος λόγος will say he is able to prevail over his adversary with new little words and concepts (11.942-43), and hence to use weak discourse τοὺς ἥττονας λόγους (1.1042) to contradict laws and justice τοῖσιν νόμοις καὶ τῇ δίκη (1.1040). Pheidippides, too, once he had learnt the lesson at the school of Socrates, in order to demonstrate to his father that it is just that he should beat him, asks him if he wants him to use τὸν κρείττον᾽ ἢ τὸν ἥττονα (1.1337) and again using weak reasoning (11.1444-45) states he is ready to prove that it is acceptable to beat one's own mother (1.1446).

In other words, Aristophanes has shifted the predominantly gnoseological meaning of the famous Protagorean proposition

τὸ τὸν ἥττω λόγον κρείττω ποιεῖν[48]

into the realm of morality, portraying the two λόγοι in opposition on the pretext that each of them represents the true δίκη

This gives rise to the attributes of the λόγοι-characters δίκαιος and ἄδικος which describe their nature and role[49], but which would also take for granted each's part in the contest if they did not appeal to a particular eristic ability capable of swaying every judgement (1.888; 1040 etc) and, hence, of causing the failure of Δίκαιος λόγος and the latter's desertion into the rival camp (1.1104).

This meaning of the terms κρείττων and ἥττων, then, conveys a malicious interpretation of the above-mentioned Protagorean quotation τὸ τὸν ἥττω λόγον κρείττω ποιεῖν from which

48. ARIST., *Rhet.* B 24 1402 a 7 in *Sofisti*, edit. UNTERSTEINER, I., *cit.*, p. 50. On the gnoseological significance of the Protagorean proposition, see UNTERSTEINER, *I Sofisti*, cit., p. 66 ff. esp. p. 69 and p. 95.

49. In the opening remarks of the contest Δίκαιος and Ἄδικος are defined by the one saying what is right, 1. 900, and the other denying that justice exists, 11. 905-902. But the denial of Ἄδικος is to be taken relatively, since it denies that there exists justice in what his adversary says or rather in his being able, with the discourses, to show at will that there is no justice.

Aristophanes satire stems and on which, after all, the entire comedy is based. And this is because, as we have already said, Aristophanes insinuates into the gnoseological nature that Protagoras credits to these terms, an eristico-moral meaning that the contest of the Reasoning-characters was to reveal as destructive of the morals of their forefathers and ancient education. Thus Aristophanes did indeed date back to Protagoras and, generally, to rhetorico-sophist education the responsibility for the corruption of youth, but at the same time he made more direct and precise the attack on Socrates, lord of the λόγος (1.244) and hence the very corruptor of youth (11.928; 1321 ff.) and despiser of the traditional gods (11.367; 381 ff.).

It is not inappropriate in this context to remember that it is precisely the moral and religious aspect of Socratic dialogue that the judicial charge of Anytus, Meletus and Lycon was intended to attack[50] and that Plato, to defend the memory of the unforget-

50. The motives for the charge and the legality of the sentence have been the object of a stark contrast among scholars of Socrates. To the radical thesis of P. FORSCHHAMMER, *Die Athener und Sokrates. Die Gesetzlichen und der Revolutionär*, Berlin, 1837, already maintained a century earlier by G.F. DRESIG, *De Socrate iuste damnato*, Lipsia, 1738 and taken up again by G. SOREL, *Le procès de Socrate*, Paris, 1889 and by H. RÖCH, *Der unverfälschte Sokrates*, cit., who embraces the view of FORSCHHAMMER, *cit.*, p. 74: "Never was a more legal sentence pronounced before a more legal court than that by which Socrates was first found guilty of disbelief in the gods of the state and of corrupting youth and was then condemned to death", in RÖCH, *cit.*, p. 129, are resolutely opposed R. PÖHLMANN, *Sokrates und sein Wolk*, München und Leipzig, 1899 and P. MARTINETTI, *Socrate*, in *Ragione e Fede*, Torino, 1942, p. 443, in whose view the judges sentenced Socrates "rappresentavano un fascio di volgari interessi politici", and by K. HILDEBRANT, *Platone*, Ital. ed., Torino, 1947, p. 81, in whose view whoever approves the judgement of the Eliasts "non ha nessun sentimento di giustizia". Between these two opposing theses lies that with which HEGEL, *Lezioni sulla storia della filosofia*, II, Ital. trans., Firenze, 1923, p. 82 ff., ZELLER, *Die Philosophie der Griechen in ihrer geschichtlichen Entwicklung*, II, I, English trans. *Socrates and the Socratic schools*, New York, 1962, p. 221 ff. and MAIER, *Socrate*, cit., II, p. 174 ff., brings the charge and sentence into the realm of the positive law of the Athens of 399 recognising the good faith of the judges and the legality of the sentence on religious, moral and political grounds. The precise grounds for the charge and the legality of the sentence as criteria for a Socratic interpretation have been the object of study in the essay: *Socrate. Dal mito alla storia*, see above, and in the *De Socrate iuste damnato. The rise of the Socratic problem in the eigtheenth century*, Gieben, Amsterdam 1981. It. ed. Roma 1981.

table master from that sentence of the Eliasts which gave grounds for seeing him as an impious man and a corruptor, and the young men who had kept company with him as corrupt men no different from Pheidippides in the *Clouds* and specifically from Critias and Alcibiades, went to great lengths to distinguish Socrates as clearly as possible from the Sophists[51], likewise conferring on the term σοφιστής[52], in contrast to Socratic ignorance[53], that pejorative meaning that it commonly has even now[54].

We would not say that Δίκαιος λόγος and Ἄδικος λόγος personify and replace in our *Clouds* the κρείττων λόγος and ἥττων λόγος of the staged comedy. We believe, however, that the

51. Not only by later Sophists, UNTERSTEINER, *Sofisti, Testimonianze e frammenti*, cit., I, p. XXII, but also by the Sophists who were contemporaries of Socrates, with the *Protagoras* and the *Gorgias*, in the first of which Plato exalts the educational system of Socrates compared with that of the Sophists, and in the second the contrast between Sophistry and Socratism is stressed in the contrast between rhetoric and philosophy. And it is certainly no mere coincidence that in the *Gorgias*, which replies to the attack of Policrates, Chaerephon, who Aristophanes had defined as the champion of the disciples of Socrates including him in the same charge, Chaerephon, we said, was opposed to Polus and Callicles in sharing and maintaining with Socrates a high ideal of ethical life in the face of which Callicles, the disciple of the Sophist Gorgias, ends by asking whether all the values in which he believes do not come out of it subverted, *Gorgias*, 481c. Just as it is certainly no coincidence that Critias and Alcibiades are aligned with Socrates precisely in the *Protagoras*, in the dialogue that deals with the teachability of political virtue.

52. On the word σοφιστής, its origin, meaning and historical evolution, see the note of UNTERSTEINER, in *Sofisti*, cit., I. p. XVI-XXIII and the relevant evidence.

53. On Socrates' profession of ignorance, both as a methodological position for every fruitful dialogue and in contrast to sophist polymathia, see Plato, *Apology* 20e, 21b-d, 23b, 33a, 41b-d-e; *Charmides* 165b-c; *Euthyphro*, 5b; *Protagoras*, 348e, 361c; *Gorgias*, 506a; *Symposium*, 117d, 216d; *Alcibiades* I, 109e; *Meno*, 70e, 80a-c-d, 83b, 90b; *Theaetetus*, 149a, 150c-d, 187d; *Republic*, 337b, 337e, 450e, 473e, 491e. For the position of Socrates towards the Sophists one should turn to Socrates' speech in the *Symposium*, in which, against any knowledge as gratifying possession, the true σοφία is defined as love and search for the beloved object, anxiety and tension towards what one misses.

54. Cf. ARISTID., 46 (II 407 DIND.) in *Sofisti*, I, ed. UNTERSTEINER, 79, p. 5: "A me pare che Platone usi sempre in senso deteriore la parola sofista e che sia colui che, in particolar modo, si sia levato contro questo nome".

Reasoning-characters, exponents of two different types of education and, afterall, of two different types of moral behaviour, make use of the eristic skill of κρείττων λόγος and ἥττων λόγος in defence of the type of education that each represents and to which each wants to attract the young Pheidippides.

And since frequent reference is made to δίκαιος and ἄδικος λόγος all in places preceding the contest scene[55], and, as we have seen, firstly Strepsiades and then the resigned Pheidippides ask of Socrates nothing other than to teach them the ἄδικον λόγον and, Socrates promises them nothing other, the argument that the terms δρείττων and ἥττων λόγος were replaced by Δίκαιος and Ἄδικος λόγος invoked in support of the innovation of the contest scene absent from the staged *Clouds* no longer stands.

5. — Still on the subject of the innovation of the scene of the contest between the Discourses, it has been observed that the staging of the debate of the two Reasonings would demand the simultaneous presence on stage of not three, nor even four, but five actors. And so, simultaneously on stage would be:
1) Right 2) Wrong 3) Strepsiades, silent during the contest, with the four lines 1107-1110 4) Socrates, silent during the contest with the three lines 1105-1106 and 1111 5) Pheidippides, also silent, with line 1112[56]. This recitative pattern of the second *Clouds*, adjustable to the usual Aristophanean practice of three actors[57] and, what is more, quite costly[58], would prove, it is said, that our *Clouds* is not recitable[59] and hence that the debate of the Reasonings was an imperfect innovation of the second *Clouds*, absent from the staged version[60].

---

55. In addition to the places cited, remember the lines 114-116 and 183-185 in which ἄδικος λόγος is always present alongside ἥττων λόγος and even identified with this.

56. Similarly RUSSO, *cit.*, p. 150 and n. 2.

57. RUSSO, *cit.*, p. 149 ff. In contrast ERBSE, *cit.*, p. 398 does not rule out the possibility of 5 actors being on the stage simultaneously. But in my view the well-founded reasons adopted by Russo seem incontestable.

58. RUSSO, *cit.*, p. 152. In the view of ERBSE, *cit.*, p. 397, however, the rule of the three actors is aesthetic and not economic in character and yet such that it would not have made a comedy impossible or difficult to stage.

59. RUSSO, *cit.*, p. 155 and 373.

60. RUSSO, *cit.*, p. 373.

But is it really true that for the Agon our text would require "the clamorous usage"[61] of a fourth and fifth actor and the simultaneous wastage of at least two principal actors[62]? In other words, are Socrates and Strepsiades really present on stage during the contest of the Discourses?

Let us say from the outset that the contest scene is strictly contained in lines 889-1104[63]. In the staged *Clouds*, this scene was introduced and concluded by two choral sections between 888-889 and 1104-1105[64], missing from our text. These two missing choruses, in the staged *Clouds*, had amongst other things the following function: the first, to relieve the two protagonist actors, Socrates and Strepsiades, for the following contest scene in which they reappeared in the masks of the two Reasonings, and the second, at the end of the contest, allowed the same actors to put their former masks back on for the brief episodic scene of 1105-1115.

In the staged *Clouds*, the two choral interludes of 888-889 and 1104-1105 therefore guaranteed full respect for the recitative practice of the three actors, whereas in our text the absence of the two choruses gives neither the coherent development, inside the Thinking-shop, of the action beginning at 886, nor relief to the protagonist actors for the next scene of the contest, nor, lastly, the re-employing of these actors for the scene of 11.1105-1115.

61. RUSSO, *cit.*, p. 151.

62. RUSSO, *cit.*, p. 151.

63. That the remark of 1. 1105 belongs to Socrates and not to Wrong, apart from any other internal reason, is the common lesson of the manuscripts, adopted by BRUNCK, DINDORF, TEUFFEL, VAN LEEUWEN, ROGERS, a.l. whereas STARKIE, COULON, CANTARELLA and DOVER, a.l. attribute it to Wrong.

64. As regards the first chorus cf. BRUNCK, BERGK, TEUFFEL, VAN LEEUWEN, COULON, CANTARELLA, DOVER, *aa.ll.* and again DOVER ed. cit., *Introd.*, pp. LXXIX and XCIII.

No mention is made in the manuscripts of the second Chorus. However that in the staged *Clouds*, from 1. 1104 onwards there was the recitation of a choral passage seems beyond doubt to BERGK, *Praefatio ad Nubes*, ed. cit., p. XX f. 1. 1105: "Ante hunc versum haud dubie addendum est χοροῦ"; to VAN LEEUWEN, a.l. and to COULON, a.l. We will give the reasons for this later on.

For DOVER, however, a.l. "There are [...] no formal grounds for positing a lost choral song between 1104 and 1105". This is because DOVER attributes not to Socrates but to Wrong the quip on 1. 1105.

This does not, however, mean that the characters on stage during the course of the contest are, in our text, five rather than three in number. Socrates, at 1.887 has left the stage: and with him Pheidippides, whom Socrates leads into the Phrontisterion to entrust him, as he had said, 1.886, to the two Discourses. Strepsiades, for his part, after the stern exhortation shouted at Socrates as he leaves with his son, that the latter should learn to contradict everything that is right (1.888), has nothing more to do on stage, since the lesson will take place inside Socrates' school.

To believe, like the grammarian of Argument I, that Socrates is calling the two Reasonings out for Pheidippides[66] denotes a

65. VAN LEEUWEN, a.l.: ἐγὼ δ'ἄπειμι, ERBSE, cit., p. 398, as for GELZER, cit., p. 66, Socrates would not leave the stage, but would stand aside during the contest of the discourses. RUSSO rightly observes: «῎Απειμι 'I go' metrically possible, would not have been so precise: it would have simply indicated a moving away from centre-stage or the intention to leave it or even a final departure, but not the complete future absence to coincide with the lesson of the special masters of Pheidippides", cit., p. 156. So why does RUSSO write, cit., p. 151, that "Socrate è senza dubbio presente" during the contest of the Discourses?
According to the reading of a manuscript, ap. COULON, a.l. the remark ἐγὼ δ'ἀπέσομαι belongs to Strepsiades and not to Socrates, and DINDORF follows this reading, the accuracy of which seems to be confirmed by the γοῦν or νῦν of the following verse common to the manuscript tradition, COULON, a.l. Reading line 887 ΣΤ. 'Εγὼ δ'ἀπέσομαι. Τοῦτό γοῦν > νῦν < μέμνησ',ὅπως, the removal of Strepsiades from the stage would turn out to be more explicit and more obvious would be the connection between the exit of Strepsiades and that of Socrates who returns to entrust Pheidippides to the two Reasonings. Anyway, it is comforting that from at least one manuscript it appears clearly that from line 888 the stage is cleared of the characters Socrates, Strepsiades and Pheidippides for the planned recitation of the choral passage and hence for the reuse of the first two in the roles of the two Reasonings.
66. So RUSSO, cit., p. 156, for whom "apparentemente ben interpretava il grammatico dell'Argomento I, 19 col dire che Socrate fa uscir fuori per Fidippide i due Ragionamenti". For RUSSO, ibid., in fact, line 886 foretold the appearance on stage of the two Reasonings as masters of the character present on stage: "Fidippide resta qui, qui verranno i due Ragionamenti" p. 157.
That the grammarian of Argument I should say that Socrates presents to Pheidippides on the stage τὸν ἄδικον καὶ τὸν δίκαιον λόγον in my view gives incontrovertible proof of the fact that the Alexandrian had before him our text of the Clouds and none other; meaning a text, like ours without the necessary choral passage between 1. 888-889, hence his erroneous inference.

failure to bear in mind two circumstances, namely:

1) that Aristophanes has clearly signalled the mysterical nature of the Socratic school[67] and the esoteric nature of the teaching imparted therein[68]. The learning of the ἄδικος λόγος, that is of the speech which is able to contradict all that is right, cannot, and indeed not come about outside, but inside the Phrontisterion, insofar as it was a secret discipline of the school and the entirely personal teaching of Socrates (1.112 ff.).

The fact is that nothing about this teaching is revealed on stage and Strepsiades will later go to show Pheidippides at the Phrontisterion asking Socrates if his son has now learnt that reasoning (11.1148-1149)[69];

2) that the contest of the Reasonings has nothing to do with the true teaching of the ἄδικος λόγος. The dispute hinges, rather, on which of the two ἄδικος λόγος will be charged with instructing Pheidippides, and the two Discourses come out into the open for each to expound the nature and merits of his own education and not the particular object of that teaching for which Socrates needs them on behalf of Pheidippides (1.886).

From these remarks it follows:

a) that Socrates does not ask the two Reasonings to come out for Pheidippides, but leads Pheidippides with him into the Thinking-shop where the two Reasonings are (1.112 ff.), and, therefore, the remark that sends Socrates away simultaneously sends away Pheidippides who is following Socrates[70]. Finally, Strepsiades, after having shouted behind Socrates the utmost recommendation (11.887-888), leaves the stage, on which his presence would now be completely unnatural, both because of the following recitation of the choral section, and because of the esoteric nature of Socratic teaching which does not make provision for the two Reasonings to rush on to the stage.

b) that when the two Reasonings come out on to the stage,

---

67. On this subject remember the scene of Strepsiades' initiation, 1. 254 ff., and the excellent observations of GELZER, *cit.*, p. 67 ff.

68. Cf. *Clouds*, 1. 140, 143 and *passim*.

69. Cf. RUSSO, *cit.*, p. 150.

70. Dissimilarly RUSSO, *cit.*, p. 157, interprets 11. 886-87: "Fidippide resta qui, qui verranno i due Ragionamenti, io sarò via''.

dragging Pheidippides behind them[71], they show that, inside the φροντιστήριον, they have already embarked upon a disagreement over who of the two should teach the young man Socrates had put in their charge[72]. This is a disagreement which naturally could not have started unless Socrates had led the resigned Pheidippides into the Phrontisterion and unless, as has been said, he had already handed him over to the two Reasonings.

In our text, therefore, from line 888 onwards up to line 1104, that is for the whole duration of the contest, Socrates and Strepsiades are off stage; appearing in their stead are Right and Wrong, dragging behind them Pheidippides for whose education they dispute the privilege.

There are therefore three actors on stage from 1.816 to 1.889: Socrates, Strepsiades, Pheidippides; three actors on stage from 1.889 to 1.1104: Right, Wrong, Pheidippides.

The only trouble is that between the simultaneous withdrawal of Socrates and Pheidippides, the exit of Strepsiades and the entrance immediately following of the two Reasonings, our text would need a recitative interlude to allow the exited characters to make their way into the action as announced in line 886, Αὐτὸς μαθήσεται παρ' αὐτοῖν τοῖν λόγοιν, and to allow the two Reasonings to begin that off-stage disagreement over which of them should educate the young man; the disagreement which will then continue outside, before the audience. The very development of the plot requires such an interlude which theatrical technique would opportunely have exploited by enabling the two protagonist actors to reappear in the sketch in the guise of Right and Wrong. This interlude, as has been said, lacking the choral passage between lines 888-889, does not appear in our text and so, even though Socrates and Strepsiades are not on stage, the recitation of the comedy in the text we are reading would have required the use of a fourth and fifth non-protagonist actor for the role of the two Reasonings.

But can we therefore say that Aristophanes had deliberately given up his plan to dispense with two of the three ordinary actors

71. For the presence of Pheidippides during the contest of the Discourses, *Clouds*, see 930 ff., 990, 1043, 1071.
72. Similarly RUSSO, *cit.*, p. 156.

for the full roles of the new characters and, therefore, that our text was no longer valid for the theatre[73]?

This seems highly unlikely to me, because, by removing Socrates and Strepsiades from the stage, Aristophanes has created the technical condition for the same actors to be used again, wearing different masks, in the roles of the two Reasonings. This is a condition the poet could opportunely have exploited by introducing the first of the two now missing choruses.

Except that, having for some reasons abandoned the plan to bring his favourite comedy back to the theatre, Aristophanes has not rewritten the choral passages which were removed from the staged comedy, and which he certainly proposed to draft at the last moment, to adapt them to the second production of his comedy.

One confirmation, both of the removal of the Chorus from the recited text and of a new draft, seems to me to be given by the intervention of the Chorus, in the course of the contest, at 1.934 ff. and, especially, at 1.952 ff., where those two Νῦν of 1.952 and 1.954, serve to indicate the imminent happening of something previously announced, as it certainly was in the recited comedy, and, as far as our text is concerned, of course, to announce, because that ἀγὼν μέγιστος (1.956), about which Right taught the young men of former times and which Wrong teaches the young of today (1.935 ff.), presupposes an adequate preparation and introduction to which the Chorus with its iteration of the Νῦν clearly refers. And the removal of the Chorus from the staged text and the related reservation of a new draft is natural, since Aristophanes had something to say to the public of the Dionysia; and the draft of the choral passage gave him the very opportunity to stress, with arguments different from those used for the first production of 423, the nature of the contest, to which the Chorus refers in 1.934 ff. and 1.952 ff., and its moral import, stressed in 1.1024 ff., and therefore the innovation of those two Discourse-characters introduced for the first time on to the stage of the theatre of Dionysus. Moreover, in the new Parabasis, expressly reworked with a view to a second production of the Comedy, Aristophanes would have liked to point out to the audience the

73. Cf. RUSSO, *cit.*, p. 156 and p. 373.

originality and merits of his comedy despite its lack of success in 423. And that Aristophanes intended to entrust to the Chorus the task of emphasizing the novelty of the contest scene, so central and decisive in the whole game of thoughts set in operation in the comedy, exemplified in the Parabasis and particularly in the hints offered by the frequent interventions of the Chorus in the course of the contest, seems to us anything but an easy supposition.

The draft of the first of the two choral passages would therefore have allowed to protagonist actors Socrates and Strepsiades, who had already been dispensed with by lines 886-889, to reappear in the masks of the two Reasonings in the scene following the contest.

Similar reasons apply, of course, for the missing choral passage at the end of the scene of the Discourses[74]. A passage which would obviously have concluded by commenting on the desertion into the Socratic camp (1.1104) of Wrong. And, in fact the Chorus, on lines 1024-1031, manifests an active participation in the reasons invoked by Right in favour of ancient education. But when the contest finishes with the defeat of Right, the immediate introduction of Socrates on to the stage with that brusque Τί δῆτα of 1.1105[75] warns of the absence of any comment on the clamorous desertion, especially after that sorrowful invocation of the honest education of the fathers (1.1024 ff.) which remained in our text without follow up, the few metres of line 1114: "you will see that you will regret it", being insufficient to comment on it. For it was without doubt to the missing choral passage at the end of the contest that Aristophanes had entrusted the expressions of his lament for that honest education that formed the generation of Marathon, now discredited and destroyed by the Sophists in general and Socrates in particular. And it was also here, certainly, that Aristophanes would have taken a stand against sophist education and have declared his final judgement on Socrates, the living symbol of that education.

---

74. That the manuscripts makes no mention, as for the choral passage of 888-889, of a χοροῦ between 1104-1105, does not seem to me sufficient grounds for saying that Aristophanes had "not even thought of" a chorus between 1104 and 1105, as maintained by RUSSO, cit., p. 158. Cf. VAN LEEUWEN, a.l.

75. Cf. ERBSE, cit., pp. 399-400 and RUSSO, cit., p. 159.

Here too the draft of the choral passage between lines 1104-1105 would have freed the two actors who appeared in the guise of Right and Wrong restoring to them their roles of Socrates and Strepsiades for the short episodic scene of 1.1105-1114. Since it is doubtless Socrates, and not Wrong, who is the character of line 1105 who asks Strepsiades whether he whishes him to teach his son to speak ἢ διδάσκω σοι λέγειν[76], for of the art of fine speaking εὖ λέγειν Socrates in fact is master and not ἄδικος λόγος, which, as a way of speaking specially intended to hold sway in judicial debate, is only part and means of that art. And, moreover, Socrates' question ἢ διδάσκω σοι λέγειν of line 1106 is connected and consequential to Strepsiades' initial question to Socrates: Βουλόμενος μαθεῖν λέγειν, I want to learn to speak, 1.239. For Strepsiades εὖ λέγειν was resolved precisely and only in learning that ἄδικος λόγος which would make him escape from the hands of his creditors (1.434, 1.739). And Strepsiades had in fact handed Pheidippides over to Socrates (1.867) in order that he should learn that discourse capable of contradicting every judgement (1.882-4); and finally to Socrates and not to the ἄδικος λόγος will he later put the question of whether Pheidippides, whom Socrates himself had introduced into the school, has learnt that famous reasoning τὸν λόγον ἐκεῖνον (1.1149).

And so let us conclude by summarizing what we have said so far:

1) Socrates, Pheidippides and Strepsiades have left the stage, the first two with the remark of 1.887, the third with the lines 887-888.

2) The contest of the Discourses, 11.889-1104, uses on stage three characters and not five, namely: Right, Wrong, Pheidippides.

3) Socrates, Pheidippides and Strepsiades return on stage from line 1105 up to line 1114.

4) The draft of the missing choral passage at 1.889 would technically have allowed the protagonist actors Socrates and

---

76. We have already said that the manuscripts attribute to Socrates this remark.

Strepsiades to reappear in the masks of Right and Wrong in the contest scene.
5) The draft of the missing choral passage at 1.1104 would technically have allowed Right and Wrong to put on the first masks again for the brief episodic scene of 11.1105-1114.

From 1.814 to 1.889 there are then three actors; three from 1.889 to 1.1114; the recitative practice of the actors would thus have been respected with the draft of the two missing choral passages and the text, completed with the two choruses, would have again been fully valid for the theatre.

If, consequently, the above considerations allow us to enclude that the contest of the Discourses constitutes an imperfect innovation of our *Clouds* not present in the staged *Clouds*[77], the same considerations give us grounds for concluding that the 45 euplidei

77. RUSSO, *cit.*, p. 373. According to RUSSO, *cit.*, p. 161 ff., in place of the scene of the Discourses, in the staged *Clouds* there must have been a similar scene between Pheidippides right — Chaerephon wrong, p. 168; whereas Socrates would have paid more attention, as hypothesised already over a century ago KOECHLY, ap. CHIAPPELLI, *Le prime Nubi*, cit., p. 294, to Strepsiades than to Pheidippides. In the second *Clouds*, however, the new duo of the discourse-characters would have sacrificed Chaerephon, p. 164, thus causing "una revisione artistica della materia delle *Nuvole prime*", p. 165. That Chaerephon acts in the first *Clouds* as a character of importance is motivated by RUSSO, *cit.*, p. 161, by his "vitale presenza prescenica" which did not subsequently materialize in his expected presence with the audience. But I wonder if it is really necessary to hypothesise that Chaerephon played an active part in the staged version and hence that it was completely transformed to exclude him from the second *Clouds*, when the central scene of the contest in our *Clouds*, in which all the previous episodic scenes are consistently resolved, is specifically prepared by the frequent references to the pair of the Reasonings and their qualities and virtues and put before the spectators' fantasy, from the first remarks onwards, as real characters having their own precise and finished individuality and a particular agonistic ability of expert wrestlers (1. 958). Remarks which to RUSSO, *cit.*, pp. 163-64, seem few. And in fact RUSSO will recall only a few, whereas in our text those references are very much more frequent. Before the contest in fact, in addition to 1. 112, the pair is recalled at 11. 244 and 883 and after the contest at 1. 1337; whereas for Wrong Reasoning one should recall the quotations of 11. 116, 657 and 885 before the contest and 1229, 1444 and 1451 after the contest. Furthermore RUSSO himself first says that those quotations are few in number and then he quotes a greater number of them than those concerning Chaerephon.

of the Parabasis (1.518-562) and the dropping of the two choral passages which, as already in 423, in the planned but not executed second production of the comedy, should have introduced and concluded the contest scene, are the only variations of our *Clouds* compared with the so-called first *Clouds*[78].

And as there is no change in the comedy known to us compared with the one produced on stage, so there is no change in Aristophanes' judgement on Socrates: the Socratic image is the same both in the staged text and in the one known to us and, consequently, the comedy of Aristophanes to which Plato refers, with or without the new Parabasis, with or without the two now-missing choral passages, was substantially the same as the one we now read.

II

1. — The results of our research into the text of the *Clouds* are confirmed in a series of Platonic remarks about Socrates' relations with Alcibiades and the first historically reliable Socratics, sufficient in themselves to set aside once and for all not only the thesis now under discussion, according to which the dual writing of the *Clouds* would evidence the change in Socratic activity from the science of nature to moral investigation[79]; but also the no less

---

78. Differently RUSSO, *cit.*, p. 170, writes: "di certo Aristofane non avrà preteso di rimettere in gara, con tutta la concorrenza che c'era di poeti comici di valore, le *Nuvole* del 423 con la sola novità dei quarantacinque euplidei, come vorrebbero i moderni credenti nella verginità testuale delle *Nuvole* seconde". And why "Aristofane non avrà preteso" if, in the new *Parabasis*, this is precisely what he said he wanted to do? Instead RUSSO may be completely right when he writes, p. 169:. "Forse fu il piano di rimettere in gara una commedia sconfitta senza una radicale e generale trasformazione a tagliare alle *Nuvole* seconde la via del teatro". We should note, however, that, if, as RUSSO believes, *cit.*, p. 164, Aristophanes had added to the second *Clouds* the scene of the contest of the Discourses and had, therefore, changed the distribution of parts of the characters, making "muto" that Chaerephon who "forse aveva chiacchierato troppo nelle *Nuvole* prime", p. 162, the comedy would have received anything but "una radicale e generale trasformazione".

79. Which is, as has been said, the thesis posited by CHIAPPELLI, in *Le*

114

ancient one, which has very frequently been taken up in recent, even very recent, times, according to which the *Clouds* reflected a period of Socratic activity both known to Aristophanes and unknown to Plato and Xenophon[80]. On the subject of Alcibiades Plato informs us that Socrates' friendship with the restless pupil of Pericles dated back to some years before the beginning of the Archidamic war[81]. In the *Ban-*

Prime Nubi, cit., p. 291 ff., esp. 293-94, and partially corrected in *Nuove Ricerche*, cit., p. 378 where CHIAPPELLI concedes to Zeller that the naturalistic phase could have ended before the second writing of the *Clouds*.

80. This is a thesis adumbrated, over a century ago now, by G.C. TYCHSEN, *Über d. Prozess d. Sokrates*, Göttingen 1786; taken up and adopted by F.A. WOLF, *Aristophanes Wolken erklärt*, Berlin, 1811 and then by A. BOECKH, *De Socratis rerum physicarum studio*, Berolino, 1838; reprinted in *Kleine Schriften*, IV, Berlin, 1874, pp. 430-436; then by CH. A BRANDIS, *Handbuch der Gesch. der griechisch-römischen Philos.*, Berlin, 1835-60, II, p. 34 ff.; *Die Entwicklung d. griech. Philos.*, I, Berlin, 1862, p. 236. E. ALBERTI, *Sokrates*, Göttingen, 1869; A. FOUILLEE, *La Philosophie de Socrate*, I. Paris, 1874, broadened and relaunched by CHIAPPELLI, opp. citt., then by G. ZUCCANTE, *Socrate. Fonti. Ambienti. Vita. Dottrina*, Milano, 1909 and by C. PASCAL, *Dioniso*, Catania, 1911 and made classic in Socratic historiography by J. BURNET, *Plato's Phaedo*, Oxford, 1911 ed. 1956, p. XXXIV ff.; *Greek Philosophy*, London, 1914, ed. 1953, p. 124 ff. *Early Greek Philosophy*, 1892, London, 1908, 2 ed. p. 192 ff.; 358; 415; *Plato's Euthyphro, Apology and Crito*, Oxford, 1924, ed. 1957 p. 91.; and by A.E. TAYLOR, *Varia Socratica*, Oxford, 1911, esp. pp. 129-177; *Socrates*, London, 1935, Ital. transl., Firenze, 1952, pp. 42 ff., to which subsequently mention has been made, with a greater or lesser degree of agreement, by E. DERENNE, *Les Procès d'impiété intentés aux philosophes à Athènes au Vme et au IVme siècle avant J.C.*, Liège-Paris, 1930, pp. 73-93; WINSPEAR-SILVERBERG, *Who was Socrates* - it. trans., *Realtà di Socrate*, 1939., Urbino, 1965, p. 78 ff.; 103-5; W. JAEGER, *Paideia, Die Formung des griech. Menschen*, Ital. ed., Firenze, II, 1954, p. 45 ff., greatly toned down, TOVAR, *Vida de Sócrates*, 1947, Madrid, 1953, p. 121 and finally R. MONDOLFO, *Sócrates*, Buenos Aires, 1955, p. 12 ff.; J. CHEVALIER, *Histoire de la Pensée*, I, Paris, 1955, p. 151 and J. HUMBERT, *Socrate et les petits socratiques*, Paris, 1967, pp. 29 ff, 79.

The volume announced by V. DE MAGALHÃES-VILHENA, *Aristophane et le Socrate historique*, does not appear to have been published. But from the same writer MAGALHÃES-VILHENA see the long note, *Socrate et la recherche scientifique*, in *Le Problème de Socrate*, Paris, 1952, p. 17 ff. and p. 446 from which I get the impression that the Portuguese writer holds a view very similar to that held by Burnet and Taylor, in the sense at least that he does not deny an early naturalistic phase in the activity of Socrates.

81. The writer is aware that the chronological data given by Plato are very

quet, in fact, Alcibiades himself dates his acquaintance with Socrates in the years immediately preceding the events of Potidaea[82].

The scene narrated by the son of Cleinias, according to the correct observation of Hatzfeld[83], must therefore not be dated before about 434-33, that is when Alcibiades, having attained his majority, eighteen years, and undergone the δοκιμασία[84], leaves Pericles' tutelage[85] and has his own house and slaves and liberally entertains his friends[86]. In fact, if the *Charmides* (153a) shows us Socrates, who on his return from Potidaea in 423 B.C. questions his friends περὶ φιλοσοφίας (153d) as if taking up a habit again that had only been interrupted for a short while; the *Protagoras* (309a ff.), set before the Potidaea campaign, shows us Socrates in the full process of his spiritual mission among men and already in pursuit of the handsome Alcibiades.

If it is true then that the friendship between Socrates and

unreliable. Regarding the relationship between Socrates and Alcibiades related in the *Symposium*, we must bear in mind the remarks of J. HATZFELD, *Alcibiade*, Paris, 1951, pp. 63-64. Furthermore, that Plato had "aucun souci de la chronologie" and that provided he wishes, "pour une raison littéraire ou philosophique" or even, we might add, for opportunist reasons or, more often, because he has no certain information, that Plato, in a word, "brouille les dates" has on several occasions been pointed out, see A. CROISET, ap. PLATON, *Gorgias*, *Notice*, Paris, 1949, p. 100, L. ROBIN, ap. PLATON, *Banquet*, *Notice*, Paris, 1951[5], XX ff.; and "le sfacciate deformazioni della verità storica" of the Menexenus, where Socrates, who died in 399, repeats the funeral oration learnt from Aspasia, who probably died before 400, in praise of the soldiers who died in the war of Corinth in 396, stands as the most strident and best known example. Despite this, I think there is no reason to doubt the report Plato gives us about the beginning of the relationship between Socrates and Alcibiades since this beginning is made to date back to the period immediately after Alcibiades left the tutelage of Pericles, *Symposium*, and Socrates' amorous interest in the son of Clinias, when the latter was still young, cf. *Protagoras*. Plato had an interest in anticipating as far as possible the breaking off of this relationship, but he could harldy have altered its beginning. And, what is more, Plato could not date this beginning earlier than he did.

82. PLATO, *Symposium*, 219e.
83. HATZFELD, *Alcibiade, cit.*, p. 33.
84. HATZFELD, *op cit.*, p. 28. On the proof of the -δοκιμασία- cf. G. GLOTZ, *La Cité grecque*, Paris, 1953, pp. 255-256.
85. HATZFELD, *cit.*, p. 30.
86. HATZFELD, *cit.*, p. 33.

Alcibiades began in 434-44 and that, as it is easy to suppose, it became more intense in 426-25 when Alcibiades was preparing to speak in the people's assembly and to enter political life[87], when the *Clouds* was produced in 423 that friendship must already have been common knowledge to the Athenians and perhaps had already for some time been the subject of evil gossip. And to me it seems highly probable[88] that in that Pheidippides, a great lover of horses[89], prodigal son of a member of the Alcmaeonidae, grandson of Megacles, son of Megacles[90], Aristophanes wanted to hint at Alcibiades himself, whose mother Deinomaché, of the γένος of the Alcmaeonidae, was none other than the daughter of Megacles[91].

However, it is certainly no coincidence, if Aristophanes has attributed to the young horse-lover of the *Clouds* the same matronimics as Alcibiades whose extravagant passion for horses was to astonish all Hellas[92], and, whether or not one whishes to believe in a hint at Alcibiades, one thing at least is certain: that Aristophanes, in 423, could not have been ignorant of the decade-old relationship between Socrates and Alcibiades and indeed he was well aware that, if Alcibiades sought Socrates, it was certainly not to measure with Chaerophon the height fleas could jump[93] or, to speak non-metaphorically, to learn from Socrates to examine the phenomena of sky and earth. In other words, if from 434-33 to 425, and beyond 423, to perhaps about 416[94], Alcibiades was the

87. For Alcibiades' entry into Athenian political life, the date and manner of that entry, cf. HATZFELD, *op. cit.*, p. 66 ff.

88. J.W. SÜVERN, *Über Aristophanes Wolken*, Berlin, 1826, p. 33 ff. first put forward the hypothesis of an adumbration of Alcibiades in the Pheidippides of the *Clouds*. This hypothesis is clearly rejected by ZELLER, *Socrates*, cit., p. 217, n. 3 and by M. CROISET, *Aristophanes et les partis à Athènes*, Paris, 1906, p. 150, n. 1; relaunched by G. SOREL, *Le procès de Socrate*, Paris, 1889, p. 51 and cautiously taken up again by HATZFELD, *Alcibiade*, op. cit., pp. 34-35 who is led to deny more the effect of that adumbration on the public of the city Dionysia than the fact itself.

89. *Clouds*, 11. 16-32.

90. *Clouds*, 1. 46.

91. References in HATZFELD, op. cit., p. 18 nn. 5 and 6.

92. THUCYDIDES, VI, 12, 2. Other references in HATZFELD, p. 130 and nn.

93. *Clouds*, 1.143 ff.

94. *Symposium*, 213c; 216b; HATZFELD, *cit.*, p. 33.

friend and disciple of Socrates, this means that Alcibiades recognized in Socrates, more than in other famous masters who were then offering their services in Athens, not the mastery of a science of nature, but that ἀνθρωπίνη σοφία[95] of which only Socrates said himself to be a sage and which for him coincided and formed one thing with political virtue[96] and, lastly, of that human and political wisdom that later will attract to him the young Plato, longing, no less than Pericles' pupil, to get involved in politics[97].

The same could be said of Critias and perhaps of Plato's elder brothers, certainly of Antisthenes, of whom it is difficult to imagine that he gave up Gorgian dialectic in favour of Socratic naturalism, provided that Socrates was at that time a physiologist, and of Eucleides who certainly in the years of the Peloponnesian War would not have gone to Athens to learn from Socrates doctrines that were already professed by Anaxagoras and Archelaus, given that he came from Megara and had been brought up in the Eleatic school.

But the most important thing to note, against the ancient and ever-returning thesis that sees in the Aristophanic satire certain proof of a first naturalistic phase in Socratic teaching, is that against the naturalists who, by examining the things of the sky and the earth, then managed to deny their own gods, as Socrates of the *Clouds* does, (1.367: *there is no Zeus!*) still prevailed, at least throughout the duration of the Peloponnesian War, that hapless decree of Diopeithes[98], which rendering liable for punish-

---

95. *Apology*, 20d.

96. The classic passage which shows how things human ἀνθρώπινα, the object of Socratic teaching, coincide with things political πρλιτικά is found in XENOPHON, *Memorabilia*, I, 1, 16,. Cf. MAIER, *cit.*, I, p. 145, according to whom "il gruppo d'idee, che a Socrate era stato accessibile e familiare, e in cui l'opera di lui era stato a suo posto, è la sfera della 'φρόνησις e delle altre virtù' che culmina nella saggezza intesa al governo dello Stato e della famiglia" and JAEGER, *Paideia*, op. cit., II, pp. 158-159, according to whom research into the single virtues find their meeting point in the *Protagoras*, which "caratterizza la direzione di tutte queste ricerche col comprenderle sotto il concetto di arte politica".

97. PLATO, *Letter* VII, 324c. For Socrates' interest in the young men destined for political life, see the dialogues *Menexenus, Charmides, Alcibiades I*.

98. In 423, R. PETTAZZONI, *La religione nella Grecia antica fino ad*

ment anyone who was busy with μετάρσια, was to open, with Anaxagoras[99], the tragic series of trials against freedom of thought brought against the philosophers of all times.

If however it were true, as Chiapelli then Taylor, and Burnet and now Humbert believe, that after 433-31, that is after the ψήφισμα of Diopeithes, in force until Euclid's amnesty Socrates had actually been Archelaus' successor in Athens and, precisely as physiologist and head of an organized school had been risen to such fame as to give grounds for the Aristophanic satire on the one hand and the Pythia's reply to Chaerephon on the other[100], it is hard to believe the son of Sophroniscus had waited 70 years to be accused, tried and sentenced.

Alessandro, Torino, 1953, p. 184, et alii, Diopeites, cf. SWOBODA, in PAULY-WISSOWA, RE, IX, 1046-47, q.v., the Athenian soothsayer and scholar of mantic science, proposed a ψήφισμα PLUTARCH, *Pericles*, 32, 2 (= DK 59A17), according to which would be brought before the assembly of the people, GLOTZ, *Cité*, cit., p. 179 ff., following the procedure of the εἰσαγγελία, GLOTZ, *cit.*, 196, DERENNE, *cit.*, p. 236; MAIER, *cit.*, II, p. 199, n. 2; U.E. PAOLI, *Studi sul Processo Attico*, Padova, 1933, p. 53 f., whoever did not believe in the gods or taught doctrines relative to celestial phenomena. Cf. DECHARME, *La lois de Diopeithès*, in *Melanges Perrot*, Paris, 1903. That the psephism of Diopeites was never *de jure* abrogated, but the more indulgent practice would have brought a *de facto* mitigation, is the opinion of GOMPERZ, *Pensatori Greci*, cit., II, 523; GLOTZ, *Histoire Grecque*, Paris, 1931, II, p. 429; A. MENZEL, *Untersuchungen zum Sokrates-prozess*, in *Sitzungsberichte der Wiener Akademie. Phil. historische Klasse, Wien*, 1903, CXLV, p. 19. At the time of Socrates' trial, this ψήφισμα was no longer in force. Cf. MAIER, *cit.*, II, pp. 198-199 and *ultra*, On the trial of Anaxagoras.

99. DIOGENES LAERTIUS, II, 3, 12-15; PLUTARCH, *Pericles*, 32, 2 (= DK. 59A17). Reasons religious and political in character in the charge brought against Anaxagoras and accusers the legend tells of and the defence of the philosopher made by Pericles — re these, cf. DECHARME, *La critique des traditions réligieuses chez les grecs*, cit., p. 158-159; DERENNE, *Les Procès*, cit., p. 25 ff.; GERNET and BOULANGER, *Le génie grec dans la réligion*, Paris, 1932, p. 346, B. SNELL, *Die Entdeckung des Geistes, Studien zur Entstehung des europäischen Denkens bei den Griechen*, Ital. ed. *La cultura greca e le origini del pensiero europeo*, Torino, 1951, p. 52, P.M. SCHUHL, *Essai sur la formation de la pensée grecque*, Paris, 1934, p. 368, PETTAZZONI, cit., p. 206 ff.

100. Cf. CHIAPPELLI. *Il Naturalismo*, cit., p. 288; BURNET, *Greek Philosophy*, cit., pp. 136 and 142 ff.; TAYLOR, *Socrate*, cit., p. 49 and p. 55.

2. — It was thought possible to overcome these objections by considering ended the naturalistic phases of Socratic teaching at the beginning of the Archidamic War and assuming, as the conscious beginning of the spiritual mission among men, the "trance" in which Socrates is said to have fallen on the fields of Potidaea following the crisis caused in him by the oracle given to Chaerephon[110].

If this were the case, one should conclude that Aristophanes had brought on to the stage the image of a Socrates engaged in research into nature which in fact he had stopped a decade earlier. And what would Aristophanes have known of this research, born as he probably was in 445[102]. How can we consider the *Clouds* to be a document of the naturalistic phase of Socratic teaching, as some believe, if Aristophanes had had no direct experience of that first phase of Socratic teaching? Also from the artistic point of view, the lack of topicality of the Socratic caricature would have been detrimental to the comic effect of the character, while the force of the satire would have diminished against a forgotten figure from the past.

In this case one might think that the very untopical nature of the Socratic caricature might be the cause of the failure in 423, whence the need for a radical change in the *Clouds*, in the revision of which the charge of moral corruption would have been stressed and instead attenuated the naturalistic nature of Socratic teaching on which the first *Clouds* had particularly insisted. But we prefer to leave to others the responsibility for such a hypothesis.

3. — All we have said so far, therefore, confirms the conclusion we had already arrived at, namely that it is untenable to claim that the alleged second version of the *Clouds* presents a different picture of Socrates from the one drawn in our *Clouds* and, hence, that between the so-called first *Clouds* and the so-called

101. Cf. TAYLOR, *Socrate*, cit., p. 58; BURNET, *Greek Philosophy*, pp. 135-136. Also worthy of attention, DERENNE, *Les procès*, cit., pp. 92-93 and MONDOLFO, *Sócrates*, cit., pp. 13-14.

102. In fact this seems the probable date of Aristophanes' birth; data gathered, among others, by M. CROISET, *Histoire de la Littérature Grecque*, vol. III, Paris, 1953[3], p. 549; by COULON, *Introduction*, cit., p. II and by Q. CATAUDELLA, *La poesia di Aristofane*, Bari, 1934, p. 1, e.a.

second *Clouds* a change of opinion had taken place in Aristophanes towards the personality of Socrates corresponding to a different direction of Socratic teaching.

Our investigation had also led us to deny that the *Clouds* evidenced a naturalistic phase in Socratic activity, making clear, on the one hand, that in 423 Socrates was no more and no less than the same man whom Plato knew and, furthermore, that if Socrates had ever been naturalist up to the beginning of the Archidamic war, Aristophanean comedy did not in fact have that dimension of historical testimony that many attribute to it, since that first phase of Socratic activity would have been as unknown to Aristophanes as it was to Plato and Xenophon[103].

4. — The truth is that Aristophanes put on the stage not a naturalist Socrates, but a sophist Socrates[104]; a Socrates master of the art of speech[105] and lord of the *Lógos* particularly effective in triumphing in judicial conflicts[106]. And as for the Sophists the analogy with the physical cosmos was the criterion for judging human, moral and social matters[106], so for the Socrates of the *Clouds*, propaedeutic to dialectics is the study of nature[108], or better, the discovery of the organizatory concepts of the science of nature transferable to the level of logic and morals; in the same way as for Plato the introduction to philosophy is mathematics, or again nature raised to a universal significance and symbol. Of

103. As it will be remembered, this is the ancient thesis, already rejected by ZELLER and yet relaunched by modern scholars.
104. *Clouds*, 11. 111; 112 ff.; 636 ff.; 658 ff.; 1308-9 and here note 172-178.
105. *Clouds*, 11. 239, 1106.
106. *Clouds*, 11 99, 245-46, 434, 445, *et passim*. Remember Critias' prohibition to Socrates about teaching young men the art of discoursing τῶν λόγων τέχνην, XENOPHON, *Memorabilia*, I, II, 34.
107. For the link between naturalism and sophistry, cf. R. MONDOLFO, *Alle origini della filosofia della Cultura* (1942), Bologna, 1956, p. 75 ff.; C. DIANO, *Il concetto della storia della filosofia dei greci*, in *Grande Antologia Filosofica*, Milano, 1954, p. 285 ff.; A. CAPIZZI, *Protagora*, Firenze, 1956, p. 12; E. PACI, *Storia del Pensiero Presocratico*, ERI, 1957, p. 254 ff.
108. In this sense Socrates deals in the *Clouds* with astronomy and meteorology, 11. 94, 170 ff., 193 ff., 200, 225 ff., 368 ff., 375 ff., 395 ff., §&* FF., with geology, 11. 186 ff., 192 ; with geography, 1. 206 ff.; with geometry, 11. 144 ff., 202 ff.; with physics, 1. 145 ff.; as he deals with metrics, with rhythmic 1. 636 ff., and with grammar, 1. 658 ff.

121

a Socratic naturalism, understood as the profession of a different objective knowledge and opposed to the humanism professed later by Socrates as a spiritual mission in the service of the god, speak in fact those critics who have failed to notice how Greek sophistry is ultimately the same Ionian naturalism taken up again from the point of view of the subject, and so they clearly distinguish a cosmological period from an anthropological one contrasting them as two absolute and impenetrable historical moments[109]. And this distinction and contrast is transferred by those same critics into the figure of Socrates in the *Clouds* who seems to them to be composed of heterogeneous and irreconcilable elements, which are on the one hand Anaxagorean and Diogenean, and on the other hand Protagorean[110]. The arbitrariness of this composition would thus reveal the poet's true intention, which would have been to attack not the real Socrates, but rather the whole illuminist movement of the time incorrectly incarnated in a historical person widely known to the Athenians of 423 B.C.[111].

109. Regarding Hegelian responsibility for this historical periodization and the errors which result from it in historiographical practice, it is particularly important to bear in mind the controvercy which has been conducted for many years by MONDOLFO, *Nota sopra il genio greco e le sue creazioni spirituali* and especially *Nota sulla divisione in periodi della Filosofia greca*, in ZELLER-MONDOLFO, *La filosofia dei greci nel suo sviluppo storico*, Florence, 1951³, I, I, p. 360 ff. and 375 ff.; *Nota sulla Filosofia presocratica*, in *op. cit.*, vol. II. *Problema umano e problema cosmico nella formazione della filosofia greca*, in *Problemi del pensiero antico*, Bologna, 1936, p. 21 ff.; *L'Infinito nel Pensiero dell'antichità classica*, 1934, Florence, 1956, p. 4 ff. and especially *Epoche e continuità nella storia della cultura*, in *La comprensione del soggetto umano nella antichità classica*, ed. Cast. 1955, Florence, 1958, Chap. I, p. 3 ff.

110. Let us remember, among others, MAIER, *Socrate, op. cit.*, p. 163, according to whom the figure of Socrates in the *Clouds* embodies two different types: the philosopher of nature and the sophist: Diogenes of Apollonia and Protagoras; C. PASCAL, *Dionyso*, cit., p. 246; F.M. CORNFORD, *The Philosophy of Socrates*, in *The Cambridge Ancient History*, VI, 1933, p. 302-303; DERENNE, *op. cit.*, p. 74-75; SCHUHL, *Essai*, cit., p. 371, n. 1; A. BANFI, *Socrate*, Milan, 1944, p. 125-126, J. ZAFIROPULO, *Diogène d'Apollonie*, Paris, 23 ff. and again DOVER, apud. ARISTOPHANES. *Clouds, Introd.*, cit., p. XXXVI-XL.

111. Of all of these MAIER, *op. cit.*, I, p. 169, according to whom Aristophanes did not intend to attack the real Socrates, but rather the leader of illuminism, "l'illuminista alla più alta potenza", the "*spiritus rector*" of all the

Deriving from this, and feeding off it, is a vast current of Socratic historiography that sees in the central character of the *Clouds* not Socrates but a symbol: the generic type of philosopher[112] to whom Aristophanes had attributed certain clear characteristics of the historical Socrates[113], attenuated however in making him a foreign sophist, a certain "Socrates of Melos"[114]. Aristophanes' comedy was thus stripped of every concrete documentary interest and the figure of Socrates in the *Clouds* rejected as a mythical and poetic figure.

This refusal of the Aristophanic source had in reality its roots in the suggestion that the image of Socrates delineated by Plato has always exercised on historians. An exact evaluation of Aristophanes as a Socratic source has in fact been harmed by the comparison with Plato, all the more so since this comparison was originally instituted when, in the neo-humanist era, Greek spirituality was rediscovered through the rediscovery of Plato and when the same Socratic problem was imposed on the presupposition of the historical reliabilty of the *Apology*[115].

5. — When in fact the Socratic problem was, for the first time, posited in all its fullness and complexity as a problem of historical knowledge[116], Aristophanes was practically excluded from the

modern disorder, and hence was able in total freedom to represent Socrates on the stage as "maestro a un tempo di filosofia della natura e di sofistica".

112. See remarks above.

113. Characteristics unanimously accepted by historians and carefully pointed out by DERENNE, *op. cit.*, p. 77.

114. *Clouds*, 1. 830. See the perceptive remarks of G. SOREL, *Le Procès de Socrate.*, cit., p. 52.

115. See what will be said more fully in the following text and in the associated notes.

116. A study into the genesis of the Socratic problem as a historical problem has not yet even been embarked upon. The few references made to it by DE MAGALHÃES-VILHENA, in *Le problème*, cit., p. 128 ff., however stimulating, are still far from laying the foundations for such a study. Furthermore, the starting point of the enquiry seems to me to lie much further on than where the Portugese scholar places it, to be precise in those patient, painstaking and illuminating researches conducted into the Greek and Latin classics from the school of Gottinga with Gesner, Heyne, Ernesti, Reiske, cf. C. ANTONI, *I dotti di Gottinga*, in *La lotta contro la Ragione*, Florence, 1942, p. 99 ff.; G.

albeit short list of those sources which are useful for the purposes of a historical reconstruction of the human and philosophical personality of Socrates. In an era, like the neo-humanist and Romantic periods, full of the classical ideal of beauty and perfection, Aristophanean comedy must have been harmed by the contrast between the prosaic and grotesque image of Socrates in the *Clouds* and the plastic evidence and humanity of the portrait of the unforgettable master painted by Plato. A comparison all the more unfavourable to Aristophanes the more vibrant enthusiasm was at that time for Plato. The cult for the "divine" Plato,

FUNAIOLI, *Lineamenti di storia della filologia attraverso i secoli*, in *Studi sulla letteratura antica*, Bologna, 1951, p. 185 ff., especially p. 321 ff.; BERNARDINI-RIGHI, *Il concetto di filologia e di cultura classica dal Rinascimento ad oggi*, Bari, 1953[2], p. 214 ff. whose research was to reveal to German culture a vision of the Greek world understood for the first time in all its totality and organic unity in the schemes of a nascent philosophy of history which that world, before Winckelmann, then with Herder and lastly an decisively with Hegel, interpreted as an unrepeatable moment and category in the history of the human spirit and together with the ideal model of classical beauty and perfection to which the Christiano-Germano spirit dreamt of returning as to its distant womb and of thus renewing in the forms of a new Humanism.

We must therefore go back to the origins and precursors of neohumanism and historicism, F. MEINECKE, *Le origini dello storicismo*. 1936, Ital. transl. Florence. 1954 and the remarks by C. ANTONI. *Lo Storicismo*, ERI, 1957, p. 17, to trace back, with the formation of modern historical consciousness, the first roots of those historiographical myths or pseudo concepts interpretative of history to which Montesquieu, E. FUETER, *Storia della Storiografia moderna*, 1955 Ital. transl. Naples, 1954, II, p. 58 ff., gave shape and life, such as the climate, the race, the spirit of the peoples, FUETER, *cit.*, B. CROCE, *Teoria e storia della storiografia*, Bari, 1943[3], p. II, c. V, and especially that unilateral vision of the Hellenic genius, MONDOLFO, *Nota sul genio ellenico*, in op. cit.: *La comprensione del soggetto umano*, cit., etc., with al the exaggerations and limits that it involved to understand then the arbitrariness of that historical periodization introduced by Hegel and raised to a system postulating a precise dialectisation of the historical eras each conceived as a different moment and degree of the development of the idea, HEGEL, *Vorlesungen über die Gesch. d. Philos.*, Ital. ed. *Lezioni sulla filosofia della storia*, Florence, 1947 ff., so that in ancient philosophy Socrates must have been situated between sophist relativism on the one hand, and Platonic idealism on the other. Since it was precisely the need to discover and reveal a thought or a philosophy or indeed a Socratic|metaphysic|that would coherently ensure the transition from one moment to the next in the course of history establishing itself as an actual fact of its own time, which suggested to the interpreters of Socrates a certain attitude already celebrated by the Humanists of the Italian Renaissance[117] and continued in England by the Cambridge School[118], had been brought back to Europe by Winckelmann who had learnt of it from the books of Shaftesbury[119] and then passed it on to Herder, Schiller and Goethe, and in general to all the creative minds of German Romanticism[120]. The rediscovery of Hellenism came to

towards the problem of sources and attempted a solution which proves consistent with the way each interpreter understands the reasons and ways of that process in which Socratic cross-questioning must finally be resolved.

A study along these lines of the first positing of the Socratic problem would, in my view, succeed in clarifying, with the genesis, the reasons for the crisis in which the very problem is debated as a crisis which affects a whole world of thoughts, and in addition would warn the modern historian of the errors of the past, experience of which could and should suggest, after the lesson of GIGON, *Sokrates, Sein Bild in Dicht. u. Gesch.*, Bern, 1947, 1979², a new criterion of research directed towards reaching the historical persona of Socrates over and above any myth, in his precise human dimensions: that is, a man in a living world of men and condemned to death as a ἀσεβής and not just a concept, imprisoned in an eternal theory of concepts, or a human ideal above any human scale, or, lastly, omnipresent spirit of the various and multiform tendencies of the Socratics, of whom the point of origin and irradiation would remain pitifully unknown. See M. MONTUORI, *De Socrate iuste damnato. The rise of the Socratic problem in the Eighteenth Century*, Amsterdam, 1981, Ital. ed., Rome, 1981.

117. For the cult professed by the Humanists of the Italian Renaissance to the "divine" Plato in contrast to that "beast" Aristotle and the significance of this preference, cf. E. GARIN, *L'Umanesimo Italiano. Filosofia e Vita Civile nel Rinascimento*, Bari, 1952, esp. *Introduzione*, pp. 18-19.

118. Cf. E. CASSIRER, *Die Platonische Renaissance in England und die Schule von Cambridge, La rinascenza platonica in Inghilterra e la scuola di Cambridge*, 1932, Ital. transl. Florence, 1947.

119. On the Platonism of Winckelmann, and how this is linked to the Cambridge school of Shaftesbury, cf. CASSIRER, *La rinascenza*, op. cit., pp. 204-205. For Winckelmann's doctrine on the art in relation to the Platonism of A., cf. B. CROCE, *Estetica*, Bari, 1946⁶, II, P., p. 291 ff. and again CROCE the essay on Winckelmann, in *Discorsi di Varia Filosofia*, II, Bari, 1945, pp. 102-112. and again C. ANTONI, *J.J. Winckelmann*, in *La lotta contro la Ragione*, cit., p. 37 ff. For the Platonism of Winckelmann in the birth of German historicism, cf. MEINECKE, *Die Entstehung des Historismus*, Ital. ed. *Le Origini dello storicismo*, cit., p. 231 ff., and also MEINECKE, *Classicismo, Romanticismo e pensiero storico nel secolo XVIII*, in *Senso storico e significato della storia*, Ital. transl. Naples, 1948, p. 45 ff.

120. Shaftesbury's influence on Herder and the mediation of Winckelmann has been clearly shown by MEINECKE, *Le Origini*, cit., p. 301 ff.: "tra coloro

coincide, precisely with Winckelmann, with the rediscovery of Plato and Plato himself was to suggest to Winckelmann that original interpretation and olympic mythification of Greek art that would finally spread with neo-humanism to all the manifestations of the classical spirit until it became fixed into interpretative historiographical canon of the Greek genius[121].

Aristophanes, on the other hand, was judged extremely negatively, both in terms of his personality and work, and the echo of this aversion has remained in the vigorous defence Hegel makes of him, which denies that Aristophanes was "a vulgar buffoon or a lowly jester who had made fun of every fine and sacred thing and had sacrified everything to his jibes just to amuse the Athenians"[122]. But a few months before his death, Goethe, extremely angry with Schlegel, that "poor simpleton" who had found fault with Euripides[123], repeated the old opinion calling Aristophanes a "clown"[124], guilty, in his eyes, of having inspired Schlegel's criticism of the ancient tragedian[125]. And, as Lessing had already denied any possible link between the Aristophanic Socrates and the real person of the son of Sophroniscus[126], so

fra i suoi predecessori e contemporanei che lo hanno avvicinato al pensiero e alla concezione platonica, bisogna annoverare anche Winckelmann [...]" "L'influenza di Winckelmann è stata rilevata financo nel vocabolario del giovane Herder" p. 302. For the Neoplatonism of Goethe, MEINECKE, op. cit., p. 376 ff. esp. 496, and Senso storico, cit., p. 45 ff. and esp. p. 55.

121. Cf. MONDOLFO, Nota sul genio ellenico, cit. and Nota sopra la Religione greca, ibid., p. 140 ff., and the works, already mentioned, L'infinito nel pensiero dell'antichità classica and La comprensione del soggetto umano nell'antichità classica, which MONDOLFO wrote in reaction to the classicistic mythicization of the Hellenic genius claiming, against the limits imposed by that mythicization, cognition of the infinite and comprehension of subjectivity.

121b. See in this regard my mémoire, "Les Philosophes" di Palissot e la fortuna di Aristofane nella storiografia socratica moderna, now in Socrate. Un Problema storico, Napoli, 1984, pp. 299-333.

122. HEGEL, Lezioni sulla storia della filosofia, cit., II, p. 86.

123. I quote from B. SNELL, La cultura greca e le origini del pensiero europeo, op. cit., p. 171.

124. SNELL, cit., ibid.

125. SNELL, cit., p. 155.

126. Cf. G. LESSING, Hamburgische Dramaturgie 1767-1769; XCI Stück, Marz, 1768; Leipzig, no date. p. 381 ff.

Goethe resolutely excluded the clumsy figure of Euripides portrayed in the *Frogs* from having anything in common with the historical Euripides[127].

Indeed this climate, as favourable to Plato as it was adverse to Aristophanes, would be detrimental to the fortune of the poet of the *Clouds* as a Socratic witness.

All the more so since one in love with Plato, educated in the school of Winckelmann and Herder, translator and exegetist of Plato, would be the first to bring to light the Socratic question, dealing with it against the background of the Platonic question and as an attempt to define the horizon of Socratic thought in the wider context of the Platonic Dialogues[128]. But in the classic statement given by Schleiermacher to the problem of Socratic sources, a problem he conceived of as harmonization to the common Socratic limit of the idealization of the Platonic portrait with the banality of the Xenophonean portrait[129], the more historically reliable appeared to Schleiermacher the drawing of the human personality of Socrates made by Plato in the *Apology* and in the speech of Alcibiades[130], all the more repulsive and unacceptable became the grotesque image of Socrates in the *Clouds*.

Hegel, on the other hand, gave Aristophanes credit for "having noticed the negative side of Socratic dialectic"[131] providing, even in the exaggerated comic expansion of the character, a largely faithful representation of the true Socrates[132]. This notwithstanding, Aristophanes' picture was then in fact excluded by Hegel

127. SNELL, *cit.*, p. 171.

128. Cf. F. SCHLEIERMACHER, *Ueber den Wert des Sokrates als Philosophen*, in *Abhandlungen der Berliner Akademie*, Phil. Kl. 1818, p. 50 ff., reissued in *Ges. Werke*, Berlin, 1838, III, 2, p. 287 ff.

129. For the famous "golden rule" cf. SCHLEIERMACHER, *op. cit.*, p. 297. It is opportune to recall, regarding Schleiermacher's methodological criterion, J. BURNET, *Plato's Phaedo*, 1911, Oxford, 1937, p. XXXVIII according to whom Schleiermacher, for the first time, posits the Socratic problem in its true light, and MAIER. *op. cit.*, I, p. 13, to whom, in contrast, it seems that that rule throws open wide "le porte ad ogni arbitrio soggettivo di combinazioni storiche".

130. SCHLEIERMACHER, *Platons Werke*, 1804-1810, *Einleitung zur Apologie*, 1861[3] p. 183 ff.

131. HEGEL, *Lezioni sull storia della filosofia*, op. cit., II, p. 89.

132. HEGEL, *loc. cit.*

from the contest of the Socratic sources and practically not used for the purposes of his interpretation of the Socratic personality. This is because for Hegel the Socratic image in the *Clouds* scarsely represented a comic imitation of the real persona of Socrates, whose dialectic Aristophanes had boldly relegated to "the extreme bitterness of consequence"[133], while to reconstruct, beyond the Aristophanic imitation, the real model that had inspired the character in the *Clouds*, Hegel believed he could restrict himself to combining together the humanity of the Platonic Socrates with the philosophical content of Xenophon's Socrates[134].

But it is with Süvern[135] that Aristophanes is finally excluded from Socratic sources. According to Süvern, in fact, the philosopher in the *Clouds* is not a real person but a symbol[136] and the Aristophanean satire was not intended to attack Socrates himself, but rather the school of sophists and rhetors flourishing in the Athens of Socrates[137]. This means that the characterization of Socrates in the *Clouds* is in fact denied any historical reliability, as it does not really deal with Socrates, son of Sophroniscus the sculptor and Phaenarete, perhaps, midwife, but rather with a symbol, a philosophical figure who represents all the others: a literary image in fact, unrelated to reality.

Zeller has vigorously refuted Süvern's hypothesis[138], pointing out how the essential features of the portrait of Socrates in the *Clouds*, far from being pure literary invention, are built on the objective foundation of an opinion widespread amongst the Athenians and honestly shared by Aristophanes[139]. To a conservative like Aristophanes, noted Zeller, that eternal debate on virtue and justice, religion and the state must have made Socrates

133. *Ibid.*
134. HEGEL, op. cit., p. 72. On the distinction and dialectization of the two moments, *human* and *philosophical*, operated by Hegel in the persona of Socrates, see the apposite remarks of PAOLO ROSSI, *Per una storia della storiografia socratica*, in *Problemi di Storiografia filosofica*, ed. A. BANFI, Milan, 1951, p. 86 ff. and esp. pp. 94-95.
135. J.W. SÜVERN, *Ueber Aristophanes Wolken*, Berlin 1826.
136. SÜVERN, op. cit., p. 19 and p. 26.
137. SÜVERN, op. cit., p. 30 ff. and p. 55 ff.
138. ZELLER, *Socrates and the Socratic Schools*, New York, 1962³, p. 217.
139. ZELLER, *op. cit.*, *ibid.*
140. ZELLER, *op. cit.*, p. 218-19.

seem like a dangerous destroyer of the traditional morality and piety of the forefathers. Hence the attack directed against Socrates by Aristophanes, who in the *Clouds* denounced the immoral, irreligious and sophist aspect of Socratic teaching[141]. Precisely this dangerously destructive aspect of Socratic dialogue later motivated the legal action and legitimated the sentence[142]. A sentence, however, which in Zeller's view proves to be legitimate only in the context of the ancient Greek concept of law and state[143], whereas, on an ethico-juridical evaluation, the same sentence, considered in the time it was pronounced, appears to be a flagrant injustice for which the Eliasts were responsible[144]

This contradiction emphasized by Zeller between traditional morality, represented by Aristophanes, and the majority of the Eliastics, to whom Socrates appeared impious and a corruptor and therefore liable to condemnation, and the moral climate of Athens at the time of the Peloponnesian War and the restoration of democracy that exculpated Socrates, also on the basis of positive law, from any possible blame, came subsequently to compromise the reliability of the portrait of Socrates in the *Clouds*. A portrait which after all was based on a misunderstanding, on a total incomprehension of the conservative poet whose ideas were extremely limited and scarsely interested in the truth[145], towards the work of moral renewal to which Socrates had devoted himself. Thus Zeller came much closer to Süvern than he thought. If in fact for Zeller the Socrates of the *Clouds* is no longer a symbol, a literary and fictitious personage as it was for Süvern, but the result of a misunderstanding or also the incapacity of Aristophanes to understand the true character of Socrates' personality and of his teaching, nevertheless the

---

141. ZELLER, *op. cit.*, p. 218.
142. ZELLER, *op. cit.*, pp. 212; 270.
143. ZELLER, *op. cit.*, p. 231.
144. ZELLER, *op. cit.*, p. 223.
145. ZELLER, *op. cit.*, pp. 218-219. Aristophanes appears to Zeller as a conservative hostile to any attempt at innovation in matters of morality and politics, religion and art, inclined as a comic poet, to have very few scruples about virtue and morality and hence practically to destroy precisely that ancient morality whose return he was calling for. Cf. also DE SANCTIS, *Storia dei Greci*, II, op. cit., p. 349.

Socratic image of the *Clouds* is no less remote from real personality of the son of Sophroniscus. Zeller found himself none the less sharing Süvern's implicit judgement about the uselessness of the *Clouds* for the purposes of a Socratic interpretation and therefore to exclude, as indeed he does exclude, Aristophanes from all consideration of Socratic sources[146].

Grote[147] accentuated and in some respects aggravated Zeller's negative judgement, which was reiterated by Labriola[148], appropriated by Schanz[149], followed by Pöhlmann and Wilamowitz[150] and so on, in over fifty years of Socratic study, by Gentile and Maier, De Sanctis and Jaeger, Banfi and Bastide, Cornford and Ehrenberg[151] and, more recently, by Cantarella[152], to whom

---

146. ZELLER, *op. cit.*, p. 105 in fact draws the figure of Socrates "from the three accounts of Xenophon, Plato and Aristotle".

147. G. GROTE, *History of Greece*, London, 1849, VI, p. 659, who compares Cleon and Socrates as Aristophanic characters, concluding that, as the Cleon of the *Knights* is a literary fiction, so the Socrates of the *Clouds* "*is not even a caricature but a totally different person*". The opposite point of view is held by GELZER, *op. cit.*

148. A. LABRIOLA, *Socrate*, Bari, 1947[4], p. 15, who yet recognizes that the *Clouds* constitute an historical testimony of the influence that Socrates already had at that time and of the consideration for his persona in Athenian society.

149. M. SCHANZ, *Platonic Apologia*, Leipzig, 1893, p. 45 ff., refuses to see in the Aristophanic Socrates the albeit caricatured traits of the real Socrates. Aristophanes, according to SCHANZ, had painted for the public what was the new science, rhetorics, the wisdom of the Sophists, concentrating the whole culture of the day into the figure of Socrates. The Socrates of the *Clouds* was therefore thought of not as an individual, but as a type: "Der Sokrates des *Wolken* ist ein Typus, kein Individuum", p. 50.

150. R. PÖHLMANN, *Sokratische Studien*, in Munch. AKSB, 1906, p 49 ff., esp. p. 70 ff. U. VON WILAMOVITZ-MÖLLENDORF, *Platon*, I, Berlin, pp. 99-100.

151. For GENTILE, cf. *La Critica*, 1909, p. 289, cit., *Storia della Filosofia. Dalle Origini a Platone*, Florence, 1964, p. 96; also C, PASCAL, *Dioniso*, Catania, 1911, p. 234 and n. 1; MAIER, *Socrate*, op. cit., I, p. 169; G. DE SANCTIS, *Storia dei Greci*, op. cit., II, p. 355; JAEGER, *Paideia*, I, op. cit., p. 625, according to whom the Aristophanic Socrates personified the whole decadent culture of his age, shown for the first time in the *Clouds* as the spiritual face of a whole era. Aristophanes had therefore accumulated in Socrates all the features of the type, amongst whose ranks he clearly was numbered, of the Sophists, rhetors and philosophers of nature or, as they were then called, the meteorologists. A. BANFI, *Socrate*, Milan, 1944, p. 125; R. BASTIDE, *Le mo-*

Socrates appears in the *Clouds* "a mask, a funny puppet", by Paci[153], for whom the Aristophanean Socrates remains "a symbol [...] the philosopher who represents all the others" and lastly by Erbse[154], who a century later echoes the view of Lessing considering the character in the *Clouds* to be a poetic figure with absolutely no relationship with the historical person of the son of Sophronicus.

6. — It is precisely to this thesis, which denies any evidential value to the portrait of Socrates in the *Clouds*, that must be attributed most responsibility for the failure in which is finally concluded a century of Socratic historiography and an endless crop of studies and research. This is because the exclusion of Aristophanes virtually excluded the only source which reflected the judgement of a large part of the Athenians on the character, intention and aim of Socratic dialogue and that harmonized with extraordinary accuracy with that bill of indictment that remains for us the only historical evidence on Socrates capable of taking us out of the mists of the myth and on to a firm historical footing. The refusal of the Aristophanic source in fact finally distracted the research from those grounds that had nurtured the view of the Athenians during the whole twenty-five year period of Socratic

ment historique de Socrate, Paris, 1939, p. 78, for whom "le grossissement caricaturale équivaut à une déformation derrière laquelle l'original nous échappe"; F.M CORNFORD, *The Philosophy of Socrates*, in *The Cambridge Ancient History*, VI, 1933, pp. 302-303. CORNFORD again, in *Before and after Socrates*, 1932, Cambridge, 1950, does not even mention Aristophanes when dealing with Socrates; V. EHRENBERG, *The People of Aristophanes*, London, 1974[2], p. 275, 276. And we might also mention, without any pretence to being comprehensive, DECHARME, *La critique*, op. cit., p. 126; M. CROISET, *Histoire de la Littérature Grecque*, op. cit., III, p. 239; VAN DAELE, *Notice* ap. *Les Nuées*, op. cit., p. 148-150; K. HILDEBRANDT, *Platone*, op. cit., p. 16; ZAFIROPULO, *Diogène d'Apollonie*, cit., p. 23 f.; G. GALLI, *Socrate ed alcuni dialoghi platonici*, Turin, 1958, p. 18; M.P. NILSSON, *Greek Piety*, Oxford, 1951[2], p. 74, and others.

152. CANTARELLA, ap. ARISTOFANE, *Le commedie*, III, op. cit., p. 23; and also in *Storia della Letteratura Greca*, Mila, 1962, p. 417.

153. PACI, *Storia del pensiero presocratico*, op. cit., p. 240.

154. ERBSE, *Sokrates im Schatten der Aristophanischen Wolken*, art., cit., p. 420.

activity, subsequently embodied in the sworn charge of Anytos, Meletus, Lycon and finally the sentence of the Eliasts.

And so, while the vast majority of interpreters allowed themselves to be seduced by the myth of the unjustly condemned[155] accepting and confirming the image of a Socrates beloved of Apollo and invested by the god of Delphi with a special religious mission among men[156] in the fulfilment of which

155. Of all we need only remember GROTE, *History of Greece*, VIII, op. cit., p. 671, to whom Socrates' sentence seems one of the many misdeeds with which the religious and poltical intolerance is tainted, awakening in men a feeling of indignant reproach *"the force of which —* writes GROTE — *I have no desire to enfeeble"*; LABRIOLA, *Socrate*, op. cit., p. 4, who sees in Socrates the "vittima innocente" of an exaggerated principle of conservation of the Athenian democracy; M. CROISET, *Histoire de la Littérature Grecque*, III, op. cit., p. 237, for whom the only thing Socrates' moral grandeur lacked was a *"condamnation injuste"* and his enemies secured this for him by making him "victim of a violent religious reaction closely connected to the recent democratic triumph", cit., p. 238; K. HILDEBRANDT, *Platone*, op. cit., p. 81, according to whom anyone who condones the verdict of the Eliasts "non ha nessun sentimento di giustizia"; P. MARTINETTI, *Socrate* in *Ragione e Fede*, Turin 1944, p. 443, for whom the judges who sentenced Socrates "rappresentavano un fascio di volgari interessi politici" the sentence of Socrates seems like this to MARTINETTI, op. cit., p. 444, as it already had to R. PÖHLMANN, *Sokrates und sein Wolk*, München und Leipzig, 1899, pp. 111-112, whose judgement he quotes: "una delle innumerevoli manifestazioni di quella violenza bestiale, con cui lo strato inferiore della spiritualità umana dappertutto recalcitra e resiste al pieno svolgimento del contenuto spirituale interiore della cultura, della ragione e della moralità. La tragedia, che qui si svolge, si ripete attraverso tutta la storia dell'umanità fino ad oggi, sotto sempre nuova forma, ma sempre con lo stesso risultato: l'oppressione dell'individualità intellettuale e moralmente libera e del pensiero autonomo per opera dello spirito elementare, in breve l'oppressione del puro elemento spirituale dell'alta cultura per opera del peso bruto del volgare, che la psiche collettiva getta nella bilancia". Cf. too BANFI, *Socrate*, op. cit., p. 139 and, among the more recent, E. TUROLLA, ap. PLATONE, *I Dialoghi, l'Apologia, le Epistole*, I, Milan, 1953, p. 470

156. The eminently religious character of Socrates' personality has been particularly stressed by GROTE, *History of Greece*, VIII, op. cit., p. 556 ff.; LABRIOLA, *Socrate*, op. cit., p. 28 ff.; TOVAR, *Vida de Sócrates*, op. cit., p. 141 ff.; R. GUARDINI, *La mort de Socrate*, 1947, Paris, 1959 and more recently by CHEVALIER, *Histoire de la Pensée*, I, op. cit., p. 170 ff. and MONDOLFO, *Socrate*, op. cit., p. 29 ff.; for whom Socratic philosophizing is identified with the seriousness and profundity of the religious sentiment which is reflected in all aspects of the activity of Socrates identifying his life with his

he aroused against him the fiercest and gravest enmity of his fellow-citizens and hence the charge, trial and sentence[157], on Aristophanes, however, though the ancient judgement[158] on the man and his work no longer applied, there continued to weigh, as a Socratic source, a censure as severe, as historically unjust and critically without foundation[159].

doctrine and assuming the character of his personality as a religious mission among men.

It is clear that the stressing of Socrates' piety as fidelity to the religion of the polis is possible only for whoever accepts the historical truth of the oracle to Chaerephon, *Apologia* 21a more precisely for whoever remains inside the *Sokratesdichtung*.

157. Cf. *Apologia* 23a. On the mortal enmity "fra la città e il suo fedele cittadino" see HILDEBRANDT, *Platone*, op. cit., pp. 66-67.

158. To a rehabilitation of Aristophanes, already under way in literary criticism, a contribution had been made, in the sphere of Socratic study, among others SOREL, *Le procès de Socrate*, cit., and particularly RÖCK, *Der Unverfälschte Sokrates der Atheist und "Sophist"*, op. cit., and he fell into the opposite excess with JAEGER, *Paideia*, op. cit., I, p. 611 who recognises in the Aristophanic work "una alta missione educativa" which is explained in the public censure the comedy exercised on politics, education and custom, p. 617 ff. hence that "straordinaria serietà", p. 616, which, according to Jaeger, was hidden under the hilarious mask of the poet. EHRENBERG, *The People of Aristophanes*, London, 1974², rightly considers "a wild exaggeration" the thesis according to which the comic poets tended to represent public criticism in Athens.

159. Alongside JAEGER's excessive faith in the duties of ancient comedy and of Aristophanes in particular, remain the negative judgements of ROBIN, *La Pensée Grecque*, op. cit., p. 179, for whom the portrait of Socrates "*atteste chez Aristophane un fâcheux défaut de clairvoyance*"; of DE SANCTIS, *Storia dei Greci*, II, op. cit., p. 349, to whom the educative work of Aristophanes seems "negativa e dissolvitrice" and such as might contribute "nella prima parte della guerra del Peleponneso a quel momentaneo infiacchimento degli animi che condusse all'infausta pace di Nicia", p. 357. The attack on Socrates seems therefore to DE SANCTIS to be inspired by the ancient aversion of the conservative poet, p. 349, to the new education, thus contributing, despite the failure on stage of the *Clouds*, "alla condanna del più degno rappresentante della educazione nuova", p. 357, hence "antichi e moderni concordi gli hanno fatto acre rimprovero", p. 355. Along similar lines is the view expressed by STEFANINI, *Platone*, op. cit., I, p. 4, for whom "Aristofane, spregiudicato e incredulo, corrompeva i giovani con le stesse opere con cui avrebbe voluto richiamarli al culto della moralità e religiosità antiche". For HILDEBRANDT, *Platone*, op. cit., p. 16 "Aristofane introduce l'errore, nemico dello spirito, cui soggiacque Socrate", making himself coresponsible for the death of Socrates *ibid*. whom he

We must therefore agree on the character and value of Aristophanes' testimony.

7. — The figure of Socrates drawn in the *Clouds* reproduces in dramatic form an image of the master of Crytias and Alcibiades already clearly defined in the imagination of the Athenian public at the beginning of the Peloponnesian War[160].

had blamed "con incomprensibile disconoscimento e in modo del tutto arbitrario" *ibid*, for every distortion and nonsense (!) that Socrates attacks in the Sophists. To NILSSON, *Greek Piety*. It. trans. *Religiosità greca*, op. cit., p. 105, it seems that "quando Aristofane con le sue caricature si attaccò agli dei, non si accorse che egli dava all'antica pietà il colpo di grazia". According to GALLI, *Socrate ed alcuni dialoghi platonici*, op. cit., p. 18, Aristophanes "non volle, e forse non ne era capace, non volle scorgere le differenze profonde che distingue-vano Socrate dagli altri, sì che questo fu da lui confuso coi Sofisti e con Euripide". Similarly too now DOVER, *Aristophanes Clouds, Introd.*, p. LIII, for whom Aristophanes "simply did not see the difference between Socrates and the Sophists" or even "he would not have regarded it as important".

160. I. BRUNS, *Das literarische Porträt der Griechen im 5 und 4 Jahrhundert vor Christi geburt*, 1896, Darmstadt, 1961, p. 181 ff., esp. p. 196 ff., was the first to point out that Aristophanes had portrayed Socrates according to the ideas that the great mass of citizens had formed about him. The sentence of Socrates would prove therefore, for DERENNE, *Les procès d'impiété intentés aux philosophes à Athènes au Ve et au IVe siècle avant J.-C.*, op. cit., p. 79, that the majority of the Athenians had a very different idea from that which we owe to his disciples. It seems therefore impossible to DERENNE, *ibid.* to attribute responsibility for that extraordinary vitality of calumny to a comedy that had been staged 24 years earlier. Necessarily, DERENNE concludes, those ideas must have been deeply rooted in the spirit of the Athenians and other reasons must have been influential.

For EHRENBERG, *The People of Aristophanes*, p. 276, however, the figure of Socrates in the *Clouds* does indeed represent the opinion that the Athenian people had formed about Socrates, but not that which Aristophanes had really formed about him "for he will have known him better", p. 274. And as the people had personified in Socratic activity the strangest and most irritating aspects of sophistry, so Aristophanes "attacked Socrates as the true sophist" as "the incarnation of all sophists", p. 277. The death of Socrates seems to EHRENBERG like the result of the resistance of the Athenians to the activity of the Sophists, p. 274, and the comedy of 423 part of the tragedy of 399. Socrates' fate was therefore the result of "a common misunderstanding" p. 276, of the Athenian people supported in their mistake by the Aristophanic comedy. According to SARRI, *Riletture delle Nuvole di Aristofane come fonte per la conoscenza di Socrate*, in the Riv. di Filosofia Neo-scolastica LXV (1973), p. 534: "Dobbiamo credere che Aristofane, lungi dal compiere sforzi per correggere l'opinione

And this Socrates already alive in the popular imagination Aristophanes has put on the stage, creating a character with features openly allusive to known peculiarities of the real person[161]. Aristophanes has in fact given back to the public what the public itself had prepared for him, presenting on stage a figure already widely known to the Athenians on which popular satire had already focused and given considerable vent to its feelings. And a spectator of the scenes in the square and gatherer of voices coming from it was Aristophanes himself, who shared that idea that the people had formed of Socrates and perhaps with its quips contributed to confirming and defining. Consequently, Aristophanes did not invent his Socrates, just as he did not invent Cleon in the *Knights* or Euripides in the *Frogs*[162]. And as he did not invent him, so his image was not distorted by the alleged conservatism of which the poet of the *Clouds*[163] is always accused.

popolare, ci abbia presentato un Socrate secondo l'immagine che di lui si era fatta l'Ateniese medio sulla base dei suoi criteri di giudizio". To L. ROSSETTI, *Le Nuvole di Aristofane; perché furono una commedia e non una farsa*, in Riv. di Cultura classica e medievale XVI (1974), p. 135, who attributes to the *Clouds* greater historical adherence, it seems that: "Le *Nuvole* riflettano assai da vicino e con discreta fedeltà la sostanza e i modi, e forse anche i contenuti, del magistero socratico degli anni 425-420".

161. The features of the historical Socrates have been clearly defined by DERENNE, *op. cit.*, p. 77.

162. GELZER, *Aristophanes und sein Sokrates*, art. cit., has studied the way in which Aristophanes deals with Cleon and Euripides to deduce the way in which that same Aristophanes deals with Socrates, p. 65, concluding that as Cleon and Euripides adhere to the real persons of the demagogue and the tragic poet, known by other sources, so the Socrates of the *Clouds* is the Socrates of history and not a poetic figure. But another of GELZER's works to note is *Der Epirrematische Agon bei Aristophanes. Untersuchungen zur struktur der att. Alten Komödien*, Zetemata XXIII, Munich 1960 and *Aristophanes*, in PW. RE, supplement Band XII, coll. 1393-1570.

163. The conservatism of Aristophanes has become a commonplace in Aristophanic criticism, blaming on the poet's inability to understand the spirit of the new times his failure to understand the work of Socrates and the responsibility for his tragic fate. And so Aristophanes is an anachronistic conservative with extremely limited ideas for a historian of philosophy like ZELLER, *Socrates*, cit., pp. 115; 218-19; for a historian of Greek literature, like A. CROISET, *Histoire de la littérature grecque*, IV, op. cit., pp. 238-239; and for a historian of the ethico-political life of the Greeks, like DE SANCTIS, *Storia dei Greci*, II, op. cit., p. 349.

Aristophanes is not a conservative nor, worse, a die-hard reactionary, just as he is neither a deprecator of the gods nor a defender of the established religion. He is not a conservative nor, worse, a reactionary, for the simple reason that Aristophanes is interested in the past only insofar as it is in contrast with the present, since he drew his laughter from none other than the opposition and contrast between past and present, old and new, tradition and fashion[164]. Moreover, when the *Clouds* was produced, Aristophanes had only just turned twenty, and at twenty people are not conservative. What sort of past would be cherished by a young man of twenty who, though he be as precocious as Aristophanes was, has only just become aware of the present? And he is not a deprecator of the gods, nor a defender of the national religion, since impiety or piety are features distinctive of the impious or pious character and not an expression of the author's own persuasion[165]. The impiety of Peisthetaerus, for ex-

164. M. CROISET, *Histoire de la Littérature Grecque*, III, op. cit., p. 561, has rightly said that "le propre de la comédie ancienne, c'est de montrer le ridicule des choses à la mode; et, encore une fois, Aristophane est la comédie faite homme". But, continues CROISET, *cit.*, p. 562, if Aristophanes praises the olden days, it is only to contrast them to the new ones, since only in this contrast can he bring out the ridiculous aspect of what enthralls his contemporaries. So it comes about that Aristophanes himself can believe in the goodness of the past; nonetheless he more than anyone would be disappointed to return to the olden days.

165. The thesis, ancient but taken up again in recent (indeed very recent) times, is the one which accuses Aristophanes of impiety, cf. C.A. BOETTIGER, *Aristophanes impunitus deorum gentilium irrisor*, Dresdae, 1837; C. BEHAGEL, *De vetere comoedia deos irridente, I, Aristophanes*, Gottingae, 1856; F. KOCK, *Aristophanes und die Götter des Volksglaubens*, Leipzig, 1857; C. HILD, *Aristophanes, impietatis reus*, Vesontione, 1880.. C. PASCAL, *Dioniso*, cit., p. 15, finally, for whom Aristophanes was "un audace spregiatore delle credenze popolari". But a correct view is held by C. DEL GRANDE, *Hybris*, Napoli 1947, p. 272, to whom it seems that "nella soluzione della irreligiosità di Aristofane abbiano avuto ragione quelli che l'hanno negata non quelli che l'hanno ammessa". Modern critics according to DECHARME, *La critique des traditions réligieuses chez les grecs*, op. cit., p. 109, not contemporary ones have accused Aristophanes of impiety. And the ancients did not do so in order to "travestir les dieux et les ridiculiser sur la scène comique, [...], rire à gorge deployée de leurs attitudes et de leurs mésaventures, était considéré comme une chose absolument inoffensive, qui ne pouvait attirer sur la cité le moindre éclat de colère céleste". p. 110. Attacking the gods, DEL GRANDE, *op. cit.*, p. 273,

136

ample, is an occasion for laughter precisely because of its enormity, but the poet's own view is far removed from it[166]. It is no mere coincidence, moreover, that no playwright, comic or tragic, unlike philosophers, has ever been accused of impiety[167].

was one of the many excesses that the festival allowed and that the rite in general largely restored. "La rappresentazione di una commedia", writes PETTAZZONI, *La Religione nella Grecia antica*, op. cit., p. 210, "era pur sempre un atto di culto. E la licenza, anche la più sfrenata, era un carattere congenito di quella celebrazione". Otherwise not only Aristophanes, but all the ancient comedy-writers, most especially Epicharmus, should have been accused of ἀσέβεια. And this did not happen because the comedy aimed at merely entertaining, and if entertainment took place at the expense of the divinities, no-one was scandalized by it, DECHARME, *op. cit.*, p. 110; DEL GRANDE, cit., p. 272.

166. ARISTOPANES, *Birds*, ll. 1199-1270. In relation to the scene of Peisetairos and Iris, DEL GRANDE, *Hybris*, op. cit., p. 267, wonders "se oggi un autore drammatico, per quanto spregiudicato, oserebbe concepire una scena nella quale una santa, venuta di Paradiso, fosse minacciata di essere scoperta e polluta lì per lì, alla presenza di tutti. Ma ammesso il caso positivo, non credo se ne permetterebbe la recita in un teatro pubblico, sotto qualunque regime onesto. Questo avveniva senza scandalo nella libera Atene" p. 268. But I believe that here Aristophanes does not intend to cause offense to the popular feeling of the inviolability of the gods, but instead to mock at the vulgar coarseness of Peisetairos and the boors like him, who were incapable of honest thoughts even in front of a goddess and in which even the most spontaneous sense of reverence was subject to an irresistible movement of instinct, to the obscene desire of an impossible contact. And the comic nature of the scene lies precisely in the absurdity of the reduction of the divine Iris to the instinctive brutality of Peisetairos. And so I agree with PETTAZZONI, *Le Religione nella Grecia antica*, op. cit., p. 212, when he writes that the "satira degli dei voleva essere innanzitutto satira di coloro che concepivano davvero gli dei come il poeta da burla li rappresentava".

167. The same Athenians "che permettevano ai poeti comici di caricaturare illimitatamente religione e dei, per giudizi della stessa natura, ma di grado più lieve, accusarono Protagora e condannarono Socrate", DEL GRANDE, *Hybris*, op. cit., p. 272: "per giudizi, però, non per intuizioni: cioè per affermazioni dovute a ragionamento non ad estro comico". "Un momento di saturnali, posti sotto il segno di Dioniso; e ufficialmente si sapeva, e tutti erano d'accordo, che quanto là si diceva era uno scherzo". All was permitted, to achieve the purpose of the merry feast, DEL GRANDE, *Hybris*, op. cit., p. 272.

For the people, writes DECHARME, op. cit., p. III, the gods, after having laughed at them, probably remained those they were before: divine beings who had to be respected and feared. This does not preclude the possibility of thoughts of a different order being kindled in some more reflective spirits; but in this case those thoughts were suggested by the frequentation of philosophers and not the

In brief, we cannot attribute to Aristophanes all that Aristophanes himself attributes to his own characters and for the same reason we cannot claim that behind the comic mask is always hidden a serious and thoughtful face of the tradition, customs, religion and laws of the native land[168]. It is a mistake to make of Aristophanes a vulgar buffoon, but it is also a mistake to take Aristophanes too seriously[169].

Aristophanes finally, is a comic author who in city contests presents his comedies, which are able to succeed only if they manage to amuse the audience more than the other rival comedies. And, in fact, does Aristophanes himself not say that his duty is that of giving to the public "little boredom, much merriment"[170]? And what else would Aristophanes have intended to do with the *Clouds* than to amuse the public? And to amuse them Aristophanes represented on stage, in a blatant comic distortion, the master of Crytias and Alcibiades as he had come to appear in the popular imagination: a Socratic image, consequently, drawn from the squares and crossroads of Athens[171] and maintained at the level of the plebs of the Dionysia. Unlike the

theatre of Dionysus, since the comedy, which no-one took seriously, was not the most suitable school in which doubts could be aroused.

168. "Faire de lui un incrédule", writes M. CROISET, *Histoire de la Littérature Grecque*, III, op. cit., pp. 563-564, "ce serait à tout prendre une plus grosse erreur que d'en faire un croyant. Pas plus en fait de religion qu'en fait de politique ou de morale, on ne se présente ce joyeux poète descendant au fond de sa conscience et se demandant à lui-même ce qu'il croyait réellement: il est très probable que cela dépendait des jours, des sujets qu'il traitait, des gens avec qui il vivait, de son humeur, mais surtout des hasards de la verve, des entrainements du style, de l'effet à produire. Avec tous ces éléments, il es bien difficile de faire ni une croyance solide ni une incrédulité bien établie".

169. "Mais ce n'est un simple bouffon", CROISET says of Aristophanes, op. cit., p. 564. "Il a un des esprits les plus prompts, les plus clairvoyants, les plus habiles qu'il ait jamais eu: il a compris ou senti qu'il n'y avait pas de haute comédie sans idées, et voilà pourquoi il s'est fait des idées. Ce sont celles de son rôle".

170. ARISTOPHANES, *Peace*, 11. 764-765.

171. M. CROISET, *Aristophane et les partis à Athènes*, op. cit., p. 22: "il n'est pas un seul de ses lecteurs qui ne sente, à chaque page de ses [Aristophane] œuvres, ce qu'il a dû à la rue, à l'agora, au port, aux rencontres et aux réunions. Tout ce qu'il y a de réalité dans son théâtre vient de là, et sa fantaisie même s'en inspire largement".

138

Apology, which presents an image of Socrates that is clearly idealized beyond any human measure.

Aristophanes presents to us a sophist Socrates[172] who has his own organized school[173] and who teaches for money[174] the art of speaking in political assemblies and tribunals to initiated disciples[176] whom he morally corrupts by making them into deniers of the national gods[178]; Plato, on the other hand, draws the figure of a Socrates beloved by the god of Delphi[179] and charged with a spiritual mission for a whole people[180]; a Socrates who has no disciples[181] to whom he would have anything to teach since he knows nothing[182]; who does not have his own school, but speaks in the squares and gymnasia of Athens to whoever wants to listen to him[183]; who takes no money[184] and who, what is more, sank into extreme poverty[185] for his mission in the service of the god and the city[186].

Two figures then that are completely irreconcilable and contradictory if confronted; but the mistake lies precisely in the confrontation of the picture of Socrates in the *Clouds* with that of the *Apology*.

8. — The *Clouds* and the *Apology* should instead be brought back within that common Socratic limit represented by the charge, trial and sentence and the historical reliability of the two sources commensurate with the possibility each of these offers of

172. *Clouds*, 1. 112 ff.; 1. 266; 1. 636 ff.; 1. 658 ff.; 1. 1111; 11. 1308-309.
173. *Clouds*, 11. 95; 133 ff.
174. *Clouds*, 11. 98; 249; 669; 856 ff.; 1146-1147.
175. *Clouds*, 11. 112 ff.; 239 ff.; 430 ff.; 486 ff.; 748-783; 874 ff.; 1149; 1229; 1339.
176. *Clouds*, 11. 140; 143 ff.; 250 ff.
177. *Clouds*, 11. 830; 1321-1453.
178. *Clouds*, 11. 367; 381, 423; 813-30; 1241; 1470.
179. *Apology*, 21a ff.
180. *Apology*, 22a; 23b; 33c.
181. *Apology*, 33a.
182. *Apology*, 19e; 21d; 22d; 23b; 33b.
183. *Apology*, 23c; 33a-b.
184. *Apology*, 19e; 31b; 33b.
185. *Apology*, 23c; 37b; 38b.
186. *Apology*, 23e; 29e; 30a; 31a-b; 36c-d.

a coherent interpretation of the human and philosophical personality of Socrates in relation to his fate in the prison of the Eleven. Since, if we only know this[187] that a Socrates existed in Athens and that this same Socrates was sentenced to death in 399, an interpretation of Socrates that aspires to being more than a mere hypothesis must move in the direction of a critical justification of that tragic consistency between Socratic cross-questioning and the death by hemlock, trying as closely as possible to link the effect to its cause. That it was only gossip, envy, calumny, the fiercest and gravest of enmities that led Socrates to court, is an argument that Zeller already had rejected, remarking how the attack on Socrates hit out especially at his political ideology and more particularly the moral, religious and political aspects of his teaching[188].

Now, in the *Clouds* there recur just those elements of the tragic consistency between the life and death of Socrates that enable us to pick out, beyond the literary fiction, the historical personage of Socrates.

187. Well known is the sceptical conclusion of GIGON, *Sokrates. Sein Bild in Dichtung und Geschichte*. Bern, 1947, 1979[2], for whom the Socrates we know is only the "zentraler Gegenstand einer philosophischen Dichtung", p. 16, Socratic literature being nothing if not *Dichtung*, p. 14, and the contradictory pictures of Socrates drawn by the Socratics of the pure simple aspects of the *Sokratesdichtung*, p. 15, destined to create the ideal model of the sage. Cf. of GIGON, *Les grands problèmes de la philosophie antique*, Paris, 1961, p. 292 ff. That a Socrates existed, that this same Socrates had taken part in certain military enterprises and that he was subsequently charged, tried and sentenced is, finally, all we know of him: seek to know more is a vain effort, p. 64.

The provocative thesis of GIGON has opened up the problem of Socrates to a new critical and methodological awareness. Of the works on Socrates, born out of the need to overcome GIGON's scepticism, let us recall DE MAGALHÃES-VILHENA, *Le problème de Socrate. Le Socrate historique et le Socrate de Platon*, Paris, PUF, p. 1952; *Socrate et la légende platonicienne*, Paris, PUF, 1952; I. LUCCIONI, *Xénophon et le socratisme* Paris, PUF, 1953; MONDOLFO, *Sócrates*, Buenos Aires, 1955; G. CALOGERO, *Socrate*, in *Nuova Antologia*, November 1955, (F. 1859) pp. 291-308; and esp. A. CAPIZZI, *La testimonianza platonica*, in *Rassegna di Filosofia*, 1. VI, f. II, pp. 205-221 and 1, VI, f. IV, pp. 309-337.

188. ZELLER, *Socrates*, cit., p. 218 l.c.

140

When, indeed, in the converstation between Socrates and Strepsiades, the singular master speaks to the slow pupil about the divinity of the clouds, Aristophanes puts into Socrates' mouth this sacrilegious statement: there is no Zeus: οὐδ'ἔστι Ζεύς[189], adding that his place had been taken by the ethereal whirligig αἰθέριος δῖνος[190], hence Strepsiades' confusion and timorous admission ὁ Ζεὺς οὐκ ὤν, ἀλλ'ἀντ'αὐτοῦ Δῖνος νυνὶ Βασιλεύων[191] which soon afterwards changes into a resolute statement following the proofs supplied by Socrates; so much so that Strepsiades himself, mocking his son Pheidippides who had sworn by Olympian Zeus[192], repeats he is convinced that there is no Zeus[193] and that Δῖνος is in his place[194] and that these things are said by Socrates and repeated by Chaerophon[195]. But when, finally, disillusioned and full of regret at having entrusted himself and his son to Socrates, he sets fire to the Phrontisterion[196], he shouts that for a thousand reasons Socrates and his disciples deserve similar punishment, but especially for their offences against the gods[197].

It is quite clear from all this that 24 years before the charge signed and sworn by Meletus had been placed in the hands of the archon-king, Aristophanes had, in precise terms, formulated his

189. *Clouds*, 1. 367.
190. *Clouds*, 1. 380.
191. *Clouds*, 1. 381 "*...que Zeus n'existe point et qu'à sa place Tourbillon règne*".
192. *Clouds*, 1. 817.
193. *Clouds*, 1. 827.
194. *Clouds*, 1. 828.
195. *Clouds*, 1. 850. It may be interesting to note the different ways in which Aristophanes and Plato characterize Chaerephon, whom Aristophanes describes as "half dead", *Clouds*, 1. 504, pale and sickly, always shut away at home, which he leaves only in the evening, hence his nickname of "bat", *Birds*, 1. 1296, 1564; whereas Plato presents him as ardent and decisive, *Apology*, 21a, ready to go into voluntary exile rather than put up with the odious tyranny of the Thirty. Might this characterization have been done on purpose to make plausible the question that Chaerephon had dared ἐτόλμησε, *Apology*, 21a, to put to the Pythia whether there was one wiser than Socrates?
196. *Clouds*, 1. 850.
197. *Clouds*, 1. 1509.

report, corresponding perfectly in its charge headings with the later legal charge[198].

- Socrates, said the legal charge, does not believe in the gods the state worships[199],
- Zeus does not exist, said Socrates in the *Clouds*[200],
- He introduces new ones[201],
- Δῖνος reigns in his place[202],
- He corrupts young men[203],
- Corruptor of youth, is said of the discourse learnt at Socrates' school[204].

And so, once the satire is stripped of all the comic alterations and all the obvious artifices used in constructing the Socrates character, there remains a specific accusation of impiety and moral corruption and a terrible death sentence which in a sinister fashion anticipate the verdict of the Eliasts.

The significance of the *Clouds* as a Socratic document lies, in my view, precisely in that charge. Aristophanic comedy thus poses a problem which is very different from that of knowing what Socrates might have been like for Aristophanes to feel authorized to present him as the head of an organized school and engaged in research on nature. We should rather wonder what

198. The reliability of the text of the charge transcribed by Favorino and quoted by DIOGENES LAERTIUS, II, V, 40 has long been discussed and often refuted, Cf. SCHANZ, *Apology*, op. cit., p. 14. The divergences, which are merely literary in nature, between Favorino's text in DIOGENES and the one quoted by Xenophon and by Plato, are not sufficient to cast doubts on Favorino's account. XENOPHON, *Memorabili*, I, I, 1, reproduces only "approximately" the text of the charge, bringing to it substitutions and omissions which are notable but not prejudicial; in PLATO, *Apology*, 24h, Socrates quotes from memory the text of the sworn charge and the shifting of the charge must be ascribed to the defensive criterion adopted by Socrates-Plato. Precisely for this GIGON, *Sokrates* cit., p. 89, rejects the reliability of the charge text which he also considers to be part of the Socratic *Dichtung*.

199. Favorino, apud. DIOGENES LAERTIUS, II, V, 40. The meaning of the word νομίζειν, which recurs in the charge text against Socrates, has been discussed supra in *Socrates. From myth to history*.

200. *Clouds*, 1. 367.

201. Favorino, apud. DIOGENES LAERTIUS, *cit*.

202. *Clouds*, 1. 379.

203. Favorino, apud. DIOGENES LAERTIUS, cit.

204. *Clouds*, 1. 928.

was the origin of the charge of impiety which is found already so precisely formulated in the *Clouds*[204a] and which for twenty-five years at least accompanies Socratic activity.

Let us finally leave aside the myths: of ancient calumnies, the just man condemned, judges who represent a bundle of vulgar interests and that whoever approves their judgement has no feeling of justice: all fine thoughts from sensitive minds, but which have nothing to do with history. History is different; the historical Socrates is a ἀσεβής[205] Socrates, specifically identified by Aristophanes and as such charged, tried and sentenced in 399.

With this ἀσεβής Socrates we must make ourselves acquainted by trying to understand the spirit, intention and aim of the eternal cross-questioning which, against the custom, mentality and law of Athens in 399, made Socrates seem impious and a corruptor, thus occasioning the charge, trial and sentence.

To me there seems no other way of overcoming the scepticism of Gigon, albeit starting out from the same sceptical conclusion as Gigon[206].

204a. In the view of GELZER, *Aristophanes und sein Sokrates*, cit., p. 84, however, the charge of introducing new divinities and, in general, that of impiety, was more for comic purposes than to indicate a precise spiritual attitude towards the divinity.

205. I am however very far from the extremism of RÖCK, *Der Unverfälschte Sokrates. Atheist und "Sophist"*, op. cit. and of PASCAL, *Dioniso*, op. cit., who, stressing Socrates' atheism, attribute its origin to the naturalistic research and the influence exerted by the physicists and particularly by Anaxagoras. The Socrates who raised enthusiasm in Critias and Alcibiades, when Plato was not yet born to philosophy, could certainly not have been the naturalist and quibbling Socrates of the *Clouds*. Socrates was ἀσεβής, but not because he was a naturalist. And it is not sufficient to say that he was naturalist and atheist in an early phase of his activity known to Aristophanes and known to Plato, because if this were the case it would no longer explain the charge and sentence which took place 24 years after the comedy of Aristophanes. Socrates was always ἀσεβής, right throughout the whole of his teaching because of a new and different intuition of man of which he was the bearer. Cf. *supra*, *Socrates. From myth to history*.

206. CALOGERO, *Socrates*, art. cit., has rightly observed how "da un punto di vista metodologico convenga tener conto il più possibile dello scetticismo di Gigon e partire, provvisoriamente almeno, dalla sua posizione, anche senza condividerne, per così dire, lo spirito di sfiducia", p. 292.

More forcibly and with a greater awareness of the complex problems aroused

And it is already a positive result to point out that the ἀσεβής Socrates of the *Clouds* coincides perfectly with the historical Socrates.

And we will see that Plato and Xenophon will confirm the truth about the historical Socrates revealed by Aristophanes in the *Clouds*.

9. — In this paper we have tried to show: that the text of our *Clouds* does not differ from the staged version except in the 45 lines of the new Parabasis and in the omission of the two choral passages that should have introduced and concluded the scene of the contest of Right and Wrong; that as there is no change in our text compared with the 423 version, so there is no change in Aristophanes' view of Socrates; that the Socrates of the Comedy, despite the openly comic distortion of the character, is the same Socrates known later by Xenophon and Plato; that the Socrates of the *Clouds* is not a physiologist, but a sophist, a master of the art of speaking in tribunals and political assemblies; that the impious and corrupting Socrates of the *Clouds* coincides perfectly with the ἀσεβής Socrates of history: with the Socrates, namely, who was tried and sentenced in 399.

The pointing out this similarity makes clear the value of Aristophanic comedy as a Socratic source, from which the enquiry must move on in an attempt to understand those elements of Socratic cross-questioning which against the custom, mentality and laws of Athens in 399 made Socrates appear impious and a

by the crisis open in the Socratic historiography of Gigon, speaks CAPIZZI, *Il problema socratico*, in *Sophia*, XXV, nn. 3-4, 1957, pp. 199-207: "Per noi sono [...] validi dal 1947 in poi quegli studi che hanno almeno tentato di battere il Gigon sul suo stesso campo, riesaminandone gli argomenti: perché solo liberandosi in modo esauriente di quegli argomenti, sarà possibile in un futuro prossimo o lontano tornare alla speranza di ricostruire in qualche modo la personalità speculativa del fondatore della filosofia ateniese", p. 205. See Capizzi's study, which is in many respects fundamental and essential, for any future attempt at an interpretation of Socrates: *Socrate e i personaggi filosofi di Platone. Uno studio sulle strutture delle testimonianze platoniche e una edizione delle testimonianze contenute nei Dialoghi*, Rome 1970, about which see mine review: *I presocratici e Socrate nella testimonianza platonica*, in G.C.F.I. III, 1971, 452-467, now in *Socrate. Un problema storico*, Naples, 1984, pp. 277-297.

corruptor, thereby occasioning and legitimizing his charge, trial and sentence.

Athens, summer 1965

ON THE TRIAL OF ANAXAGORAS

*Περὶ δὲ τῆς δίκης αυτοῦ διάφορα
λέγεται*

D.L. II 6, 12

1. It is an *opinio recepta* among the great majority of historians[1] that Anaxagoras was accused of ἀσέβεια because of his teachings concerning the nature of the stars. But although this

1. I shall only refer here to a selection of the modern historians of Greek civilization, philosophy and religion, as follows: T. Stanley, *The history of philosophy*, 4th ed., London, 1743, p. 67; J. Brucker, *Historia critica philosophiae*, I, 2nd ed., 1767, p. 496; G.G.F. Hegel, *Vorlesungen über die Gesch. d. Philosophie*, Italian ed. *Lezioni sulla Storia della Filosofia* I, Perugia-Venezia, 1930, p. 360; cf. Renouvier, *Manuel de philosophie*, I, Paris, 1844, p. 230; E. Zeller, *Die Philosophie d. Griechen*, 5th ed., 1892, Italian ed. E. Zeller & R. Mondolfo, *La filosofia dei greci nel suo sviluppo storico*, pt. 1, vol. V, *Empedocle, Atomisti, Anassagora*, ed. by A. Capizzi, Firenze, 1969, from which edition I shall be quoting, p. 359; E. Zeller-Lortzing, *Grundriss der Gesch. d. Griech. Philos.*, Leipzig, 1914, p. 38, which confirms that Anaxagoras was accused of "denying the gods of the State (Staatsgötter)"; G. Grote, *History of Greece*, IV, London, 1849, pp. 135-6; E. Curtius, *Griechische Geschichte*, 1857, II, 6th ed., Berlin, 1888, p. 394; T. Gomperz, *Griech. Denker*, 1896, Italian ed. *Pensatori Greci*, 5th ed., I, Firenze, 1950, p. 317; P. Decharme, *La critique des traditions religieuses chez les Grecs, des origines au temps de Plutarque*, Paris, 1904, p. 159, according to whom Anaxagoras was brought before the judges, on the denunciation of Cleon, "pour avoir dit que le Soleil est une pierre incandescente, quand tout le monde à Athènes croyait que le soleil était un dieu"; J. Geffcken, *Die ἀσέβεια des Anaxagoras*, Hermes, 1907, pp. 127-133; J. Burnet, *Early Greek Philosophy*, 2nd ed., London, 1908, p. 297; *Greek philosophy, Thales to Plato*, 1914, London, 1953 ed., p. 76; K. Joël, *Gesch. d. Antiken Philos.*, Tübingen, 1921, p. 568; R. Pettazzoni, *La religione nella Grecia antica fino ad Alessandro*, 1921, 2nd ed., Torino, 1953, p. 178 ff.; 183-184; L. Robin, *La pensée grecque et les origines de l'esprit scientifique*, 1923, Paris, 1948, p. 147; F. Ueberweg & K. Praechter, *Grundriss d. Gesch. d. Philos.*, I, 14th ed., *Die Philos. d. Altertums*, Basel-Stuttgart, 1957; M. Nilsson, *A history of Greek*

147

common belief is supported by a long doxographic tradition², the ψήφισμα of Diopeithes³, which provided the legal basis for the

religion, 1925, Oxford, 1963, who believes that "the prosecution of Anaxagoras was based upon a charge of atheism, because he declared the sun to be a glowing mass and the moon a lump of earth no bigger than the Peloponnese"; *Greek piety*, Oxford, 1948, p. 80; E. Derenne, *Les procès d'impiété intentés aux philosophes à Athènes au Ve et au IVe siècle a. J.-C.*, Liège-Paris, 1930, p. 25, according to whom Anaxagoras was accused of impiety because he had dared to say that the sun was an incandescent stone, larger than the Peloponnese, and that the moon was an earth; L. Gernet & Boulanger, *Le génie grec dans la réligion*, Paris, 1932, p. 345; A. Covotti, *I Presocratici*, Napoli, 1934, p. 206; P.M. Schuhl, *Essai sur la formation de la pensée grecque*, 1934, 2nd ed., Paris, 1949, p. 368; E. Brehier, *Histoire de la philosophie*, 1938, 7th ed., I, Paris, 1960, p. 71; G. De Sanctis, *Storia dei greci*, 1939, II, Firenze, 1954, p. 137; O. Gigon, *Zu Anaxagoras*, Philol., 1936, pp. 1-41; F. Enriquez & G. Santillana, *Compendio di storia del pens. scient.*, Bologna, 1946, pp. 66; C. Del Grande, *Hybris*, Napoli, 1947, p. 319; J. Zafiropulo, *Anaxogore de Clazomène*, Paris, 1948, p. 247; E.R. Dodds, *The Greeks and the irrational*, Berkeley, 1951, p. 189 ff.; A. Davison, *Protagoras, Democritus and Anaxagoras*, Cl. Quart., 1953, pp. 35-45; J. Chevalier, *Histoire de la pensée*, I, Paris, 1950, p. 120: E. Paci, *Storia del pensiero presocratico*, ERI, 1957, p. 104; F. Adorno, *La filosofia antica*, 1961, vol. I, 2nd ed., Milano, 1972, p. 85; F. Romano, *Anassagora*, Padova, 1965, p. 15; W.K.C. Guthrie, *A history of Greek philosophy*, vol. II, Cambridge, p. 286; V. Ehrenberg, *From Solon to Socrates*, London, 1968, p. 244; E. Hussey, *The Presocratics*, London, 1972, p. 133; F.M. Cleve, *The philosophy of Anaxagoras*, The Hague, 1973, p. 3.

2. Cf. Sotion and Satyrus, in Diog. Laert. II III, 13 = DK 59 A 1; Suid. = DK 59 A 3; Diodor. XII 39 = DK 59 A 17; Ioseph. *c. Ap.* II 265 = DK 59 A 19; Olympiod. in *Meteor.*, p. 17, 19 Stüve = DK 59 A 19; Plato, *Apol.* 26d = DK 59 a 35, which is the predecessor of all the other sources, all of which are based on it; Irenaeus II 14, 2 (D.171) = DK 59 A 113.

The source material on Anaxagoras, collected in Diels & Kranz, *Die Fragmente der Vorsokratiker*, Berlin, 1956, referred to here as DK, has recently been edited, with an Italian translation, additions, introduction and commentary, by D. Lanza in vol. LII of the "Biblioteca di Studi Superiori" published by La Nuova Italia, *Anassagora, testimonianze e frammenti*, Firenze, 1966, and has also appeared in an Italian translation by R. Laurenti, in *I Presocratici, testimonianze e frammenti*, 2 vols, ed. by G. Giannantoni, vol. II, n.d. (1969).

3. Diopeithes, a soothsayer and practitioner of mantic science, cf. K. Swoboda, in Pauly-Wissowa, *RE*, IX, 1046-47, proposed and obtained approval for a decree, Plut., *Pericles*, 32, 2 = DK 59 A 17, according to which anyone who did not worship the gods or who taught doctrines concerning celestial phenomena would be brought before the popular assembly, in accordance with the procedure of εἰσαγγελία, Caillemer, in Daremberg-Saglio, *s.v.*; G. Glotz, *La*

accusation, trial and conviction of the Clazomenian⁴, does not appear to give sufficient evidence for the view that the ασέβεια of which Anaxagoras is supposed to have been convicted, consisted in the naturalistic reduction concerning the stars propounded by the "greatest natural philosopher" from Clazomenae. It is even doubtful whether Anaxagoras could have been accused of ασέβεια and thus have been the first victim of the series of impiety proceedings brought against the philosophers⁵ in Attica in the 5th and 4th centuries B.C. If these doubts are justified, it will be necessary to seek reasons for the conviction of Anaxagoras in spheres outside that of religion, for although in the latter sphere reasons have always been found, convincing proof has consistently been lacking.

If, however, Anaxagoras was not accused tried and convicted of ασέβεια, then of which offence, of those covered by Diopeithes' ψήφισμα, was he convicted? And how important is it to the historian of philosophy to establish the precise nature of the offence supposedly committed by the Clazomenian, and what is the significance of his consequent conviction in Attica?

This study is an attempt to answer these questions. It will, however, also have to cover further aspects of the problem, such as the date of the trial⁶ and the name of the accuser; not because

cité grecque, Paris, 179 et seq.; U.E. Paoli, Studi sul processo attico, Padova, 1933, p. 53.

Cf. P. Decharme, La loi de Diopeithès, in Mélanges Perrot, Paris, 1903. On the fact that the trial of Anaxagoras took place before the court of the Heliasts, cf. Caillemer, s.v. eisangelia, in Daremberg-Saglio and also s.v. asébeia in the same work.

The decree of Diopeithes will be examined in greater depth in the course of this study.

4. Ὁ κλαζομένιος. "Clazomenius vocatur Anaxagora unanimi consensu totius antiquitatis", notes Schaubach, Anaxagorae Clazomenii fragmenta quae supersunt, Lipsia, 1827, p. 7 and the reference therein. For the epithet ὁ μὲν φυσικώτατος, see Sext. VII 90 = DK 58 B 21.

5. For these trials, see Derenne, Les procès d'impiété, cit., and P. Decharme, La critique des traditions réligieuses, op. cit.

6. I cannot agree with Raven, in Kirk & Raven, The Presocratic philosophers, Cambridge, 1957, p. 364, who holds that the exact determination of the date of the trial or trials of Anaxagoras, cf. J.A. Davison, Protagoras, Democritus and Anaxagoras, in CQ, n.s., 3, 1953, pp. 33-45, esp. 39 f., is of little importance to the historian of philosophy. Leaving aside any other consideration concerning

of any desire for comprehensiveness as such, but because the clarification of these two controversial points is essential for an accurate assessment of the historical and political situation in which it was possible for the ψήφισμα to be approved and for the Clazomenian physicist to be convicted.

2. The date of the trial of Anaxagoras is closely connected with the date of his birth and that of his arrival in Athens.

As far as his date of birth is concerned, sufficient information is available to ensure the universal acceptance of the data provided by Apollodorus[7].

The date of the Clazomenian's arrival in Athens is, however, still disputed

Diogenes Laertius[8], following the *Chronicle* of Apollodorus, notes that Anaxagoras "was born in the 70th Olympiad" (500-497) and "died in the first year of the 88th Olympiad" (428)[9]; and since Diogenes also informs us that "at the invasion of Xerxes" (480)[10] Anaxagoras was "twenty years old" and that

the biography of Anaxagoras, cf. Taylor, *cit.*, p. 81, the trial of the Clazomenian has a bearing on a rather important element of the problem of Socrates, the clarification of which led to the necessity of undertaking the present study.

7. Apollodorus, in Diog. L. II III, 7 = DK 59 A 1, supported by Cyril, *c. Jul.* I, p. 12b = DK 59 A 4, and, less directly, Marm. Par. *ep.* 60 & 57 = DK 59 4a. On the credence given to Apollodorus rather than Eusebius = DK 59 A 4, who gives the date of Anaxagoras' death as 460, cf. Zeller, *cit.*, p. 351, n. 2, who rejects the earlier date accepted by Hermann and Unger; see Lanza, *Anassagora*, note on p. 4.

8. Diog. L. *loc. cit.*

9. The emendation to the text, replacing ἑβδομηκοστῆς by ὀγδοηκοστῆς, cf. Meursius, *Attic. Lect.* II, 27, in Schaubach, *cit.*, p. 3, has been generally accepted since the time of Cobet and Diels, cf. Hicks, in Diog. L., *Lives of eminent philosophers*, London & New York, 1925, 1950 ed., *a.l.*; M. Gigante, in Diog. L., *Vite dei filosofi*, Bari, 1962, *a.l.*; Raven, *Anaxagoras*, in Kirk & Raven, *Pres.*, *cit.*, XV, 487, p. 362; Lanza, *cit.*, A.l p. 4, and has been accepted by all historians since the time of Zeller, *cit.*, p. 351, n. 2, Capizzi, *cit.*, p. 455.

It is likely, according to Burnet, *EGP*, *cit.*, p. 290, that the chronology of Anaxagoras' life was constructed by Apollodorus from information about the trial supplied by Demetrius Phalereus; cf. Diels, *Rhein. Museum*, XXXI, p. 28; F. Jacoby, *Apollodors Chronik*, Philos. Untersuch. XVI, Berlin, 1902, p. 244; Derenne, *cit.*, p. 30, n. 4.

10. Cf. Herodotus, VIII, 50; G. Glotz and R. Cohen, *Histoire ancienne*, II,

he died at the age of "seventy-two years", the philosopher must have been born in the first year of the 70th Olympiad, namely 500 B.C.

Diogenes[11] also tells us that Anaxagoras stayed for "thirty years" in Athens, but does not give a definite date for his arrival. According to Diogenes,[12] Anaxagoras began to devote himself to philosophy in Athens, ἤρξατο δὲ φιλοσοφεῖν Ἀθήνησιν, under the archonship of Callias, ἐπὶ Καλλίου[13], at the age of twenty,

Histoire grecque, II, Paris, 1931, p. 73.

11. Diog. L., *loc. cit.*

12. *Ibid.*

13. On Callias, see Schoeffer, in Pauly-Wissowa, *RE,s.v. Kallia*, 20, 1612. That the name of Callias, Archon in 456, should be replaced by that of Calliades, Archon 480, was the opinion of Meursius, *Attic. Lect.*, IV, 15, cf. Schaubach, *cit.*, p. 14, followed, among others, by Cobet, in Diog. Laert., *De Clar. Phil. Vitis*, Firmin-Didot, Parisiis, 1850, II 3, 7; II 5, 45, and Hicks, in Diog. Laert., *Lives, cit., al.*, but rejected by Zeller, *cit.*, p. 352, to whom it appears that Callias and Calliades are nothing "se non due forme diverse dello stesso nome". Present-day critics appear to be united in their agreement with Zeller's conjecture, which has been accepted by, *int. al.*, Jacoby, *cit.*, p. 244 f.; Burnet, *E.G.Ph.*, p. 290; Derenne, *cit.*, p. 31; Diano, *La data di pubblicazione della Syngraphè di Anassagora*, in *Antemon. Scritti in onore di C. Anti*, Firenze, 1955, p. 236 & n. 2; and recently by Lanza, *cit.*, p. 5, in a note.

It appears to me, however, that Zeller's conjecture, unsupported as it is by any valid examples, is the cause of all the confusion in the biography of Anaxagoras, a confusion aggravated by the editors of Diogenes. Although the emendation of Meursius, *cit.*, which harmonizes the dates of the Diogenes text thus: Anaxagoras aged 20 = Archonship of Calliades, 480, has been accepted by some older historians, such as B. Capasso, *Historiae Philosophiae Synopsis.*, Napoli, 1728, p. 74; Stanley, *cit.*, p. 63; Brucker, *cit.*, I, p. 493, yet Tenneman, in Hegel, *cit.*, p. 355, gave a date in the 81st Olympiod, therefore 456 B.C., ἐπί καλλίου, to Anaxagoras' journey to Athens, while Schaubach, *cit.*, p. 14, rejected Meursius' reading; Cobet, *cit.*, on the other hand, read, *a.l.*, ἐπὶ Καλλιάδου,, and it was only later that, as has been seen, the two names Callias and Calliades became confused, which resulted in the disruption of the biography of Anaxagoras and the evidence of Diogenes, without any historical justification.

We may observe here that, while Diels, DK 59 A 1, gives both names,ἐπὶ Καλλίυ (456; oder = Καλλιάδου 480), Gigante, in Diog. Laert., *a.l.*, agrees with Wehrli in writing Καλλίου, but moves the year of his archonship to 480, as does Lanza, *cit., a.l.*, p. 5, who, agreeing with Zeller and others that "a Callia può sostituirsi senza correzione Calliade perché si tratta dello stesso nome", gives the translation "arconte Callia (480)". We know, however, from the Table of the Archons, cf. Schoeffer, *Archonten-Tafel*, in Pauly-Wissowa, *R.E.* 1, vols,

ἐτῶν εἴκοσιν ὤν, as Demetrius of Phalerum states in his *List of the Archons*. However, Callias was Archon in 456-55[14], and if Anaxagoras "began to devote himself to philosophy"[15] in Athens ἐπὶ

581-589, that a Calliades was Archon in 480, cf. Jacoby, *cit.*, p. 405, and we can rely on the evidence of both Diodorus Siculus, Schoeffer, *cit.*, and Herodotus, VIII, 51, who mentions a Calliades who was Archon at the time of the passage of the Persians, the same Archon, in other words, as the one referred to by Diogenes Laertius, *loc. cit.*, when he states the date at which Anaxagoras was 20 years old, and when he mentions, II 5, 45, that Euripides "was born in the first year of the 75th Olympiad, ἐπὶ Καλλιάδου".

In 456, however, the Archon was Callias, cf. *Archonten-Tafel, cit.*, and there were two later Archons of the same name, in Ol. 92, 1 = 412-411 and in Ol 93, 3 = 406-405. The names of the Archons Callias and Calliades are always well distinguished and the alternative spelling was not given for either of the other Archons bearing the name Callias, except in the *vita Euripidis*, 133, 3, in Jacoby, *ict.*, p. 244 I, which is the only text in which Callias stands for Calliades, Diano *cit.*, p. 236 & n. 2.

Moreover, no other Callias known to us through the history ever seems to have had his name spelt in the alternative way. See, for example, Callias the soothsayer of Elis, Herodot. V 44, 45, Callias the Spartan, Xenoph., *Ages.* VIII 3, and Callias son of Hipponicus, mentioned by Herodot. VII, 151, and Xenophon, *Hell.*, IV 5, 13; 5 4, 22; VI 3, 2; *Symp.* I 5; IV 62, etc, cf. J. Bruns, *Das literarische Porträt* (...), 1896, Darmstadt, 1961, p. 40 ff., and especially by Plato, *Prot.* 311a; *Ap.* 20s; *Crat.* 39c; *Theaet.* 165e; *Phil.* 19b; these names are always transcribed in a uniform way, without any possibility of confusion with the name Calliades.

We may, in fact, mention that the names Callias and Calliades are clearly distinguished in references to Callias, son of Calliades, who became wise and illustrious through hearing Zeno of Elea, Plat., *Alc.* I 119a, and who was the victorious Athenian general at Potidaea, as recounted by Thucydides, I, 61-63.

Therefore it seems most unlikely that Callias and Calliades are different forms of the same name, and so we shall read ἐπὶ Καλλίου, referring to the Archon of 456 B.C., and ἐπὶ Καλλιάδου, referring to the Archon of 480; the alternative hypotheses that Anaxagoras arrived in Athens under the archonship of Calliades in 480, or under the archonship of Callias in 456, will be discussed separately.

14. Cf. *Archonten-Tafel*, in *RE*, I, 581-598, *cit.*, and Schoeffer, in *RE*, *cit.*, *s.v. Kallia*, 20, 1626.

15. Diog. Laert. II III, 7. I do not agree with R.D. Hicks, in Diogenes Laertius, *Lives of eminent philosophers*, London, 1925, 1980 ed., vol. I, p. 137, who translates: "began to study philosophy"; neither with Raven, *The Presocratic Philosophers*, cit. xv, 487 (p.362) for whom "he [Anaxagoras] began to be a philosopher."

Καλλίου, then Anaxagoras must have been 44 years old, [16] and not 20 as Demetrius of Phalerum states.

It is true that there is an alternative reading of this text, followed by Cobet, Jacoby and Hicks[17], which is of equal antiquity and in which ἐπὶ Καλλίου is replaced by ἐπὶ Καλλιάδου.

A Calliades was, in fact, Archon in 480[18], when Anaxagoras, was, indeed, twenty years old, as Diogenes says.

Consequently, if we read "under the archonship of Calliades", Diogenes' text would indicate that Anaxagoras, born in 500 B.C., began his philosophical studies in Athens in 480 B.C., at the age of 20[19]; and since he is supposed to have stayed in Athens for 30 years, the date of his trial must be 450 B.C.

This, in fact, is the opinion held by Taylor[20], Burnet[21], Adcock,

16. Schaubach, *Anax. Frag.*, *cit.*, p. 15, followed by C. Zévort. *Dissertation sur la vie et la doctrine d'Anaxagore*, Paris, 1843, p. 10 *et seq.*, had already suggested to read μ' (τεσσαράκοντα) instead of κ' (εἴκοσι), without changing the Archon's name which would mean that Anaxagoras came to Athens at around forty years of age, when Callias was Archon, in 456. Cf. Zeller, *cit.*, p. 352.

Lanza, cit., p. 5, notes that "l'ipotesi non è stata piu ripresa perchè occorrerebbe spiegare un noviziato filosofico a quarant'anni". However, it should be pointed out that, if it is accepted that ἤρξατο δὲ φιλοσοφεῖν Ἀθήνησιν ἐπὶ Καλλίου (456) gives us the date of his arrival in Athens, then the statement does not refer to an initiation into philosophy, but rather to the beginning of the Clazomenian's teaching activity in Athens, when he was forty years old, in the time of the Archon Callias; see Schaubach, *loc. cit.*

17. For C.G. Cobet, see Diog. L. *De Clarorum Phil. Vitis*, *cit.*, *a.l.*; Jacoby, *Apollodors Cronik*, *cit.*, p. 244. and *Fasti Apollodorei*, *ib.*, p. 405; Hicks, D.L., *Lives*, *cit.*, *a.l.*

18. Cf. the previously cited *Archonten-Tafel*, in *RE*, I, 581-598. On Calliades, Schoeffer, in Pauly-Wissowa, *RE*, *s.v. Kalliade*, 20, 1612.

19. Later in this study we shall see that the thesis, accepted by some scholars, that Anaxagoras was initiated into philosophy in Athens in the year of Calliades when the Persians took and destroyed the Acropolis, is untenable.

20. A.E. Taylor, *On the Date of Anaxagoras' Trial*, in "Class. Quart.", 1917, pp. 81-87, esp. p. 86. The arguments of Taylor are summarized well by Lanza, *cit.*, 5-6. But even before Taylor, M. Swoboda, *Ueber den Prozess des Perikles*, in "Hermes", XXVIII, 1893, p. 589 *et sqg.*, and under the heading *Diopeithes*, in Pauly-Wissowa, *RE*, IV, 1, cols. 1046-1047, had cast doubt on the accounts of Plutarch, *Pericles*, 32 = DK 59 A 17, and Diodorus, XII, 39 = DK *loc. cit.*, according to whom the trial of Anaxagoras took place around the outbreak of the Peloponnesian war (under the Archon Euthydemus, 431 B.C.). According to Swoboda, Plutarch and Diodorus had a common source in Ephorus, who altered

and Peck[22], and partly shared by Davison[23], all of whom believe that Anaxagoras was accused, tried and convicted at the outset of Pericle's political career rather than at its end.

the facts to fit his case, and the events actually occurred before the outbreak of the Archidamian war. Burnet, *Early Greek philosophy, cit.*, p. 290, n.l, agrees. There is a discussion of Swoboda's proposition in Derenne, *Les procès, cit.*, p. 36 *et sqg.*

21. J. Burnet, *EGPh, cit.*, p. 290, n.l, pointed out, however, that "the Athens of 480 would hardly be a suitable place, to 'begin philosophizing'", although he was inclined to believe, p. 296, n. 3, that the series of trials of Pericles' friends took place some time before the Peloponnesian war. Later, however, accepting the reasoning of Taylor, *cit.*, Burnet, in a note of 1918 to *L'Aurore de la Philosophie Grecque*, Paris, 1952 (the French translation of *EGPh*), said that he was "convaincu que la date réculée impliquée par Diogène est exacte et que l'accusation fut portée contre Anaxagore au moment où Périclès commençait sa carrière politique".

Strangely enough, there is no substantial alteration to *Greek Philosophy, Thales to Plato*, 1914, London, 1953 ed., p. 76, as a result of Burnet's change of opinion regarding the date of the trial; while in the note to *Apol.*, 18b5, in Plato's *Euthyphro, Apology of Socrates and Crito*, Oxford, 1924, 1957 ed., he again makes use of Taylor's arguments in giving the date of Anaxagoras' trial as 450; cf. also *Platonism*, Berkeley, 1928, p. 33. Through Taylor, Burnet, *Aurore, cit.*, actually goes back to the arguments of Swoboda, but without naming him: "l'opinion que le procès d'Anaxagore eut lieu immédiatement avant qu'éclatât la guerre du Péloponnèse est due à la façon dont Ephore arrangea son récit de ces évènements, et non à une tradition chronologique authentique. Elle ne s'accorde nullement avec le fait bien attesté que Périclès fut l'élève d'Anaxagore, comme il le fut de Damon". On this point, however, Derenne has justly observed, *Les Procès, cit.*, p. 32, that if Pericles was the disciple of Anaxagoras, it does not necessarily follow that Anaxagoras was the teacher of the young Pericles. The word μαθητής does not necessarily signify a young person. Anyone who visited a philosopher regularly could be described as a disciple, regardless of age. Plutarch's account *Pericl.* 4 = DK 59 A 15, does not in any way suggest that it was a question of education first received at an early age, while the reference of Plato, *Phaedr.* 269e = DK 59 A 15, to the meeting with Anaxagoras implies, through the use of the term προσπεδών, that Pericles was no longer young, since otherwise, as Derenne *cit.*, p. 33, notes, Plato would not have said that Pericles "met" Anaxagoras, but that his parents took the latter on as a teacher for their son.

22. Adcock, in *Cambridge ancient history*, V, Cambridge, 1926-27, p. 477; A. Leslie Peck, *Encyclopeadia Britannica*, I, 1960, *s.v. Anaxagoras*, and also E. Paci, *Storia del Pensiero Presocratico*, ERI, 1957, according to whom Anaxagoras left Athens for Lampsacus "prima del 445, anno nel quale fu intentato il processo di Aspasia", p. 105. With regard to Paci's arbitrary dating, it should

154

It must, however, be pointed out that the earlier dating, implied by the altered reading of Diogenes's text (ἐπὶ Καλλιάδου instead of ἐπὶ Καλλίου), while having the merit of harmonising the explicit reference to the age of Anaxagoras on his arrival in Athens — twenty years — with the name of the Archon Eponymos — Calliades — also runs into a series of severe difficulties.

It seems fairly improbable that Anaxagoras could have moved to Athens and commenced or completed his philosophical education[24] in such a disastrous year for Athens as that of Calliades' archonship.

be observed that if Anaxagoras left Athens "prima del 445", after thirty years of residence in Athens, the well-chosen expression of Glotz, repeated by Paci, p. 104, according to which philosophy entered Athens with Anaxagoras at a time when Athens was the soul of Greece and Pericles was the soul of Athens, would no longer make sense.

23. J.A. Davison, *Protagoras, Democritus and Anaxagoras*, in "Class. Quart." n.s., 1953, pp. 33-45, esp. p. 39 f., suggests an ingenious way of combining the evidence of Satyrus and Sotion, in Diog. L. II, III, 12 = DK 59 A 1, by assuming that each source gives half of the truth. According to Davison, Anaxagoras arrived in Athens at the age of twenty in 480, under the archonship of Calliades, but in 456/55 was accused of impiety and medism by Thucydides, son of Melesias, and was condemned to death by default, as Satyrus relates. In 445/4, however, he returned to Athens, thanks to an amnesty granted after the thirty years of peace, only to be accused of impiety once more, by Cleon, because, as Sotion relates, he had declared the sun to be a mass of incandescent metal; consequently, he was fined 5 talents and banished from Athens. Cf. Raven, in Kirk & Raven, *cit.*, p. 364, and Lanza, cit., p. 10. The supposed amnesty, on which the whole of Davison's argument depends, is not mentioned in any of the sources, although a reference by Olympiodorus, in *Meteor.*, p. 17, 19 Stüve = DK 59 A 19, incidentally not recorded by Davison, cf. Lanza, cit., p. 30, n., may be taken as suggesting that the Clazomenian underwent two trials. In the interests of establishing the truth, we should also note that the hypothesis of a double trial had already been proposed by P. Bayle, *Dictionnaire historique et critique*, 1820 ed., II, *s.v. Archelaus, rem.* A; with this hypothesis the philosopher of Rotterdam attempted to resolve "une assez grande difficulté" arising from the assertion that Socrates studied under Archelaus, which, according to Bayle, could only have occurred in the interval between Anaxagoras' two periods of residence in Athens. The thesis of Davison is now accepted by Capizzi, in Zeller & Mondolfo, I V, *cit.*, pp. 458-59.

24. If we read ἐπὶ Καλλιάδου, then we must interpret the phrase ἤρξατο δὲ φιλοσοφεῖν, following Jacoby, *Apoll. C.*, and Diels, "Rhein. Mus.", 1827, p.

In the first place, we must ask ourselves what Anaxagoras could have hoped to find in a city abandoned by all its most able men, who were engaged in resisting the Persian menace[25], a city with neither pupils to teach nor masters from whom to learn. Besides, how could Anaxagoras have found a master there, at a time when no philosopher worthy of the name was living in Athens? Whereas in Ionia, although it had fallen under the sway of the Persians[26], rich scientific tradition, spreading from its roots in Miletus, still survived, in Athens the great flowering of art, thought and literature, which was to make it "the school of Hellas"[27] under Pericles, was still far off in the future.

It seems inconceivable that Anaxagoras should have sought in Attica what he already had or could easily find in Ionia; similarly, it is inconceivable that Anaxagoras' spiritual development could have taken place outside Ionia, since his thought appears so closely connected to the philosophy of the Milesian school[28], which

28, as meaning "Anaxagoras beginnt seine philosophischen Studien".

Cobet, *a.l.*, also takes the phrase as referring to the philosophical initiation of the young Clazomenian: "Philosophari Athenis coeperat Calliada archonte"; in Athens, that is, and Gigante, *cit.*, agrees with this, although he puts Callias' archonship in 480, and translates *a.l.*: "Cominciò ad attendere alla filosofia in Atene sotto l'arcontato di Callias, all'età di venti anni". On the other hand, Lanza, *cit.*, translates *a.l.*; "Incominciò a filosofare quando in Atene era arconte Callia (480)", understanding, as do Diels, Jacoby and consequently Zeller, Derenne and others, that Anaxagoras began his philosophical studies in 480, not in Athens, but in Ionia. Accepting the conventional reading, Raven, in Kirk & Raven, *cit.*, *Anaxagoras*, XV, 487, *a.l.*, translates: "He began to be a philosopher at Athens in the Archonship of Callias [ἐπὶ Καλλίου (i.e. 456/5)] at the age of twenty [ἐτῶν εἴκοσιν ὤν"], and thus fails to match the year to the age, since Anaxagoras was well over 20 in 456; moreover, if the date of 456 is given to the archonship of Callias, we cannot ignore the emendation of Schaubach, *cit.*, p. 14, and Zevort, *cit.*, p. 10, who correctly read τεσσαράκοντα for εἴκοςι and consequently M for K: see above. Remaining faithful to the text, R. Laurenti, *Anassagora*, in *I Presocratici, cit.*, vol. II *a.l.*, translates in the same way as Diels: "Cominciò a filosofare sotto l'arcontato di Callia (456 oppure di Calliade 480) all'età di 20 anni".

25. Herodot. VIII 40-42; Glotz, *HG*, II, p. 72.

26. Herodot. V 31 *sqq.*; Glotz, *cit.*, p. 26.

27. Thuc., II 41.

28. Zeller, *cit.*, p. 357, n. 2, did not accept the doxographic tradition according to which Anaxagoras was the disciple and successor of Anaximenes, and which is now generally rejected. In fact, the Ionian basis of Anaxagoras' thought

was the principal inspiration and source of his successful teaching activity[29].

On the other hand, Derenne[30], picking up a remark of Zeller's[31], asks how Anaxagoras could have thought of travelling to Athens in a year when Xerxes' fleet was at large in the Aegean, and Athens itself was besieged by the Persians.

Moreover, we must remember that, Xerxes' fleet included, together with Egyptian and Phoenician squadrons, one from Ionia comprising 200 ships[32]. At Salamis, also in the year 480, the Ionians fought most fiercely against the Aeginetan squadron, which was in danger of being overwhelmed until the Athenians came to the rescue[33].

One wonders, therefore, how Anaxagoras, an Ionian from Clazomenae, could have entered and remained in Athens, when Ionia, and Clazomenae itself, had sided with the barbarians against Greece and Athens. Furthermore, the city of Athens, evacuated earlier in the face of the advancing barbarians[34], besieged, and desperately defended by a handful of men left to garrison the Acropolis, was eventually taken, plundered and destroyed by the Persians[35]. Nor did the victory of Salamis, which forced the invaders back to the north[36], entirely remove the threat of another barbarian attack on the Acropolis[37].

It was, perhaps, only after the victories of Plataea and Mycale[38], when the Ionians rebelled against the Persians and join-

---

has become increasingly apparent; it was clearly pointed out by Burnet, *EGPh*, *cit.*, p. 292 *et sqq.*, and later recognised by Zeller, *cit.*, p. 429 ff.; cf. Burnet, *cit.*, p. 293, n.1, according to whom the ancient Ionian philosophy formed a kind of background to the thought of Anaxagoras. For Zeller's view, see also his *Grundriss*, *cit.*, p. 83.

29. See the explicit evidence in Plat., *Phaedr.*, 269e, and Plutarch, *Pericl.* 4 = DK 59 A 15.

30. Derenne, *cit.*, p. 31.

31. Zeller, *cit.*, p. 352, n. 2; also in the earlier Schaubach, *cit.*, p. 14.

32. Herodot. VII, 93-94, 97; Glotz, *cit.*, p. 50.

33. Herodot. VIII, 84-91; Glotz, *cit.*, p. 78.

34. Herodot. VIII, 40-42, 71; Glotz, *cit.*, p. 72.

35. Herodot. VIII, 50 *et sqq.*; Glotz, *cit.*, p. 73.

36. Herodot. VIII, 113 *et sqq.*; Glotz, *cit.*, p. 77 *et sqq.*

37. Glotz, *cit.*, p. 80.

38. Herodot. VII 59-70; 90; 96-106; Glotz, *cit.*, pp. 90-92; 94-95.

ed forces with the Panhellenists, and Attica was finally freed from the invaders, or possibly even after the formation of the Delian League[39], that the opportunity of entering Athens presented itself to the Clazomenian. But the battle of Mycale took place at the end of August, 479, when Calliades' archonship was already over[40].

3. It would appear, therefore, that the reading ἐπὶ Καλλίου, as accepted, in opposition to Meursius, by Schaubach and Zévort[41], is to be preferred to ἐπὶ Καλλιάδου; this, however, still leaves us with problems no less serious than those discussed above. The first of these problems is bound up with the explicit reference to the age at which Anaxagoras began to philosophize in Athens. Demetrius of Phalerum, in Diogenes, says "at the age of twenty years", but Callias, as stated above, was Archon in 456, when Anaxagoras was 44.

The second problem is concerned with the length of Anaxagoras' stay in Athens, which, according to Diogenes Laertius, was thirty years. If Anaxagoras began to devote himself to philosophy in Athens when Callias was Archon, in other words

39. Herodot. IX, 105; Thuc. I, 98; Glotz, *cit.*, p. 114 *et sqq.*

40. On the election, the duties, and the length of service of the Archons, cf. Schoeffer, in Pauly-Wissowa, *RE*, *s.v. Archontes*, I, cols, 565-580; G. De Sanctis, *Atthis, Storia della Repubblica Ateniese dalle origini all'età di Pericle*, 1911, facsimile ed., Roma, 1964, p. 120 *et sqq.*; Glotz, *La Cité Grecque*, 1928, Paris, 1953, pp. 108-109; 145 *et sqq.*; 242, 244-48; P. Cloché, *La Démocratie Athénienne*, Paris, 1951, pp. 27-29; 226-228.

41. Schaubach, *cit.*, p. 14; Zévort, *cit.*, p. 10.

Diels, in DK, 59 A 1, reads ἐπὶ Καλλίου, but gives the alternative reading in parentheses: (oder = Καλλιάδου = 480); similarly, Lanza, *cit.*, *a.l.*, p. 4, although his Italian translation is "arconte Callia (480)", like that of Gigante, in Diog. L., *cit.*, *a.l.* and p. 655, with the difference that while Lanza implicitly accepts Zeller's emendation, as suggested again by Derenne, *cit.*, p. 31, to which we shall return shortly, Gigante, *cit.*, p. 655, clearly implies that Anaxagoras began his philosophical activities in Athens in 480, when Callias was Archon; see above, note 24.

Raven, in Kirk & Raven, *cit.*, XV, 487, p. 362, also reads ἐπὶ Καλλίου, i.e. 456/5, but notes, p. 363, that the archonship of Calliades, 480/79, agrees more closely with the chronology of Anaxagoras' life given in the passage from Diogenes; Raven considers it "approximately right" that Anaxagoras "came to Athens and began his philosophical activities" then.

in 456 B.C. then, following for an interval of thirty years, the date of the accusation, trial and conviction would be 426, which was three years after the death of Pericles. Yet we know from many sources[42] that Pericles was present in court and that he vigorously defended his friend and teacher.

Derenne[43], in line with Zeller[44] and most historians after him, believes that this difficulty in the passage by Diogenes can be resolved by accepting, out of the three items under discussion (the name of the Athenian Archon, Callias or Calliades; the age of Anaxagoras at the time, twenty years; the length of his stay in Athens, thirty years), only the one which, in fact, appears to be the least reliable, since, unlike the others for which sources are given, it is introduced by the vague φασίν, tradunt: "and at Athens they say he remained for thirty years"[45]. And since Derenne correctly assigns the date of 433-32 B.C.[46] to the trial of Anaxagoras, this would make the year in which he arived in Athens neither that of Calliades' archonship, 480, nor that of Callias' archonship, 456, but rater 463-62 B.C.[47]

In order to make this dating plausible, Derenne[48], following a suggestion of Zeller's[49], makes an emendation in Diogenes' text,

42. The accounts in DK 59 A 1, 17, will be discussed in the following section
43. Derenne, cit., 13.
44. Zeller, cit., p. 387, n.l, first proposed the hypothesis that Anaxagoras arrived in Athens in about 463 or 462, so that the trial in 433 or 432 coincided with the end of his thirthy years in Athens.
45. Diog. L. II, III, 7 = DK 59 A 1, tr. Hicks, p. 137. According to Burnet, EGPh, pp. 290-291, "This may be a genuine tradition". Zeller, cit., p. 358, n. 6, although he was the originator of the common belief that Anaxagoras arrived in Athens in 463 or 462, was extremely cautious about accepting this assertion of Diogenes', and emphasized the uncertainty implied by the φασίν; later, however, he disregarded this problem.
46. Derenne, cit., p. 36 et sqq.
47. Derenne, cit., p. 31. The hypothesis of Zeller, cit., p. 358, n. 2, and partially amended in Grundriss, cit., 83, that the date of arrival in Athens was 463-62, has been widely accepted by historians; see Praechter, in Überweg, Grundriss, I, cit., p. 98; Schuhl, cit., p. 323; Diano, cit., p. 238 and 249; Adorno, cit., p. 84; Lanza, cit., p. 4-6 n.; although some are inclined to avoid the issue or leave the question open, e.g. Robin, cit., p. 147; Brehier, cit., p. 71; Chevalier, cit., p. 120; De Ruggiero, I, cit., p. 176.
48. Derenne, cit., p. 31.
49. Zeller, cit., p. 351, proposes ἤρξατο φιλοσοφεῖν ἐπὶ Καλλίου, or the more

une simple transposition des mots[50], which, nonetheless, radically alters the original meaning.

Diogenes Laertius or his source, writes Derenne, probably misunderstood Demetrius, who must have written something like: ἤρξατο φιλοσοφεῖν Ἀθήνησιν ἄρχοντος Καλλίου (= Καλλιάδου), in other words: *Anaxagore commença à s'adonner à la philosophie à l'époque où à Athènes était archonte Callias*[51]. In this way Diogenes' passage would be interpreted not as an explicit reference to Anaxagoras' arrival in Athens, but as an incidental reference to Anaxagoras' initiation as a philosopher, not in Athens, but in Clazomenae, in 480, when Callias (= Calliades) was Archon in Athens[52].

It seems unlikely, however, that Demetrius of Phalerum, in his List of Athenian Archons, should have referred, under the name of the Archon Eponymos of 480 B.C., to the insignificant fact of the twenty-year-old Anaxagoras' initiation into philosophy, particularly if it did not take place in Athens, but in Clazomenae or Ionia[52a].

It is hard to see why Demetrius should have wished to make such a reference concerning a year which saw the battle of Salamis and the destruction of the Acropolis by the Persians, assisted by Ionias, including the Clazomenians.

Besides, it is conceivable that Anaxagoras could have decided to devote himself to philosophy at a time when the Persians were recruiting the able-bodied men in Clazomenae for the fleet which was to be sent out against Athens?[53] Was it really Anaxagoras' in-

probable ἤρξατο φιλοσοφεῖν Ἀθήνησιν ἄρχοντος Καλλίου; in this reading, the phrase ἤρξατο φιλοσοφεῖν would mean, not that Anaxagoras opened a school, an unlikely thing for a youth of twenty to do, but simply that he began his philosophical studies, at the time when Callias or Calliades was Archon in Athens, 480 B.C.

50. Derenne, *cit.*, p. 31 and n. 2.

51. Derenne, *cit.*, *ib.*

52. Derenne, *ib.*, adds that "il faut évidemment comprendre avec Taylor, Calliades" and, consequently, 480 B.C.

52a. On this point, we should note the objection of Diano, *cit.*,p. 238, who states that only for the philosophers of the Hellenistic period "l'inizio dell'attività filosofica poteva costituire un fatto degno di ricordo (...). Trasportata agli inizi del V secolo la cosa è affatto anacronistica".

53. On the foregoing, see section 2 and notes thereto.

itiation into philosophy in Clazomenae — and in a year so disastrous for Athens — that Demetrius was talking about, while Diogenes failed to understand this?[54] Quite frankly, this does not seem possible to me, especially since, without recourse to arbitrary hypotheses which would change both the name of the Archon and the whole meaning of the passage, it is quite possible to read, as Schaubach did, *Athenis sub Callia coepit docere philosophiam*[55], understanding by this that Anaxagoras arrived in Athens in 456, under the archonship of Callias, and began teaching there[56].

If this were so, it would make the reference by Demetrius of Phalerum in the list of Archons entirely reasonable, since Anaxagoras, "eminent for wealth and noble birth"[57], in his prime, and already famous[58], could justly be considered to be the heir to a

54. This is the opinion of Zeller, *cit.*, p. 382, n. 2, Derenne, *cit.*, p. 31, and all other historians who accept 463 as the date of arrival in Athens; cf. Lanza, *cit.*, p. 6.

55. Schaubach, *cit.*, p. 15, who adds the note: "*sic intelligenda sunt verba* ἤρξατο φιλοσοφεῖν Ἀθήνησιν Diog. L. II, 7. '*Nam jam ante philosophiae operam dederat, cum adhuc Clazomenis versaretur*'".

56. The emendation to the passage from Diogenes, suggested by Schaubach, *cit.*, p. 15, which would replace K(20) by M(40), would thus be quite reasonable, indicating, rather than the Clazomenian's initiation into philosophy at the age of forty (as, *int. al.*, Diano, *cit.*, p. 236 and Lanza, *cit.*, pp. 4-5, understand it), the beginning of Anaxagoras' philosophical teaching in Athens.

In my view, it is impossible to agree with the opinion of those scholars such as Guthrie, *cit.*, II. p. 322, who interpret Diogenes' phrase ἤρξατο δὲ φιλοσοφεῖν Ἀθήνησιν ἐπὶ Καλλιάδου (480) in the same way as Diels and Cobet, *cit. supra*, p. 110, n.1, taking it to mean "Anaxagoras beginnt seine philosophischen Studien", and who hypothesize that Anaxagoras began his philosophical studies in Athens when he arrived there as a conscript in Xerxes' army. Leaving aside the considerations already referred, and the no less relevant observation of Diano, it is still difficult to believe that by ἤρξατο φιλοσοφεῖν Ἀθήνεσιν Demetrius Phalereus meant that Anaxagoras, a twenty-year-old recruit in the Ionian contingent of the Persian army, took up philosophy in Athens at the time of the plundering and destruction of the city by the Persians.

57. Diog. L. II, III, 6 = DK 59 A 1, tr. Hicks, p. 137.

58. In my opinion, it is not unlikely that, before his move to Athens, but after 467-6, Marm. Par. cp. 57; Plin. *N.H.* II 149 f.; Eus. *Chron* (= *Hieron*) = DK 49 A 11, cf. Schaubach, *cit.*, p. 40; Zeller, *cit.*, 358, n. 5; Diano, *cit.*, p. 237; Guthrie, *cit.*, II, pp. 266 & 302, and before 456, Diog. Laert. II 7 = DK 59 A 1; Schaubach, *cit.*, p. 15, Anaxagoras published, in Ionia, his work on nature,

great philosophical tradition, which he was bringing into the heart of Hellas by moving to Athens, possibly at Pericles' invitation. Consequently, his arrival in Athens could have been an event well worth mentioning under the name of the Archon Eponymos of 456.

4. However, the assumption that Anaxagoras arrived in Athens under the archonship of Callias, and began teaching philosophy then, raises questions as to the duration of the Clazomenian's residence in Attica.

Diogenes Laertius[59] states that Anaxagoras remained for 30

which, being the first example of a scientific text, Diano, *cit.*, p. 344 f., whether or not it was accompanied by diagrams, was bound to gain renown for the Clazomenian. Consequently it is probable that Pericles invited him to Athens and that he moved there ἐπὶ Καλλίου, thus introducing philosophy into Athens from Ionia; see Clem., *Strom.* I 63; Gal. *Hist. Phil.* 3 = DK 59 A 7; Diog. Laert. II IV, 16 = DK 60 A 1.

However, Diano, cit., p. 247, linking the πρῶτος συγγραφῆς ἐξέδοκε βιβλίον, Diog. Laert. II 11 = DK 59 A 1, with the ἤρξατο φιλοσοφεῖν Ἀθήνησιν ἐπὶ Καλλίου, Diog. Laert. II 11 = DK 59 A 1, suggests that ἐπὶ Καλλίου indicates the date of publication in Athens of Anaxagoras' συγγραφή, which, being "il primo libro che in quel genere apparisse in Atene", *ib.*, became worthy of a mention in the Table of Archons of Demetrius Phalereus. But although Diano's proposition appears to Capizzi, *cit.*, p. 458, "ineccepibile per quanto riguarda la natura e la data della pubblicazione del libro di Anassagora", I would still maintain, in oppositon to Diano, that the ἐπὶ Καλλίου in the passage in Diogenes indicated the year in which Anaxagoras, preceded by the fame achieved through the publication of his book on nature, moved to Pericles' Athens, under the archonship of Callias, and began to teach philosophy. This thesis is in closer agreement with Diogenes' text, as emended by Schaubach, *cit.*, p. 14, and does not conflict with Diano's accurate observation that the Clazomenian's doctrines were already known in Athens before 456; however, whereas Diano, *cit.*, p. 248 ff., thinks it possible that Aeschylus became acquainted with some of Anaxagoras' doctrines by conversing with him in Athens before the publication of the συγγραφή, I believe that Aeschylus may well have acquired the elements of Anaxagoras' thought that appear in his tragedies from Anaxagoras' book, which arrived in Athens before its author. This would provide grounds for the conjecture that the arrival of the Clazomenian in Athens, where he was already famous, was important enough to be recorded by Demetrius Phalereus under the name of the Archon Eponymos; and for the hypothesis that it was Pericles himself who invited Anaxagoras to Athens.

59. Diog. L. II, III, 7 = DK 59 A 1.

years in Athens, ἔνθα καί φασιν αὐτὸν ἐτῶν διατρῖψαι τριάκοντα, and this statement has become, for historians throughout the ages, an incontrovertible *point de repère* for the biography of Anaxagoras[60], according to which the dates of his arrival and of his trial have been fixed.

However, if the date of his arrival is accepted as being 456, ἐπὶ Καλλίου, then the trial, which ended the thirty years spent in Athens, would have to be dated to 426, three years after the death of Pericles, whereas in fact, Pericles was, as previously stated, present in court.

According to Plutarch[61], in fact, the attack on Anaxagoras was intended as a blow against his disciple and protector, during the troubled period of Athenian civil life immediately before the Peloponnesian war, when the opposition was attempting in every possible way to damage Pericles' personal prestige by having a series of decrees passed which would strike at those nearest and dearest to Pericles[62].

If, on the other hand, Taylor's date of 450 is accepted for the trial of Anaxagoras,[63] Plutarch's reference to the motives for the proceedings taken against the Clazomenian becomes totally out of place in his discussion of the position of Pericles and the attacks of the opposition on the eve of the Peloponnesian war.[64] In fact, Plutarch's dating is confirmed by Diodorus Siculus and by

---

60. See Burnet, *EGPh*, *cit.*, pp. 290-91, for whom the thirty years' residence in Athens comes from a "genuine tradition"; this is accepted, as seen above, by all those who take the date of arrival in Athens to be 463 B.C., not to mention Taylor, *cit.*, and those who share his view that the thirty years' stay in Athens lasted from 480 to 450.

61. Plut., *Pericl.* 32 = DK 59 A 17 and Diodor. XII, 39, *ib.*

62. Derenne, *cit.*, p. 18, n. 3, has pointed out that it is an impossible task to establish the chronological order of these trials. However, Decharme, *La Critique*, *cit.*, p. 161, believes that the trial of Anaxagoras took place before that of Aspasia: "Périclès", writes Decharme, *cit.*, *ib.*, "intervint pour Aspasie comme il était intervenu pour Anaxagore; il plaida pour elle comme il avait fait pour lui". In Plutarch, *Pericl.* 32, the accusation against Aspasia is earlier than that against Anaxagoras, which, according to Diodorus, XII, 39 = DK 59 A 17, was made after the charge against Phidias.

63. Cf. Taylor, *On the Date*, *cit.*, p. 81 *et sqq.*, see above, p. 000.

64. As has been rightly pointed out in a note by Cloché, *La Démocratie*, *cit.*, p. 114, n.l.

Sotion[65], and is also in accordance with the earlier indirect evidence provided by Aristophanes and Plato.[66] However, if the date of the trial is accepted as being 433-31, and if, as Diogenes claims, Anaxagoras spent thirty years in Athens, the date of arrival cannot have been 456, ἐπὶ Καλλίου. This has led to the notion, first proposed by Zeller, that the date of arrival was 463.[67]

But can the evidence of Diogenes, preceded in context by a φασιν, without any source being named, really be taken literally? Could it not be taken to mean "about" thirty years? If this is so, then the passage under discussion may be read as follows: *Anaxagoras began teaching in Athens* (ἤρξατο δὲ φιλοσοφεῖν Ἀθήνησιν) *under the archonship of Callias* (ἐπὶ Καλλίου, 456 B.C.), *at the age of forty-four* (τεσσαράκοντα τέσσαρας) *and stayed in Athens for about* (περίπου) *thirty years* (τριάκοντα).

This variant reading would leave the name of the Archon, Callias, unaltered, and would only alter the length of Anaxagoras' stay in Athens in a minor way, from thirty years to "about" thirty years. It would also offer a plausible date for the

65. Diodor. XII, 38, *et sqq.*, investigating the causes of the Peloponnesian war, observes that the difficulties in which Pericles found himself as a result of his administration of the federal treasury were aggravated by other matters, such as the trial of Phidias and that of Anaxagoras, which both he and Ephorus, XII, 41, 1, believe to have taken place in 431, under the archonship of Euthydemus, DK 59 A 17.

Sotion, in Diog. L. II, III, 12 = DK 59 A 1, records, as we shall see later, that Pericles was present in court and defended Anaxagoras.

66. Zeller, *cit.*, p. 351, n. 2, was the first to point out that both Xenophon, *Mem.*, IV, 7, 6, et seq., and Plato, *Apol.*, 26d, describe Anaxagoras as a physicist whose doctrines were familiar in Athens towards the end of the 5th century; and he is referred to as such by Aristophanes in *The Clouds*. Neither Aristophanes nor Plato would have brought Anaxagoras into their texts if, as Taylor believes, Anaxagoras' trial had taken place in 450; this applies especially to Plato. If Taylor was right, the trial of the Clazomenian would have been held 51 years before that of Socrates: Meletus might not have been born then, Plato, *Apol.*, 25d, *Euthyphro*, 2b, and it would have been difficult for Socrates to make the objection to him that in accusing him he was accusing Anaxagoras, *Apol.* 26d. The fact that Aristophanes, *Av.*, v. 988, refers to Diopeithes, originator of the *pséphisma* of 432, as still being alive at the date of the performance (= 414 B.C.), does not seem particularly significant to me, since it would be equally consistent with the presentation of the *pséphisma* in 450.

67. Zeller, *cit.*, p. 358, n. 6.

Clazomenian to have begun teaching philosophy in Athens, i.e. 456, when he had reached maturity and felt qualified to be a representative of Ionian learning in Attica, and could therefore present himself as a master to the Athenians and find disciples among them.[68]

Thus, too, the date of the accusation and conviction would still be that for which Plutarch, Diodorus and Sotion, and, as we shall see, Satyrus, provide ample evidence: a date at the end of Pericles' political career, namely 433-31 B.C., which is generally accepted, and which allows for Anaxagoras' thirty years' stay in Athens.

5. The problem of the reasons and the legal grounds for the accusation against Anaxagoras has been resolved without difficulty hitherto, but only because it has never been seriously examined.

According to Sotion[69], Anaxagoras was accused of ἀσέβεια "(because) he declared the sun to be a mass of red-hot metal". Satyrus[70] agrees with Sotion concerning the accusation of impiety, but adds to it, οὐ μόνον ἀσεβείας, that of medism, ἀλλὰ καὶ μηδισμοῦ[71].

---

68. On Anaxagoras' Athenian disciples, see Schaubach, *cit.*, p. 17 *et sqq.*, esp. p. 22; on Euripides, see Zeller, *cit.*, p. 458, n. 9 & p. 41 *et sqq.*

69. In Diog. L. II, III, 12 = DK 59 A 1. The translation of the following passage in quotation marks is by Hicks, Diogenes, *Lives*, *a.l.* On Sotion of Alexandria, cf. Stenzel, in Pauly-Wissowa, *RE*, III A cols, 1253-37. Still useful is Jonsius, *De Scriptoribus Historiae Philosophicae*, Francofurti, 1659, II, p. 165 et seq., who mentions some of the works modelled on the *Successions*. See also Dal Pra, *La Storiografia filosofica antica*, Milan, 1950, p. 148 *et sqq.* For the quotations from Sotion in Diogenes, see Gigante, *cit.*, p. 642.

70. In Diog. L. *loc. cit.* On Satyrus the peripatetic, see under this heading in Pauly-Wissowa, *RE*, II A 1, cols, 228-229; Jonsius, *cit.*, p. 169 *et sqq.*; for the quotations in Diogenes, Gigante, *cit.*, p. 640.

71. This additional statement by Satyrus, notes Zeller, *cit.*, p. 359, n. 11, "resta del tutto isolata" among the rest of the evidence that has reached us concerning the Clazomenian; to Decharme, *cit.*, p. 259, it is surprising; to Diano, *cit.*, p. 246, it appears "assolutamente priva di senso"; to Capizzi, cit., p. 456, it is "inesplicabile". However, Derenne, *cit.*, p. 29 *et seq.*, considers the accusation of medism not at all improbable. In fact, the Athenians were highly sensitive to two particular offences, which were always classed together, namely μηδισμός and τυραννίς, cf. Aristoph., *Thesm.*, v. 335 *et sqq.*; Jacoby, *Apoll, Chronik*, *cit.*, p. 428, n. 7, in Derenne, *cit.*, p. 29, n. 3; so much so that, half a century

Thus both of Diogenes' sources agree that the offence of ἀσέβεια, of which Anaxagoras is supposed to have been accused, is to be identified with his teachings concerning the nature of the stars.

Plato[72] appears to confirm the reasons provided by Sotion and Satyrus, and they have been repeated by all the ancient doxographers and biographers, and accepted by modern historians[73].

However, Diopeithes' ψήφισμα[78], which, as has been said

after the victory over the Persians, the Thebans again had to defend themselves against the traditional accusation of Persophilia, Thuc. III, 62-63; Isocrat., IV, 157. But in the case of Anaxagoras we must ask whether such an accusation, made in 433-31, fifty years after Salamis, could be upheld under the law. Moreover, at the time of the passage of the Persians Anaxagoras, as Diogenes Laertius, II III 7, records, was twenty years old; could he really have been accused 50 years later, and after 30 years of residence in Athens, of being or having been a Persophile? We may accept, by way of hypothesis, the possibility that Anaxagoras had fought with the Ionias on the Persian side at Salamis, cf. Herodot, VII 93-94, 97,VIII, 84-91 and section 2 above, but nevertheless half a century has passed since then, and Anaxagoras had been living in Athens for thirty years: would Thucydides, son of Melesias, and Cleon (especially the latter) have failed to remember the military escapades of the elderly philosopher until 433/31? Furthermore, if there was really a desire to attack Pericles through Anaxagoras, Plut., Pericl., 32 = DK 59 A 17, it would have been quite pointless to accuse Anaxagoras of medism in an attempt to cast suspicion on Pericles, which is what Derenne, cit., p. 29, and others believe to have happened: for Pericles was the son of Xanthippus, who had won the victories at Mycale and Sestos, Herodot. IX, 96-196; 108 et sqq.; Glotz, HG, II, p. 94 et seq., and who had thus crushed the Persians and freed Greece from the barbarians. Moreover, Pericles himself had, in 472, led the chorus in Aeschylus' tragedy, Plut., Themistocles, 15, which celebrated the victory over the Persians and eulogized both Athens and Hellas as a whole as victors over the barbarians. Thucydides and Cleon, therefore, could never have thought of attacking Pericles in such a way. Neither can I accept the suggestion of Parmentier, Euripide et Anaxagore, p. 35, in Derenne, cit., p. 29 & n. 7, that the accusation of μηδισμός was based on Anaxagoras' cosmopolitanism. I do not believe that the Athenians, who pardoned and recalled Alcibiades and Xenophon, could have been so insistent on this point.

And yet the accusation of medism is not as strange as it may appear. We shall return to this question in section 8, giving conjectural evidence for our argument.

72. Plat., Apol, 26d. On this point, however, we should bear in mind the observations of Burnet, Plato's Apology, cit., a.l., p. 111, and the remarks made in the rest of this section.

73. A small selection of these are listed on p. 147 f.

74. Given by Plut., Pericl., 32 = DK 59 A 17, who has retained the spirit if

already, provided the legal basis for the accusation and conviction of Anaxagoras, clearly distinguishes between ἀσέβεια and astrology, μετάρσια, identifying two different kinds of offence: 1) τὰ θεῖα μὴ νομίζοντας; 2) λόγους περὶ τῶν μεταρσίων διδάσκαντας, separated in the original context by the disjunctive ἤ[75].

Only the first of these offences can strictly be classed as a form of ἀσέβεια[76]; the second is an offence previously unknown in Athens, namely the teaching of doctrines relating to celestial phenomena[77].

This distinction is lost in Sotion and Satyrus, however, and the offence of ἀσέβεια with which Anaxagoras is supposed to have been charged is, in practice, identified with his naturalistic reduction of the sun to a mass of incandescent metal. Admittedly, such reduction would deny the divinity of the sun, but only if the sun

not the letter of the decree, which he probably obtained from the anthology of Craterus, cf. Cobet and Krech, in Derenne, *cit.*, p. 22, n. 2. See also Decharme, *La loi de Diopeithes*, in *Mél. Perrot*, Paris, 1903. On Diopeithes, see above, p. 000.

75. In M.P. Nilsson, *A history of Greek religion*, 2nd ed., Oxford, 1963, p. 266, and *Greek Piety*, Oxford, 1948, p. 80, ἤ is translated as "and", thus concealing the dilemmatic nature of the decree.

76. On the concept of ἀσέβεια, see Caillemer, in Daremberg-Saglio, *s.v.*, where there is a thorough survey of the various offences of impiety. Cf. also Decharme, *La Critique*, *cit.*, p. 141 *et sqq*; Derenne, *cit.*, p. 9 *et sqq*. On the meaning of ἀσέβεια in Diopeithes' decree, see my observations on p. 170 f.

The political nature of the offences of *asébeia* has been demonstrated clearly by Pettazzoni, *La Religione*, *cit.*, p. 184, and by Glotz, *HG*, II, p. 429: "les Athéniens ne recherchèrent jamais d'autres crimes contre les dieux que ceux qu'ils estimaient en même temps des crimes contre l'Etat". Nilsson, *Greek Piety*, *cit.*, p. 78, and H. Maier, *Sokrates*, Tübingen, 1913, Italian ed. *Socrate*, Firenze, 1943, II, p. 199: "Lo stato si era posto sotto la protezione della divinità ed ogni offesa alla divinità, potendo divenire per esso esiziale, finiva con l'essere un'offesa ai fondamenti dell'ordine statale". On the political motive for the impiety trials, B. Snell, *Die Entdeckung des Geistes*, Hamburg, 1946, Italian ed. *La cultura greca e le origini del pensiero europeo*, Torino, 1951, p. 52; Gernet & Boulanger, *Le génie grec dans la réligion*, Paris, 1932, p. 346. On the γραφή ἀσέβεια, Plutarch, *Pericl.*, 32; U.E. Paoli, *Studi sul processo attico*, Padova, 1933, pp. 16, 58-59, 86.

77. This innovation introduced by Diopeithes' decree had already been pointed out by Lipsius, Schöman-Lipsius, *Das attische Recht u. Rechtsverfahren*, Leipzig, 1905, II, p. 360.

was really accepted as divine in the first half of the 5th century B.C. In fact, we know that, at least until the Hellenistic period, the sun and moon, Helios and Selene, ἐπιφανεῖς Θεοί, received no particular worship in Greece⁷⁸; nor, in the classical period, were they ever looked on as true divinities by the Greeks, who rejected astral divinities and their worship as barbaric⁷⁹. Athens had her own national gods, the sacred triad of Athena, Zeus and Apollo⁸⁰, who were officially worshipped; other gods were the

78. W.K.C. Guthrie, *The Greeks and their Gods*, London, 1950, p. 211 ff., together with Nilsson, *HGR*, *cit.*, p. 74, shows clearly that Helios and Selene, as apparent divinities, had no else contact with mankind, see Wilamowitz-Moellendorf, *Der Glaube*, I, p. 253, in Guthrie, *ib.*, and that consequently they did not receive the honour of temples and worship: "They move to an instinctive awe, but they do not demand temples and sacrifices, for they do not come down to reward piety or avenge neglect."

As Farnell notes, *The Cults of the Greek States*, 5 vols., Oxford, 1896-1909, II, 457 *et sqq.*, IV, 136 *et sqq.*, at the time of the trial of Anaxagoras, Helios and Selene were not yet identified with Apollo and Artemis, cf. Burnet, Plato's *Apology*, *cit.*, 26d.

79. Pettazzoni, *cit.*, p. 180, notes that "l'adorazione diretta delle forze e degli elementi naturali come divinità (non antropomorfe) era caratteristica della aborrita religione persiana, cui la greca opponeva le figure umanamente vere dei suoi iddii". See also Guthrie, *The Greeks and their Gods*, *cit.*, p. 211.

Although it has been noted, as in Decharme, *La Critique*, *cit.*,p. 157, that Socrates, after spending the night in a trance, prayed to the rising sun, Plat., *Symp.*, 220c-d, yet Socrates says in *Crat.*, 397c-d, "I suspect that the sun, moon, earth, stars, and heaven, which are still the gods of many barbarians, were the only gods known to the aboriginal Hellenes. Seeing that they were always moving and running, from their running nature they were called gods or runners (θεούς, θέοντας); and when men became acquainted with the other gods, they proceeded to apply the same name to them all" (transl. by B. Jowett), which is a more accurate reflection of Socrates' thought as it apears in Plato, cf. *Euthyphro*, 6b-c; a way of thinking shared by Aristophanes, *The Peace*, V, 414 *et sqq.*, who accuses Helios and Selene of betraying the nation to the barbarians, cf. Pascal, *Dionisyo*, Catania, 1911, p. 3 *et sqq*, esp. p. 8, who defines the attitude of Anaxagoras towards the introduction of barbaric cults into Athens, barely a generation after the trial of Anaxagoras.

80. On the sacred triad, which first appears in Homer, *Iliad*, II, 271, and recurs in *Scol. ad Nub.*, vv. 1468-69, see Nilsson, *A History of Greek Religion*, *cit.*, p. 125 *et sqq.*, and especially Pascal, *Dioniso*, *cit.*, p. 9 *et sqq.*, who re-examines the question of the state gods and provides a list of sources.

subjects of myth and poetry, and could even be laughed at in comedy[81].

It seems most unlikely, therefore, that Anaxagoras could have been convicted of denying a divinity that did not receive any particular devotion in Athens. The case of Protagoras was quite different[82], as was that of Diagoras, who had profaned and divulged mysteries[83], and that of Socrates, an Athenian citizen, whose ἀσέβεια involved the denial of the gods who were recognized by the state[84]

What is more, Anaxagoras was an Ionian from Clazomenae, and was therefore a metic in Athens. Metics, like slaves, were not citizens, and were not normally bound by the state religion, nor by the official rituals of worship[85]. How could an accusation of

81. On the parody of religion in the ancient comic poets, and in Aristophanes in particular, see Pascal, *cit.*, and Del Grande, *Hybris*, Napoli, 1947, esp. ch. VI. On the controversial question of the piety or impiety of Aristophanes, see my *Socrates between the first and second Clouds.*

82. See Diog.L. IX, 51, in *Sofisti, Testimonianze e frammenti*, ed. by M. Untersteiner, I, 2nd ed., Firenze, 1961, pp. 18-19, 78-79. On Protagoras' περὶ θεῶν see Untersteiner, *I Sofisti*, Torino, 1949, p. 38, *et sqq.* On the condemnation of Protagoras, see my *Socrate. Fisiologia di un mito*, Firenze, 1974, p. 211, n. 23.

83. On the accusation and conviction of Diagoras, not for his religious ideas but for his having profaned and divulged the mysteries of Eleusis, cf. Decharme, *cit.*, p. 131 *et sqq.*, and Derenne, *cit.*, p. 57 *et sqq.*

84. According to Plato, *Apol.*, 24c. Favorinus' description of the specific charge, in Diog. L., II, V, 40, may be accepted as authentic, and is in accordance with that of Xenoph., *Mem.*, I, I, 1. For my opinion regarding the accusation, trial and conviction of Socrates, see *infra Socrates from Myth to history.*

85. On the status of metics, see M. Clerc, in Daremberg-Saglio, *s.v. Metoikoi.* According to Aristophanes of Byzantium, in Clerc, *cit.*, a metic is a foreigner who has established his permanent domicile in a city, who performs certain public duties and pays certain special taxes. Clerc observes that, out of these three conditions, it was the financial obligation that attracted most attention from the ancient lexicographers, and consequently that the fiscal position of the metic was the best definition of his status. However, this definition, while it may be valid for the post-classical period, is hardly appropriate for the Periclean age, in which Pericles himself, Plut., *Pericl.*, 37; Arist., *Pol.*, III, I, 9, *Athenian Constitutions*, 26, 3; Glotz, *Cg, cit.*, p. 316, 150, by basing the legal definition of citizenship on the *jus sanguinis*, implicitly defined as metics those residents not having Athenian fathers and mothers. According to Arist., *Pol.* II, III, 1275b, however, a citizen is one who has "the right to take part in the deliberative or

disbelief in the divinity of the sun and moon be brought against a foreigner who was not even obliged by law to believe in the gods recognized by the state, at a time, moreover, when the sun and the moon were not even accepted as true divinities? Even if Diopeithes' ψήφισμα extended the concept of ἀσέβεια to cover dogma as well as ritual, to cover belief in the gods of the state as well as the practice of worship and respect for sacred things[86], it

judicial administration''; a metic, on the other hand, is a foreigner who does not have this right. Similarly a metic could be defined as one who does not have the right to possess fixed or movable assets, or who, as a foreigner, does not have the right to become a strategos. In short, the concept of metic may be defined in various ways depending on the multilateral nature of the relationships between it and the concept of citizen. The most important of these relationships was that concerning religious rights. Fustel de Coulanges, *La Cité Antique*, 22nd ed., Paris, 1921, p. 226 states that slaves and metics did not participate in the state religion: ''être admis parmi les citoyens, cela s'exprime en grec par les mots μετεῖναι τῶν ἱερῶν entrer en partage de choses sacrées. L'étranger, au contraire, est celui qui n'a pas accès au culte'', p. 227. Pettazzoni, *La Religione, cit.*, p. 172, notes that although the metics were, in principle, not involved in the practice of the official religion, they were not excluded from public religious festivals: ''non vi partecipavano di diritto, ma vi assistevano di fatto, insieme con tutto il popolo''. ''Exclus [...] des sacerdoces'', writes Clerc, *cit.*, ''les métèques participaient aux cérémonies les plus importantes des cultes de la cité''.

On the other hand, the metics enjoyed greater religious freedom, being permitted to practise the religions of their homelands; see R. Flacelière, *La Vie quotidienne en Grèce au Siècle de Périclès*, Paris, 1959; Pettazzoni, *cit.*, ch. IX.

86. The definition of ἀσέβεια, given by p.Aristot., *De Virt. et Vit.* 7, see Caillemer, in Daremberg-Saglio, *s.v. asébeia*, and generally accepted as a description of impiety in the ancient world, fails to bring out the new meaning given to the concept of impiety by Diopeithes' ψήφισμα. Whereas the ancient γραφὴ ἀσεβείας, De Sanctis, *Atthis, cit.*, p. 146, introduced by Solon, Plutarch, *Solon*, 23-25; Grote, *A History of Greece, cit.*, III, 1847, p. 171, & n.l; Glotz, *HG*, II, p. 248, punished sacrilege in particular and offences against sacred things in general, Diopeithes defined a new form of ἀσέβεια, namely disbelief in the gods. Consequently, the verb νομίζειν, which in the ancient law had meant ''to give the gods their due honours as laid down by tradition or custom'', cf. Liddell-Scott, *s.v.*, Snell, *La cultura greca, cit.*, p. 62 *et seq.*, Burnet, Plato's *Apology, cit.*, note to 24c, acquired, in the decree of 433/31, the meaning ''to believe''. However, Schöman-Lipsius, *Das Attische Recht, cit.*, II, p. 63, and Maier, *Socrate, cit.*, II, p. 198, n. 2, do not accept that the law in force before Diopeithes' decree applied only to offences connected with the practice of worship and not to disbelief in the abstract; but we must remember the fact that any new decree that was proposed had to make up for a recognized deficiency in the

still did not revoke the right of religious freedom granted to foreigners in Athens. If this right had been revoked, it would have been necessary to banish all the foreigners from Athens, and this did not happen, even when the spread of barbarian religions and the introduction of new gods into the city by metics and slaves threatened to betray the state to the barbarians[87].

Consequently, I would not accept that Anaxagoras was convicted of ἀσέβεια because of his teachings concerning the nature of the stars. Furthermore, an accusation of this kind against a metic such as Anaxagoras would have provided Pericles, the προστάτης and therefore the judicial defender of the Clazomenian metic[88], with the opportunity to make an objection or even

law, and that extremely severe penalties could be imposed on the unwary presenter of a decree concerning a matter already provided for by the law, Glotz, *Cité Grecque, cit.*, p. 194 *et seq.*, p. 210 *et seq.*; Paoli, *Studi sul Processo Attico*, Padova, 1933, p. 56. The same objection can be raised against those such as Menzel, *Untersuchungen zum Sokrates-pozess*, Wien, 1903, p. 19; Tovar, *Vida de Sòcrates*, 2nd ed., Madrid, 1957, p. 336, who maintain that the only effect of Diopeithes' *pséphisma* was the introduction of a new form of procedure, namely εἰσαγγελία, into trials for ἀσέβεια. On the other hand, Pöhlmann, *Sokrates und sein Volk*, Munich & Leipzig, 1899, Decharme, *cit.*, p. 155, and Derenne, *cit.*, p. 23, correctly state that it was only after the acceptance of Diopeithes' decree that disbelief in the gods could be the object of public accusation in Athens.

Finally I would point out that when historians have discussed the verb νομίζειν it has nearly always been in the context of the indictment of Socrates, in which the word is to be found, cf. Eckermann, Menzel, Frese, Taylor, in Derenne, *cit.*, p. 217 *et seq.*, Maier, *Socrate, cit.*, Snell, *La cultura, cit.*, p. 53, Nilsson, *Greek Piety, cit.*, p. 82; in many cases, these historians are led astray by the double meaning of the verb, on which Plato plays in *Apol.* 26c *et sqq.*, cf. Burnet, *Greek Philosophy, cit.*, p. 180, n. 2. At the time of Socrates' trial, however, the *pséphisma* had been rescinded by Eucleides' amnesty, and, in the strictly legal sense, the verb reverted to its original meaning.

87. Attacking the introduction of barbaric divinities and cults into Athens, Aristophanes' satire *The Peace*, vv. 406-413, accuses the Sun and Moon of envying the gods of the state and of betraying Greece to the barbarians. Cf. Pascal, *Dioniso, cit.*, p. 15 *et sqq.*; Pettazzoni, *cit.*, p. 165 *et sqq.*, esp. p. 172.

88. On the nature and function of the προστάτης see below, p. 000. We should mention here that Anaxagoras being a metic, unlike Socrates, had no right to defend himself, cf. Glotz, *Cité Grecque, cit.*, p. 287: "chacun [in the court] doit parler pour son compte, sauf les incapables, femmes, mineurs, esclaves, affranchis et métèques, qui sont représentés par leur tuteur légal, leur

a counter-accusation[89], a danger which always threatened those who accused others illegally or unjustly; the accuser of Anaxagoras, however, shrewdly avoided this danger by making a well-founded accusation which could not be objected to.

But if the Clazomenian metic could not have been accused of ἀσέβεια, his teachings concerning the celestial phenomena could certainly have formed grounds for his accusation and conviction.

We have already mentioned that Diopeithes' decree had, for the first time in the history of Attic law, declared the pursuit of astrology to be a crime in itself, whether or not the μετάρσια involved the offence of ἀσέβεια.

Admittedly, the ψήφισμα was drawn up in a slightly ambiguous way, so that many ancient and modern commentators were led to believe that the terms μετάρσια and ἀσέβεια were used interchangeably, and therefore simplistically concluded that the trial of Anaxagoras was based on the impiety which the ψήφισμα had surreptitiously made implicit in scientific investigation. The proof of this is seen in Plato[90], who, seizing on an opinion widely held, no doubt, by the people of his own day,[91] makes Socrates say in court that the people jumped to the conclusion that anyone who occupied himself with natural science did not believe in the gods[92].

maître ou leur patron" (προστάτης). See also Clerc, in Daremberg-Saglio, s.v. Metoikoi, cit., and Flacelière, La vie quotidienne, cit., p. 290.

89. On the παραγραφή in its wider meaning and on the part it played in trials, cf. Paoli, Studi sul Processo Attico, cit., p. 80 et sqq., and Glotz, Cité Grecque, cit., p. 284 et sqq.

90. Plato, Apol., 18c.

91. I refer here to the Athenians' deep-rooted aversion (described in the text) to physicists and meteorologists, who were called, according to Plut., Nic., 23 = DK 59 A 23, "Charlatan of the sky" this aversion was encouraged by soothsayers like Diopeithes, who were anxious about the status of their art, based as it was on the interpretation of celestial phenomena as signs from the gods, Nilsson, Greek Piety, cit., p. 80; the physicists traced these phenomena back to necessary causes, Plut., Nic., 23, cit.

92. Plato, Apol., 18c: οἱ γὰρ ἀκούοντες ἡγοῦνται τοὺς ταῦτα ζητοῦντας οὐδέ θεοὺς νομίζειν.

Burnet, Plato's Apology, cit., a.l., translates: "that they also do not worship the gods", but I do not believe that this is entirely accurate, since in this case νομίζειν is related to the popular opinion, originated and confirmed by Diopeithes' pséphisma, according to which naturalistic research was suspected of

172

In fact, it appears to me that Plato himself[93] is at the root of the philosophical tradition according to which ἀσέβεια formed the grounds for the conviction of the Clazomenian physicist, while the denial of the divinity of the stars formed the specific account of the indictment. Even in modern times, Burnet[94] declared that Plato indicated the true nature of the accusation made against Anaxagoras.

It should be pointed out, however, that, when Meletus charges Socrates with having no belief in the gods[95] or in the divinity of the sun and moon[96], the accusation is not identical with the one made against Anaxagoras in court, but is merely one that might have been made against the Clazomenian by anyone who had

being equivalent to a denial of the gods. This is confirmed in *Apol.*, 26c, where the νομίζειν is logically connected with the νομίζειν of 18c and is used in the development of Plato's defence of Socrates, in which it is shown that Socrates was not engaged in research into the celestial phenomena and the secrets of the subterranean world, *Apol.*, 18b, and therefore that it is possible to reject the accusation of disbelief in the gods, *Apol.*, 26c, based on Socrates' supposed naturalism; see below.

93. Plato, *Apol.* 26d = DK 59 A 35.

94. Burnet, *EGP*, *cit.*, p. 297, writes: "Now we know from Plato what the accusation was. It was that Anaxagoras taught the sun was a red-hot stone, and the moon earth", an opinion accepted for many years, appearing in Schaubach, *cit.*, p. 39, in Zeller, *cit.*, p. 359, n.1, in Diels, in Derenne, *cit.*, p. 25, n. 2, and in the writings of all those who have investigated the trial of Anaxagoras.

95. Plato, *Apol.*, 26c. It has already been said, n. 86 above, that in this passage νομίζειν means "to believe", as it does in *Apol.* 18c, and in the intermediate passage 26b, which logically connects the other two. On the double meaning of the verb, see n. 86.

96. Plato. *Apol.*, 26d. The artifice used by Plato is evident here: attributing to Socrates the opinion of Anaxagoras concerning the divinity of the stars, he makes the reasons for Socrates' trial identical with those which, according to the common belief, *Apol.*, 18c, lay behind the trial and conviction of the Clazomenian. If Plato had really wanted to demonstrate Socrates' belief in the gods, he could have used many other gods for his examples, rather than the sun and the moon, to which at that time no temples were built and no worship was given. Plato could also have refrained from making Meletus' reply so inept: Meletus was by no means as ill-equipped as Plato portrays him. After Meletus' interrogation, it is hard to believe that any of the judges would have voted against Socrates. But we are not dealing here with an account of the actual trial of 399, so much as a free dramatic reconstruction of it by Plato, who in this, his least successful passage, reveals the literary and imaginative nature of the *Apology*.

173

read his books[97]. In other words, Plato does not say that Anaxagoras was convicted by the court for saying that the sun was a mass of incandescent metal and that the moon was an earth, but that these opinions about the nature of the stars are found in the books of Anaxagoras.

Only in later sources[98], from the time when astral cults had become more widespread in Attica and when Apollo had been finally identified with the sun[99], is it possible to find a judicial accusation made out of what Plato had merely mentioned in passing as a statement of the obvious for anyone who was not incapable of reading and writing[100].

Whereas Anaxagoras' denial of the divinity of the stars could, at a later period, truly have been seen as an offence of ἀσέβεια,

97. See above, p. 166 f., note 58.

Plato, *Apol.*, 26d, implies that Anaxagoras' work could be bought cheaply in the orchestra of the agora, and that consequently it had a wide distribution at the time of the trial of Socrates; this appears to contradict Plutarch, *Nic.*, 23, who describes the suspicion surrounding the doctrines of Anaxagoras and the extremely cautious way in which the work of the Clazomenian was circulated among a trusted few. It should be borne in mind, however, that Plutarch is referring to the time of the lunar eclipse of 27-28 August, 413, Plutarch, *ib.*, Thucydides, VII, 50, which excited the superstitious Nicias and hastened the irremediable disaster of Sicily, and that he is therefore discussing a work published after Diopeithes' decree of 433/1 and before Eucleides' amnesty of 404/3, which rescinded all the decrees previously issued, Glotz, *HG*, III, p. 70 *et sqq.* From this I believe it is possible to deduce that Anaxagoras' work was condemned together with its author in the trial of 433/31, and that it was officially removed from circulation as a result. When Diopeithes' decree was rescinded in 404/3, the ban on the Clazomenian's work was lifted and the book was again allowed to circulate, so that in 399 it was on sale in the orchestra of the agora, Plat., *Apol.*, 26 d = DK 59 A 35, possibly under a single title, Gigante, *cit.*, pp 549-50, together with other later writings, Plat., *Apol.*, 260; Plutarch, *De Esil.*, 17, 6077 = DK 59 A 38; Vitruv. VII, p. 2 = DK 59 A 39.

98. In addition to the previously cited sources of Diogenes (Sotion and Satyrus), see Joseph, *c. Ap.* II, 265, and Olympiod. in *Meteor.* p. 17 = DK 59 A 19.

99. On the question of whether Apollo was ever identified with the sun, cf. Guthrie, *The Greeks., cit.*, p. 74, or was thought of by the Greeks as the god who presided over the Delphic oracle rather than the sun, cf. Farrington, *Science and politics in the ancient world*, 2nd ed., London, 1965, p. 75; Nilsson, *Greek Religion*, p. 196 *et sqq.*

100. Plato, *Apol.*, 26d.

this could not have been so at the time of Anaxagoras' trial, especially since he was a metic from Clazomenae. In spite of this, an obvious anachronism, representing certain religious beliefs which spread into Attica much later as belonging to the Periclean period, formed the basis for a literary tradition which, beginning with Plato and continuing in later doxographers, has become *communis opinio* among modern historiographers of philosophy. This erroneous tradition, by reducing the trial of Anaxagoras to a matter of religion, radically alters the significance which this trial had for the history of Greek thought and of human civilization in general.

While the grounds of ἀσέβεια might have satisfied popular opinion, which tended to simplify the reason for and outcome of the trial[101], the religious implications of the Clazomenian metic's naturalism were, as far as the judicial accuser and the judges were concerned, not only legally insignificant, but actually to be carefully avoided for the purposes of the trial. It was unnecessary to bring in the religious implications, since under the new decree Anaxagoras was rendered eminently indictable by the blatant openness of his work on nature[102], which, although it was later banished together with its author[103], must have had a wide circulation in Athens up to the time of the trial, since the comic poets, as we shall see, were able to make fun of it.

Present-day historians would have been better employed in spending less time on expressing amazement at the Clazomenian's audacious speculations which led up to his denial of the divinity of the stars[104], and more time on attempts to understand how the

---

101. As has been seen, Plato, *cit.*, set the example for this, and was supported by the doxographers, and, in the first place, by Aristophanes, *Nub.*, v. 367.
102. See above, p. 161 f. and section 8 below.
103. See above, p. 161 f.
104. Out of the many historians in question, we may record Decharme, *cit.*, p. 157: "Quel scandale ce fut donc, à Athènes, d'entendre Anaxagore contredire une opinion si ferme et si bien établie, dépouiller hardiment le soleil et la lune de leur divinité [...]", and Pettazzoni, *cit.*, p. 179, "Anassagora [...] negava [...] la divinità, concependo come divino soltanto il *noûs*, che è pensiero [...] e il sole è natura; e percio il sole non è divino [...] non è Helios né Apollo: non è un dio: arditi concepimenti e nuovi a udirsi per il popolo di Atene e, in genere, della Grecia propria ancor tutto aderente alla fede negli antichi numi", etc.

Athenian popular assembly could have passed a decree which practically banished scientific investigation from Athens. For this is the truly significant feature of the trial of Anaxagoras: the fact that Anaxagoras was condemned merely for discussing about celestial phenomena.

The denial of the divinity of the stars, the attack on Pericles, personal enmity, etc., were also, no doubt, factors leading to the accusation; but from the strictly legal viewpoint, it was only Anaxagoras' alleged offence of μετάρσια that could be the basis for his conviction.

We must therefore re-examine the significance of this conviction, not as an event in a savage political struggle carried on in a climate of religious intolerance[105], but as seen in the cultural context of resistance and opposition towards Ionian naturalism; at the same time, we must seek to understand what effect the Athenian assembly's ban on scientific investigation had on the later development of Greek thought.

This is what we shall seek to achieve in the remaining pages of this essay, if only to open up the discussion of the subject.

6. Sotion and Satyrus, in Diogenes[106], refer to two separate judicial accusers of Anaxagoras, namely Cleon[107] (Sotion) and

105. According to Decharme, cit., p. 177 et sqq., the Greek religion was characterized by a rigid intolerance, at least where public displays of atheism or disrespect for the state religion, or profanation of the mysteries, were concerned; a more moderate view is taken by Derenne, cit., conclusion, and Pettazzoni, cit., p. 184, who see the offences of asébeia as primarily offences against the state, with the motives or pretexts supplied for political reasons, cf. Gernet et Boulanger, Le Génie grec dans la Religion, cit., 346.

This view is shared by the vast majority of historians, including Lanza, cit., p. 28-29 n.: "Che invece l'accusa ad Anassagora fosse piuttosto una manovra politica ostile a Pericle è ormai quasi unanimemente riconosciuto".

106. Diog. L., II, III, 12 = DK 59 A 1.

107. On Cleon, in addition to what is said below, see Kahrstedt, in Pauly-Wissowa, RE, XI, col. 714. There is a well-documented description by Grote, cit., VI, p. 332 et sqq.; see also Glotz, HG, cit., II, 633 et sqq.

There is a penetrating analysis of Cleon as a character in Aristophanes' comedies, and of the attitude of the comic poet towards the hated demagogue, in M. Croiset, Aristophane et les partis à Athènes, Paris, 1926, chs, 1-3, and in G. Murray Aristophanes, 2nd ed., Oxford, 1965, ch. II. On the historicity of Aristophanes' Cleon, see T. Gelzer, Aristophanes und sein Sokrates, in "Mus.

Thucydides, son of Melesias[108] (Satyrus). Since we know that Cleon entered Athenian political life when Pericles' fortunes were past their peak or already in decline[109], while the son of Melesias, ostracized in 443[110], is known only through a few scraps of unreliable information[111], it would seem that we ought to agree, in accordance with the joint testimony of Plutarch and Diodorus[112], that Sotion followed a more reliable tradition than that of Satyrus, and that Anaxagoras was, therefore, accused by Cleon at the outbreak of the Peloponnesian war, not by Thucydides, son of Melesias, who opposed Pericles in the first years of his political career.

This view is opposed by Taylor[113], who, together with Burnet, Adcock and Peck, brings the date of the trial forward to 450, as mentioned above, and accepts Satyrus' account rather than that of Sotion, although the great majority of historians prefer the latter.

But the acceptance of either of Diogenes' sources does not necessarily imply the rejection of the other. Their divergence will, in fact, be found to be only apparent, even if it cannot be resolved

Helv." 13, 1956, who studies the way in which Aristophanes treated Euripides and Cleon, who are also described in other sources, in order to deduce how Aristophanes went about portraying Socrates. For a recent rehabilitation of Cleon, see Cloché, *La Démocratie Athénienne*, Paris, 1951, pp. 149-60, 171-77, and esp. S. Mazzarino, *Il Pensiero Storico-classico*, 2nd ed., Bari, 1966, II, p. 249.

108. Thucydides, son of Melesias, will be discussed more fully further on in this section. For more information on him, in addition to what is in Grote and Glotz, see H.T. Wade Gery, *Thucydides the son of Melesias, in "J. of Hell. Stud."*, *1932, p. 205 et sqq.*, and Gigante, *La Costituzione degli Ateniesi, Studi sullo pseudo-Senofonte*, Napoli, 1953, p. 67 *et sqq.*

109. On Cleon's entry into Athenian political life on the eve of the Peloponnesian war, see Plut., *Pericl.*, 32; Cloché, *cit.*, p. 141.

110. Plut., *Pericl.*, 12; Grote, *HG, cit.*, VI, 25; Glotz, *HG, cit.*, II, p. 187 & no. 80. "The date is not absolutely certain, but the probability is strong", according to Wade Gery, *Thucydides, cit.*, p. 206.

111. "How little we know of Ephialtes or Thucydides son of Melesias!" complains Burnet, Plato's *Euthyphro, Apol., cit.*, Preface, p.V.

112. Plut., *Pericl.*, 32; Diodor, XII, 39 = 59 A 17, already quoted several times.

113. On Taylor and the historians who share his view, see p. 153 f.

in the way in which Davison attempts the task[114], provided that the accounts of Satyrus and Sotion are re-examined in the light of the historical and legal facts of the sensational trial of 433-31 B.C.

I should like to point out that no-one has yet remarked on the fact that two separate legal procedures were involved in the trial of Anaxagoras. The first of these, a legislative act, was the approval by the ἀκκλησία of ψήφισμα presented by Diopeithes[115]; the second, a judicial act, was the accusation, trial and conviction of the Clazomenian.

It is an established fact that Diopeithes proposed the ψήφισμα which bore his name to the popular assembly[116]; but it is impossible to believe that Diopeithes could have hoped to see his proposed decree passed by the ἐκκλησία without first securing the support of those men who could ensure a large majority in the assembly.

Paoli[117] has observed *"come nella vita pubblica di Atene veri detentori del potere politico fossero coloro i quali, non solo per l'eloquenza, ma anche per la conoscenza della legislazione fossero in grado di presentare all'Assemblea una concreta proposta di decreto e di saperla eventualmente difendere nei tribunali contro*

114. On Davison, see p. 155.
115. On the legislative power of the ἐκκλησία, see De Sanctis, *Atthis, cit.*, p. 355 *et sqq.*, 441 *et sqq.*; Glotz, *CG, cit.*, p. 192 *et sqq.*, and Paoli, *Studi, cit.*, p. 55 *et seq.*: "Le deliberazioni dell'Assemblea popolare", writes Paoli, "assumevano la forma di ψήφισμα [decree]. Quanto era varia l'attività dell'Assemblea, altrettanto vario poteva essere il contenuto delle ψήφσμα, mediante il quale potevano anche essere stabilite delle norme generali; e siccome in questa ipotesi le decretate norme si imponevano obbligatoriamente a tutti i cittadini, lo ψήφισμα era assimilato alla legge e, come tale, poteva essere allegato davanti al magistrato e al giudice".
116. Plutarch, as stated on p. 166 probably obtained the name of Diopeithes as the proposer of the decree which bore his name from Craterus' collection; cf. Derenne, *cit.*, p. 22, n. 2. On the right of each Athenian citizen to propose a decree, see Glotz, *CG, cit.*, p. 188.
117. Paoli, *cit.*, p. 56. ("that in Athenian public life, the true holders of political power were those who, thanks to their eloquence and knowledge of the legislation, had the ability to present a proposal for a decree to the Assembly and to defend it, if necessary, in the courts against charges of illegality, and who could also contest the proposals of their adversaries in the ἐκκλησία and before the judges").

le accuse di illegalità e che al tempo stesso sapessero combattere e nelle sedute dell'ἐκκλησία e davanti ai giudici le proposte degli avversari".

We may therefore rule out the possibility that the villainous Diopeithes — an inept fanatic, the object of popular derision, crudely mocked by the comic poets[118] — could reasonably have hoped, on the basis of his own power in the assembly, to see his proposed decree approved, especially since this legislation would, by its very nature, be to the detriment of the Athenian democratic system[119].

Further (and more importantly), while Diopeithes' proposal, which had been accepted by the βουλή and passed to the ἐκκλησία[120], was clearly designed to strike at Pericles through Anaxagoras, it should not be forgotten that Pericles himself sat in the assembly, and must therefore have been ready, with his supporters[121], to present a united front against a decision which he undoubtedly realized would be used against him.

Nevertheless, Pericles lost the vote, and the ψήφισμα was passed. Who, then, could have challenged Pericles so openly, contending with him for the favour of the assembly? Certainly not Diopeithes. Could it have been Cleon or Thucydides, son of Melesias?

To answer this, we need to know if Cleon was already a political opponent of Pericles in 433-31, and if the son of

118. On Diopeithes, see the previously cited article by Swoboda in Pauly-Wissowa, *RE*. For the attacks of the comic poets, see Aristoph., *Equ.*, v. 1085 & *schol.*, *Vesp.*, v. 380 & *schol.*, *Av.*, v. 980 & *schol.*; Phrynichus, fr. 9 Kock; Telecl., fr. 6 & *schol.*; Ameipsias, fr. 10 Kock & *schol.*, in Swoboda, *cit.*

119. Aristot., *Polit.*, IV, 4, 7, p. 129a, condemns the habit of legislating by decree, which subverts the very foundation of a proper political constitution; cf. Paoli, *cit.*, p. 56, n.l.

120. Paoli, cit., p. 56: "Non è concesso procedere alla discussione e alla votazione di una proposta di decreto, se questa non sia stata anteriormente in discussione nella βουλή e posta all'ordine del giorno in una successiva adunanza dell'Assemblea". Glotz, *CG.*, *cit.*, p. 186 *et sqq.*, 192 *et sqq.*, and for the procedure, *ib.*

121. Aristoph. *Ecc.*, 289 *et sqq.*, implies that party leaders habitually persuaded their followers to form a united group in the assembly. Thucydides, son of Melesias, seems to have obliged his followers to do so, Plut., *Pericl.*, 11. Cf. Grote, *HG*, *cit.*

Melesias was really absent from the Athenian political scene at the outbreak of the Peloponnesian war.

Thucydides, son of Olorus, the historian of the Peloponnesian war, first mentions Cleon in connection with events which took place after Pericles' death, when Cleon, in 428-7, proposed and stubbornly insisted on the merciless punishment of the Mytilenaeans[122]. Admittedly, other sources inform us that Cleon had already been working his way towards a position of power for some time[123], attempting to gain popular favour; he had begun his agitation at the time of Aspasia's trial[124], then in 431 he criticized the tactics of Pericles, who was attempting to gain time when faced with the Archidamian invasion[125], and finally he became the direct accuser of Pericles[126]. At the time of Anaxagoras' trial, however, when Pericles was still alive, Cleon, who had been overwhelmed in the struggle with his great rival, had yet to win the rather dubious power which he enjoyed in Athens after Pericles' death[127].

It seems, therefore, most improbable that Cleon, still unsure of popular support, would have dared to put forward, or persuade others to put forward, proposals which required the consent of the assembly.

With Thucydides, son of Melesias, it was a different matter. Thucydides was an Athenian, from the deme of Alopece, and

122. Cf. Thucydides, III, 36 et sqq.

123. Plut., Pericl., 33.

124. There is no direct evidence for the active participation of Cleon in the trial of Aspasia, but as he was a friend of Hermippus, who encouraged his hostility towards Pericles, Plut., Pericl., 33, it seems likely that Cleon would have done his utmost to uphold the comic poet's case against the beautiful Milesian.

125. Plut., Pericl., 32.

126. Plut., Pericl., 35. Cf. Croiset, Aristophane, cit., p. 35, n. 3.

127. Aristot., Athenian Constitution, 28, observes that Cleon seems to have done more than any other to corrupt the people by pandering to their baser instincts. The verdict of Thucydides, II 65, 10, although indirect, is in acordance with that of Aristotle and that which may be inferred from Anaxagoras. Croiset, Aristophane, cit., n. 2, p. 39, finds that "le jugement d'Aristote et celui de Thucydide sont justifiés".

was a relative of Cimon[128], being either his son-in-law[129] or his brother-in-law[130]. He succeeded Cimon as the leader of the oligarchic faction, which he turned into a well-organized and tightly disciplined party[131]. As leader of the oligarchic party, the son of Melesias was inflexible in his opposition to the politics of Pericles. Thucydides campaigned skilfully against his great rival, with an initial indirect attack which brought about the ostracism of Damon of Athens in 444[132], followed by a direct attack on Pericles himself, whom he accused in public of squandering the contents of the league's treasury[133]. The contest between Thucydides and Pericles, wich deeply divided the city[134], was settled in 443 by an appeal to the people, who voted in favour of Pericles and decreed the ostracism of Thucydides[135]. The son of Melesias left Athens within the stipulated ten days[135] and nothing more is known of him[137]. It is certain, however, that after his ten

128. Plut., *Pericl.*, 8; Grote, *HG, cit.*, VI, p. 20; Curtius, *cit.*, II, p. 25.
129. Grote, *HG*, VI, p. 21; Glotz, *HG*, II, p. 185 *et sqq.*
130. De Sanctis, *Storia dei Greci, cit.*, II, p. 130.
131. Glotz, *HG*, II p. 185.
132. Aristot., *Athenian Constitution*, 27, 4; Glotz, *HG*, II, p. 186.
133. Plut., *Pericl.*, 12; Grote, *HG*, VI, p. 21 *et sqq.*; Glotz, *HG*, II, p. 186 *et sqq.* Pericles' defence was that Athens, having taken it upon herself to ensure the independence of the Greeks from the barbarians and to safeguard the freedom of the sea, owed no further debt to the allies, and could therefore dispose of the tribute as she pleased, Plut., *Pericl.*, 12. Grote, *cit.*, *ib.*, maintains that Pericles' reply was "perfectly satisfactory".
134. Plut., *Pericl.*, 11.
135. Plut., *Pericl.*, 12; Grote, *HG*, VI, p. 25; Glotz, *HG*, II, p. 187 & n. 80; Wade-Gery, *cit.*, p. 206.
136. Glotz, *CG*, p. 202.
137. Grote, *HG*, VI,p. 38, observes that from this moment the biography of the son of Melesias is "involved in complete obscurity". However, the historian of the Peloponnesian war, I, 117, mentions a Thucydides who was a navarch together with Hagnon and Phormion, on whose orders a fleet of 40 ships was sent to assist Pericles in his siege of Samos in 440. Does this refer to the son of Melesias? If so, this would mean that Thucydides was allowed to return to Athens after only three years, and at a time when Pericles was in considerable difficulties. In fact, most historians, following J. Cacorpino, *L'ostracisme athénien*, 2nd ed., Paris, 1935, p. 210 *et sqq.*, accept that this was the case; Glotz, with some reserves, agrees with this view, *CG*, p. 203, but is firmly rejected by Grote, *HG*, VI, p. 38, n.l, and by Wade-Gery, *cit.*, p. 219.

years in exile[138] Thucydides returned to Athens[139], to take up once more his remorseless struggle against Pericles. The political decline of Pericles was thus accompanied by the improvement in the position of the son of Melesias, who had once again become the leading spirit and the mouthpiece of the opposition, which had gradually been growing in size and strength in the years preceding the war[140].

It was no coincidence, therefore, if the series of trials designed to strike at those nearest and dearest to Pericles began in 433-32, precisely at the time of Thucydides' return[141]. The first of these trials was that of Aspasia[142], who was accused by the comic poet Hermippus and defended in court by Pericles himself[143]; this was followed by the trial of Phidias, who is also said to have been accused of impiety, for having been so astonishingly reckless as to portray himself and Pericles among the warriors in the scene of the battle with the Amazons on the Parthenon metopes[144].

Since Thucydides had already attacked a member of Pericles' entourage, namely Damon[145], it would not be surprising if

138. On the duration of the penalty of ostracism, see Glotz, *CG*, p. 202.

139. Cf., *inter al.*, Glotz, *HG*, II, p. 621; Wade-Gery, *cit.*, p. 218 & references given there.

140. Glotz, *HG*, *loc. cit.*; Curtius, *cit.*, II, p. 394. According to Glotz, *CG*, p. 203; Cloché, *cit.*, p. 26, an ostracized citizen did not lose his civil rights.

141. Plut., *Pericl.*, 31.

142. Personally I am not convinced that these trials were religious in nature, and it seems even less likely that, as has been suggested, they were used as a pretext. It is hard to believe that Pericles would have allowed such people as Aspasia, Phidias, and Anaxagoras to be brought before the courts without making all the objections allowed under Athenian law against accusations that were not completely substantiated and that concerned offences not envisaged in the law. On the accusation against Aspasia, see my *Aspasia of Miletus*, in this volume.

143. Concerning the difficulty to establish a chronological order of those trials, see above note n. 62.

144. Plut., *Pericl.*, 31. "L'accusation a de quoi étonner", observes Decharme, *cit.*, p. 161. In fact, the whole series of trials of Pericles' friends "a de quoi étonner", if we continue to believe that we are dealing here with religious trials.

145. On Damon's relationship with Pericles and the influence of the former on the latter, cf. Plut., *Pericl.*, 4. Damon is praised in Plato, *Lach.*, 180d; *Alcib.*, I, 118c. On the ostracism of Damon, Aristot., *Const. At.*, 27, 4; Carcopino,

Thucydides had also instigated the accusation and conviction of Anaxagoras in 433-31, in order to strike another blow at the protector and disciple of the Clazomenian philosopher. But this would not have been done by accusing Anaxagoras in court, but by defeating Pericles in the assembly to ensure the acceptance of the ψήφισμα presented by Diopeithes. Thucydides was, in fact, the only Athenian at that time who could oppose Pericles with any reasonable hope of success[146]. It may, indeed, be reasonable to conjecture that the ψήφισμα was put forward by Diopeithes (clearly with the support and encouragement of others) precisely in order to furnish the pretext for a final resolution of the conflict between the two rivals, through a vote in the assembly which would clearly indicate which of the parties had the support of the people. Pericles was defeated, and the ψήφισμα approved by the ἀκκλησία not only endorsed the sad decline of Pericles, but also provided the legal basis for the conviction of Anaxagoras. In this way, the son of Melesias can be said to have initiated the conviction of Anaxagoras, and this explains why the tradition recounted by Satyrus represents him as the true accuser of Anaxagoras, meaning that he had a decisive part in preparing the necessary conditions for the trial and conviction of the philosopher.

Once the legal foundations had been laid, the conviction of the Clazomenian became a foregone conclusion. There was now far less uncertainty about the outcome of the proceedings in court, unlike the debate in the assembly where Thucydides had faced considerable dangers[147]. While the encounter with Pericles in the assembly had to take the form of a frontal attack, with, at first,

---

Damon a-t-il été ostracisé?, in "Rev. Et. Grecs", XVIII, 1905, p. 95 *et sqq*. On the action taken by the oligarchs against Damon, cf. Glotz, *HG*, II, p. 186.

146. On this point, we should bear in mind what Glotz writes, *CG*, p. 187: "il était licite à tout Athénien de soutenir son opinion devant l'Ecclèsia: une égale liberté de parole [...] paraissait la condition essentielle du régime démocratique. Mais, comme on s'en doute bien, un tres petit nombre usait de cette faculté. C'était d'ordinaire les chefs de parti et leurs lieutenants qui soutenaient le poids de la discussion".

147. On the γραφὴ παρανόμος, public proceedings for illegality, which could be taken against those who proposed illegal decrees, see Paoli, *cit.*, p. 56, and Glotz, *CG*, p. 209 ff., De Sanctis, *Atthis*, cit., p. 439 ff. On the risk of παραγραφή, which always threatened anyone who accused others unlawfully or unjustly, see Paoli, *cit.*, p. 80 ff.

no guarantee of victory, it would have been impossible to exculpate Anaxagoras, in court, from the charge of μετάρσια brought against him on the basis of the recent decree.

Indeed, the trial itself, and the predictable conviction of the Clazomenian, offered the opportunity for another resounding victory over Pericles.

It should be pointed out that the trial of Anaxagoras was held in the court of the heliasts[148], and that consequently the Clazomenian metic had to be represented in court by his προστάτης[149].

It is true that many authorities today tend to see the function of the προστάτης as limited to that of presenting the metic to the Demos and having his name inscribed in the demotics lists[150]. However, the trials of Aspasia and Anaxagoras, who were both Ionian metics, would seem to indicate that the προστάτης was legally obliged to appear in court. If the aim of these trials was, in fact, to attack Pericles, this could have been achieved by bringing him before the court to account for the conduct of his protégés. Pericles did indeed act in this way for both of these metics.

In my opinion, therefore, the harm done to Pericles by these trials consisted in the fact that, as προστάτης, he became, in the eyes of the Athenian people, morally responsible for the conduct of his metic protégés, publicly condemned by the sentence passed by the court of the heliasts.

If this were not the case, it would be hard to understand why Plutarch[151] should have made the quite explicit remark that the conviction of Anaxagoras was intended to throw some suspicion on Pericles, or why it was necessary for Pericles to appear in court, when he had not been present at the trial of the Athenian Phidias[152], and why he played the role attributed to him by tradition in each of the trials of the two metics.

148. Cf. Caillemer, in Daremberg-Saglio, *s.v. eisangelia* and *s.v. asébeia*.
149. See above, p. 176 f.
150. This was the opinion of Wilamowitz-Moellendorf, *Demotika der Attischen, Metöken*, in "Hermes", XXII, 1887, p. 107, accepted as the conventional view in M. Clerc, *Les métèques Athéniens*, Paris, 1893, and *Metoikoi* in Daremberg-Saglio, *cit,*; De Sanctis, *cit.*, p. 216 *et sqq.*; Glotz. *HG*, II, p. 251-2; U.E. Paoli, *Studi di Diritto Attico*, Firenze, 1930, p. 88 *et sqq.*; H. Hommel, *Metoikoi*, in Pauly-Wissowa, *RE*, XV, col. 1413 *et sqq.*
151. Plut., *Pericl.*, 32, *cit.*
152. Plutarch does not state that Pericles was present at the trial of Phidias;

184

In the case of Anaxagoras, then, the opposition scored two victories over Pericles: the first being in the assembly, where Thucydides wrested the people's favour away from Pericles, obtaining the approval of a ψήφισμα which was clearly intended to damage one of Pericles' protégés; and the second being in the court, where the accuser secured the conviction of the Clazomenian in the presence of, and in spite of the defence of, Pericles himself.

Without doubt, it was Cleon who humiliated Pericles before the jury of the heliasts, as Sotion tells us. This was certainly a task that suited Cleon well; the ambitious tanner was given a fine opportunity to create effect with an easy victory.

If I am not mistaken, therefore, the two versions of the trial of Anaxagoras, that of Sotion and that of Satyrus, which both appear in Diogenes, are not mutually exclusive but complementary; they indicate the different parts played by Thucydides and Cleon in the conviction of the Clazomenian. Thucydides laid the legal foundation by winning popular favour from Pericles over the ψήφισμα presented by Diopeithes, while Cleon was responsible for the accusation, and consequently the trial and conviction of the metic philosopher, which occurred in the presence of Pericles and despite his defence[153].

7. Something remains to be said concerning the penalty imposed on Anaxagoras.

Sotion states that he was fined five talents and condemned to exile; according to Satyrus, however, he was sentenced to death by default[154].

It is difficult to say which of the two authors has followed the better tradition. There is a possible confirmation of Satyrus' evidence in the story related by Diogenes Laertius: "When news was brought him that he was condemned [...] his comment on the

nor, as far as may be ascertained, is this stated in other sources.

153. Cf. Plut., *Pericl.*, 32, and Diog. L., III, II, 13.

It is hardly necessary to point out that this does not rule out the possibility that Cleon supported Thucydides in the assembly, and that Thucydides helped Cleon in some way to win his case in court. My emphasis here, however, is on the leading parts played in each case, as passed down to us by tradition.

154. Sotion and Satyrus, in Diog. L., II, III, 12 = DK 59 A 1.

sentence was, 'Long ago nature condemned both my judges and myself to death'"[155]. But Satyrus also says that Anaxagoras was guilty of default, while we know from other parts of this tradition that Pericles was present in court[156], acting as the προστάτης of the metic philosopher[157]. I believe that a solution to the problem of the differences between the sources may be found in Paoli's[158] statement: "*anche nei processi capitali l'accusato, presentandosi a piede libero, aveva la facoltà di allontanarsi indisturbato prima della sentenza, dopo aver pronunziato la propria difesa*"[159]

If this was the case, it is possible that, as Satyrus says, the death penalty was imposed by default.

Paoli[160] adds:"*Il reo di delitto capitale è un uomo che, divenuto incompatibile con la società di cui faceva parte, deve essere eliminato; se provvede ad eliminarsi da se con la fuga e con l'esilio volontario, l'effetto che si voleva raggiungere con l'esecuzione capitale si ottiene lo stesso*".

This being so, we may reasonably hypothesize that Anaxagoras was present in court and that Pericles defended him, but that he fled before the sentence was passed and was therefore condemned to death by default. This hypothesis would again reconcile Sotion's version with that of Satyrus, since the former could be taken as indicating the end result, namely exile, and the latter the cause, namely the death sentence.

But regardless of whether Sotion or Satyrus was right about the

---

155. Diog. L. II, III, 13, tr. Hicks, p. 143.

156. See Sotion and Hermippus, in Diog. L., II, III, 12, 13; Suda = DK 59 A 3; Plut., *Pericl.*, 32.

157. See above, p. 183.

158. Paoli, *Studi sul Processo Attico*, *cit.*, p. 191.

159. ("in capital proceedings, too, the defendant was considered to be on bail, and was free to leave the court before the sentence was pronounced, once he had made his defence statement")
We have, however, already seen that the metic, unlike the citizen, had no right to defend himself in court; this will be borne in mind in the following passage, the hypothesis being that Pericles arranged for his metic protégé to leave Athens as soon as he realized that his defence was unsuccessful.

160. Paoli, *cit.*, p. 191. ("The man who is guilty of a capital offence has become incompatible with the society of which he is part, and must be removed from it; if he takes steps to remove himself, by means of flight and voluntary exile, the ultimate purpose of capital punishment will have been achieved")

186

outcome of the trial, or whether, as seems more likely, they were both right, it is established beyond argument that Anaxagoras escaped the penalty imposed on him by retiring to Lampsacus[161], where he is known to have friends such as Metrodorus[162], and where he knew that he would be received with honour[163]; it is also known that he continued to teach philosophy in Lampsacus for several years, and that on his death his school was taken over by his Athenian disciple Archelaus, who had followed him into exile[164].

These facts will probably suffice as far as the biography of Anaxagoras is concerned.

8. The present enquiry has shown the Athenian popular assembly, by approving the *pséphisma* proposed by Diopeithes, effectively decreed the banishment of μετάρσια, and scientific investigation in general, from Athens, and how, regardless of any religious implication, scientific investigation was condemned in the person of Anaxagoras and his work.

We have also examined the part played by Pericles, both in the

---

161. The evidence in Diogenes L., II, III, 13 = DK 59 A 1, confirmed by Suda, DK 59 A 3, and indirectly by Eus., *P.E.*, 14, 13 = DK 59 A 7, has been accepted unanimously by Schaubach, *cit.*, p. 53, Zeller, *cit.*, p. 360 & n. 13, Burnet, *EGP*, *cit.*, p. 297, *et al.*

162. Diog. L., II, III, 11 = DK 59 A 1. On Metrodorus of Lampsacus, Zeller, *cit.*, pp. 423 and 441 ff.; Praechter, in Ueberwegs, *cit.*, pp. 113 and 49.

163. Diog. L., II, III, 14, 15 = DK 59 A 1. Cf. Schaubach, *cit.*, p. 53 *et sqq.*

164. Eus., *E.P.*, X, 14, 13 = DK 59 A 7. Burnet, *EGP*, *cit.*, p. 415, maintains that there is no reason to doubt that Archelaus succeeded Anaxagoras as director of the school of Lampsacus; but this information should only be accepted with caution, see Zeller, *cit.*, p. 360, n. 12. There is still no general agreement on the significance which is to be given to the word "school". Lanza, *cit.*, p. 18-19, correctly notes that "Anassagora non poté avere una scuola organizzata istituzionalmente e il suo primato nel gruppo doveva essere quindi legato solo al prestigio personale".

On the passage in Eusebius, *cit.*, to which Lanza adds "e passato in Atene vi tenne scuola", signifying that Archelaus brought the Ionian philosophy of Anaxagoras' school back to Athens, see the note by Lanza, *ib.*, and also Zeller, *cit.*, p. 442, n. 33. However, it schould be remembered here that the decree of 433/31 was applied in all its rigour throughout the Peloponnesian war, which makes Archelaus' scholarchate in Athens, in the sense in which Eusebius understood it, unlikely.

assembly, when Diopeithes' proposal was debated and approved, and in court, when Pericles defended his metic protégé.

It is precisely Pericles' presence and defeat at both the legislative and the judicial stages that cast doubt on the view that Anaxagoras' conviction was the result of an outburst of religious fanaticism caused by the Clazomenian physicist's naturalistic reductionism concerning the stars, or petty personal or factional interests hidden behind a religious façade. It is difficult to believe that Pericles, shortly to be re-elected to the council of the *strategoi* by the same assembly[165], would not have used every available means to avoid such humiliating defeats; the fact that he was unsuccessful implies that, in the eyes of the majority of Athenians, the reasons for the conviction of Anaxagoras were far more serious than the flimsy pretexts which are usually accepted at the present time.

In opposition to the common view which tends to reduce the importance of the conviction of Anaxagoras, it should be pointed out that the long series of trials of philosophers in Athens, which occurred throughout the history of philosophy in the 5th and 4th centuries B.C., began with Anaxagoras, in other words with the first appearance of philosophy in Attica[166]. It might even be said that, from the time of Anaxagoras onwards, the history of Greek thought becomes the history of the trials against freedom of thought.

It will be appropriate, therefore, to examine this long series of trials more closely and in greater depth, in an attempt to understand how and why such a serious incompatibility arose between Athens and philosophy. This incompatibility was dramatically manifested in the conviction of Anaxagoras, but must have

165. Cf. Thucydides, II, 65; for the final election of Pericles to the supreme magistrature of the city, in the spring of 429, a few months before his death, see Glotz, *HG*, II, p. 629 *et seq*.

166. It will be remembered that after Anaxagoras' conviction Diogenes of Apollonia was put in danger of death and Protagoras was condemned, followed by Socrates and the young men who associated with him and who were described by the judgement of the court as corrupt and no different from Critias and Alcibiades, then by Aristotle, Theophrastus and finally Stilpo. This series of trials came to a conclusion at the time of the decadence and extinction of Greek freedom and independence. On these trials, see the increasingly often cited Decharme, *La critique, cit.*, and Derenne, *Les procès, cit.*

already been keenly felt before then. It is certainly no coincidence that Pythagoras moved from Samos to Croton, that Xenophanes did not attempt to stay in Athens during his long journeys throughout Greece, and that Pythagoreans, fleeing from the violent destruction of their school in the land of the Italiotes, retired, not to Athens, but to Thebes, which welcomed them. Evidently, there was a circulation of ideas around the periphery of the Hellenic world, which avoided, or was repelled by, the centre. Thus, when Anaxagoras moved to Athens, bringing with him the rich scientific tradition which he had inherited and of which he was the figurehead, Athens condemned him. The sophist, Protagoras, received no better treatment. Naturalism and sophistry were thus denied the right of citizenship in Athens[167]. The naturalists were greeted with unvarying mistrust[168]; the sophists

167. I am increasingly inclined to take the opposite view to that of Jaeger, who, limiting himself to a single example, believes, *Paideia*, Oxford, 1945, I, p. 339: "the democratic state tolerated all intellectual movements and was even proud of the new freedom of its citizens", as a result of which it "attracted to it all the intellectuals in the country", p. 339, and "the foreign, intellect, once a metic, was naturalized in Athens", *ib.* This optimistic view of Athenian liberalism is refuted by the condemnation of Anaxagoras and Protagoras, which had the effect of virtually driving naturalism and sophistry out of Athens.

168. The general antipathy towards the physiologists, as shown by Diopeithes' *pséphisma*, was clearly pointed out by Plutarch, *Nicias*, 23, who records that scientific investigation was reproached for reducing divine phenomena to necessary causes; this theme has been constantly emphasized in modern works, especially those dealing with the effects of physics on religion; see Decharme, *cit.*, p. 39; Gomperz, II, p. 124; Pettazzoni, p. 128 *et sqq.*; Derenne, p. 15; Nilsson, GP, p. 92 *et sqq.*; W. Jaeger, *The Theology of the Early Greek Philosophers*, 1948, Oxford, ch. X, p. 172 et sqq.; what has been completely overlooked, though, is the way in which Ionian physics, through its political and other consequences, contributed to the development of the antipathy in question. Up to now, in fact, there has been no serious attempt to describe, even in outline, the political stance of the ancient cosmologists. T. Sinclair, *A history of Greek Political Thought*, London, 1952, G. Sabine, *Storia delle dottrine politiche*, Milano, 1953, and K. Schilling, *Storia delle idee politiche e sociali*, Milano, 1965, for example, entirely omit any mention of the Presocratics, while B. Farrington's brief survey, *Science and politics in the ancient world*, 2nd ed., London, 1965, provides no more than some useful guidelines for further research, although it does have the merit of calling the attention of scholars to "the interactions between Natural Philosophy and Political Philosophy", p. 8.

were regarded with suspicion[169]. Aristophanes also pointed to naturalism and sophistry as the cause of Socrates' impiety and corruption[170], and consequently Plato was careful to make a clear distinction between Socrates and the sophists and naturalists, contrasting him with both schools[171]. Thus, several decades after

169. For the suspicion with which the Sophists were regarded, cf. Gomperz, *cit.*, p. 214 *et seq.*, who shows how after the naturalistic philosophers were brought into disrepute the same thing happened to the new speculation "relativa tanto ai problemi della conoscenza che alle questioni attinenti al costume, alla morale e al diritto".

On the aversion of the ancients to the Sophists, see the evidence in *Sofisti, Testimonianze e Frammenti*, I, ed. by M. Untersteiner, 2nd ed., Firenze, 1961, 1 (79) 1, 2, 2a, 3, and the note on the word "sofista", p. XVI *et sqq.*

170. Being the interpreter of popular feeling, comedy was bound to express the antipathy with which the physiologists and Sophists were regarded; both groups were the target for Aristophanes' scorn in *The Clouds*, although in my view it is a hazardous undertaking to try to identify exactly who professed which of the parodied doctrines, Pascal, *Dioniso, cit.*, p. 219 et sqq. However, it seems indisputable to me that Aristophanes had Anaxagoras and Protagoras particularly in mind, together with Socrates.

171. It is my opinion that this sharp distinction, drawn by Plato in his polemic, between the naturalists, the Sophists and Socrates, has led historians from the time of Aristotle. H. Cherniss, *Aristotle's Criticism of Presocratic Philosophy*, Baltimore, 1935, to that of Zeller, I, p. 366 *et sqq.*; Mondolfo, *Nota sulla divisione in periodi*, in Zeller, I, p. 375 *et sqq.*; *Nota sulla Filosofia presocratica, ib.*, II, p. 27 *et sqq.*, and almost up to our own times, to distinguish in the history of Greek philosophy an initial cosmological phase and a later anthropological phase, linked by a period of sophistry in which the older tradition decayed while the newer one developed. But the characterization of the whole of the older philosophy as natural philosophy, or more precisely as "dogmatismo naturalistico" (Zeller, *cit.*, I, p. 374, II 17), contrasted with a later, humanistic phase, had the practical effect of blurring or completely denying the distinctions between individual philosophers or schools of thought; while the one-sided nature of this historical picture discouraged any investigation into the links between the naturalists, the sophists and Socrates: C. Diano, *Il concetto della storia nella filosofia dei greci*, in *Grande Antologia Filosofica*, Milano, II, 1954, esp. p. 282 *et sqq.* Only when the progress of modern historical science and the growth of research into Greek philosophy have overturned the traditional view of the sequence of these periods and the differences between them, and have shown that reflections on the nature of man cannot be separated from those on the physical world, Jaeger, *Paideia*, I, p. 150 ff. Mondolfo, *Nota sulla filosofia presocratica*, in Zeller & Mondolfo, I, cit.; *Problema umano e problema cosmico nella formazione della filosofica greca*, in *Problemi del pensiero antico*, Bologna,

190

the condemnation of Anaxagoras and Protagoras, Athens was still not disposed to accept the cultural heritage brought into the city by the physiologists and sophists.

This constant and unwavering hostility which all forms of philosophy encounterd in Athens may indeed, as is commonly believed, have been the result of ignorance, fanaticism or intolerance, assuming that these are not all aspects of the same phenomenon; but it was not only the result of these, and certainly not in the case of Anaxagoras. Anaxagoras' cosmology, like all forms of Ionian naturalism, not only provided a new conception of the structure and order of the universe, but also suggested a new idea of man, both as an object of knowledge[172] and as part

1936, p. 21 et sqq., and that the problem of man was historically antecedent to *Isonomía* is well defined in M.P. Nilsson, *Religiosità Greca*, Firenze, 1961, translated from the original by C. Diano, which is to be preferred to the English edition when dealing with the matter under discussion in the present study: "un termine sotto il quale si intendeva non solo l'uguaglianza dinanzi alla legge, ma anche il diritto di aver parte uguale in tutti i beni che lo stato assicura ai cittandini, sia nel campo materiale che in quello spirituale. L'idea aveva radici profonde e fu la forza propulsiva di tutte le battaglie costituzionali e il principio animatore della tendenza alla livellazione che era la meta dela democrazia", pp. 71-72.

172. Diano, *Il concetto della storia, cit.*, p. 282, has demonstrated most clearly that Anaxagoras can be considered to be the father of humanism because "fu il primo a liberare l'uomo dalla sfera delle potenze e a collocarlo al centro del mondo [...] a dargli coscienza della sua libertà e della sua dignità, a considerarlo non più come 'anima' emigrante in un corpo, ma come essere intelligente, capace di sapienza e d'arte, e che mentre di questa si serve a completare l'opera della natura, esalta quella della contemplazione dei cieli".

As regard any direct influence of Anaxagoras on Protagoras, however, Diano, *cit.*, p. 281, points out that, although Arist., *Metaph.* XI, 6, 1063b, had already established a relationship between Protagoras' proposition of the *homo mensura* and Anaxagoras' ἐν παντὶ πάντα, Simplic., *Phy.*, 164, 25 = DK 59 B 6, the idea of a direct influence seems unacceptable to Zeller, in Mondolfo, *La comprensione del soggetto umano nell'antichità classica*, Firenze, 1958, p. 241, n.1, because Anaxagoras' book would not have been available to the public when Protagoras began his career. This argument appears to be rather weak, and besides it is possible that Anaxagoras' book was published before 456, as suggested above, and won so much fame for its author that he was invited to Athens by Pericles. But whether or not Anaxagoras had any direct influence on Protagoras, it is still possible to agree with Mondolfo, *La comprensione, cit.*, pp. 240-41, that "l'aspetto soggettivistico della gnoseologia anassagorea permette di porla tra gli antecedenti del soggettivismo protagoreo".

of an extensive network of ethical, legal and political relationships.

Man, society and nature were, in fact, never seen as independent entities in the ancient Ionian cosmology, which conceived the universe as being governed by the same rules as those which governed ethical and social behaviour. There is, in fact, reason to believe that the Clazomenian physicist was primarily interested in the problem of man in all his various aspects and relationships, and that this was much more evident to his contemporaries[173] than it is to us, who must rely on fragments of his writings and a distorting literary tradition[174]. If this were not so, it would be impossible to understand why a man such as Pericles would have wanted him at his side as a teacher[175] for almost the whole of his political career. However, the Clazomenian metic's political teaching was based on ethical and legal assumptions that had already been rejected by the Athenian mind.

Indeed, Anaxagoras' doctrine of the Noῦς, the infinite and autonomous Mind or Intelligence which is omniscient and omnipotent, and is the supreme ordering and regulating force in the universe[176], came into conflict, through its obvious legal and political implications, with the deep-rooted desire for *isonomia*[177], or equality, seen as equivalent to justice, which,

173. The great ethical value of scientific research had been publicly celebrated by Euripides, fr. 910 = DK 59 A 30, a friend or disciple of Anaxagoras, and perhaps it might be not unreasonable to conjecture that it was in response to Euripides' celebration of the physiologist, according to which no intention of unjust action was born in the heart, that Aristophanes produced his satire *The Clouds*, in which impiety v. 367, comes precisely from meteorological speculation.

174. I refer to the anecdotal material based on the ideal model of the θεωρηρικὸς βίος, of which Anaxagoras was considered to be one of the best examples. Cf. section 9.

175. Anaxagoras is described as Pericles' political adviser, τῆς πολιτείας σύμβουλον, by Plutarch, *Pericl.* 16 = DK 59 A 32.

176. According to the broad interpretation by Simpli., *Phys.*, 156, 13 = DK 59 B 12. For an exhaustive critical inquiry into the *Noûs* of Anaxagoras, see Lanza, *Anassagora, cit.*, p. 221, *et sqq.*, and the more recent account by Capizzi, in Zeller & Mondolfo, *cit.*, p. 393 ff.

177. On the concept of *isonomía*, cf. Herodotus, III, 80, where Otanes, in his discourse on the best form of government, praises government by the people and

from the time of Solon, had formed the basis of public and private law in the Athenian Republic, and of the democratic system[178]. Moreover, this doctrine of Anaxagoras, which was to earn its creator the nickname of "Mind" (perhaps more than just a soubriquet attached to him in jest by the comic poets)[179], had

says that it has the most beautiful of all names, *isonomía*, or equality as a principle of justice, which inspired Solon's legislation: "E leggi in modo uguale al plebeo e al nobile, applicando a ciascuno retta giustizia, prescrissi", in G. Fassò, *La Democrazia in Grecia*, Bologna, 2nd ed., 1967, p. 38.

Isonomía is well defined in M.P. Nilsson, *Religiosità Greca*, Firenze, 1961, translated from the original by C. Diano, which is to be preferred to the English edition when dealing with the matter under discussion in the present study: "un termine sotto il quale si intendeva non solo l'uguaglianza dinanzi alla legge, ma anche il diritto di aver parte uguale in tutti i beni che lo stato assicura ai cittandini, sia nel campo materiale che in quello spirituale. L'idea aveva radici profonde e fu la forza propulsiva di tutte le battaglie costituzionali e il principio animatore della tendenza alla livellazione che era la meta della democrazia", pp. 71-72.

178. On Solon's legislation, see especially De Sanctis, *Atthis, cit.*, chs. VI-VII, pp. 193-259; Solon's democratic ideal and the way in which it formed an essential and characteristic element of Greek thought are well described by Fassò, *op. cit.*, ch. I, who provides translations of the fragments of Solon's poetry set in their ciritical and historical context.

179. On the nickname given to Anaxagoras, cf. Plut., *Pericl.*, 4 = DK 59 A 15; Diog. L. II, III, 6 = DK 59 A 1 and Timon in the same work. Aelian., *V.H.* VIII 19 = DK 59 A 24, states that an altar was erected to Anaxagoras with the inscription "Intelligence" "Truth". There is an allusion, albeit an ironic one, in Plato, *Hipp. M.* 283a = DK 59 A 13, as was pointed out by A. Covotti, *Un filosofo soprannominato "Intelletto"*, in *I Presocratici*, Napoli, 1934, p. 219. Zeller, in Zeller & Mondolfo, *cit.*, I, V, p. 358, n. 8, *cit.*, I, II, p. 382, n. 2, followed by Burnet, *EGP*, p. 295, and Derenne, *cit.*, p. 14, n. 4, believes that the epithet *Noûs* "è da considerare più come un nomignolo ironico che come un titolo onorifico". This is a plausible hypothesis; perhaps this joking nickname, originated by the comic poets, was designed to bring out the theological and political implications of the concept of *Noûs*. Diano, *cit.*, p. 280, has clearly shown how the *Noûs* of Anaxagoras "fatto principio cosmogonico diventa immediatamente Dio", as is proclaimed by Euripides, fr. 1018 = DK 59 A 48: "The *Noûs* which is within us, is within each one, god". This may, perhaps, be the reason for the nickname of Οὐλύμπιος given to Pericles, Anaxagoras' disciple, by another comic poet, namely Aristophanes, *Arch.*, v. 530, whose wrathful Pericles is likened to the Olympian Jupiter, hurling bolts of lightning and shaking all Hellas with his thunder. The two nicknames, Νοῦς and Οὐλύμπιος, may reveal, therefore, that public opinion was not unaware of the subversive theological and political implications of Anaxagoras' doctrine. Finally, it should

to find a practical evidence in the political activities of Pericles, who, while leaving the democratic structure of the state unaltered, substituted government by one man for government by the people[180]; as a result of this, he was, quite reasonably, compared to Pisistratus and named a tyrant[181].

It was, perhaps, this blatant transformation of *isonomia* into its opposite, *pleonessia*, that lay behind the accusation of medism which, according to Satyrus[182], was made against Anaxagoras, among the people, if not in the court. The accusation was based on the similarity of Anaxagoras' doctrine of the Νοῦς, in its political aspects, to the tyranno-monarchical ideology of the Persians[183], and on the political orientation consequently perceived in Pericles' assumption of pre-eminence in Athens. The accusation of medism or Persophilia came to be inseparably identified with that of tyranny[184], and could be made against not only a tyrant, but also anyone who instigated, or in any way supported, tyrannical action[185].

be added that the fact that the comic poets used these names, and especially that applied to Anaxagoras, in their comedies, implies that the cosmological theory of the Clazomenian, far from being secret, Derenne, *cit.*, p. 15 *et seq.*, was common knowledge; otherwise it could not have formed a target for satire. This confirms what has already been stated, and means that Plutarch, *Nic.*, 23 = DK 59 A 18, in remarking on the secrecy with which Anaxagoras' work was circulated, was referring to a period following Diopeithes' decree, namely the time of the eclipse, 411, and not to the period of Anaxagoras' teaching activity before 433/31.

180. Cf. Thuc., II, 65.

181. He is described as such by De Sanctis, *Atthis, cit.*, p. 477 *et seq.*, who speaks with justice of a princedom set up by Pericles in Athens.

182. Satyrus, in Diog. L. II, III, 12 = DK 59 A 1.

183. It should be borne in mind that, in the previously cited *logos tripolitikos* in Herodotus, III, 80-83, Megabyzus describes government by the masses as stupid and insolent, and concludes that democracy is the form of government of Persia's enemies; and that Darius praises monarchy as the best form of government.

Opposition to the Persians, seen as the opposition of democracy to monarchy, is a recurring theme in classical literature, being found in Plato. *Leg.*, III, 693d ff., and again in Plutarch, in Fassò, *cit.*, . 252.

184. See supra p. On the Asiatic origin of the word τύραννος, cf. S. Mazzarino, *Tra Oriente ed Occidente*, Firenze, 1947, pp. 200, 202, as cited by M. Untersteiner, *Senofane, Test. e Framm.*, Firenze, 1956, note to B3, pp. 117-118.

185. The law on tyranny, in Aristotle, *Resp. Athen.*, XVI, 10, cf. A. Levi,

This all caused great concern in the Athenian democracy, a concern that was far more serious and well-grounded than anything arising out of the naturalistic reductionism propounded by the Clazomenian metic about the stars.

Of course, this does not man that the threat which Anaxagoras' cosmology posed to the Athenian democratic order was not equally evident in the sphere of the state religion and popular belief, whose mythical and poetic roots were more directly laid bare and undermined by the rationalism of the scientific tradition. But although the interchange and interpenetration of theological and religious concepts with those of ethics and politics[186] gave the political constitutions a sacred character, so that offences against the state were seen as offences against religion[187], the fact remains that Anaxagoras' cosmology was condemned, as has been shown, not so much for its religious implications (for which the Clazomenian metic could not, in any case, have been indicted) as for its alarming political and social consequences.

It was precisely these political and social consequences of Anaxagoras' doctrine that led to the approval of Diopeithes' *pséphisma*, which was supported in opposition to Pericles by the son of Melesias, and with which the majority in the Athenian popular assembly meant to condemn, through μετάρσια and scientific investigation in general, not science or free thought as

---

Comm., p. 178, punished with *atimia* anyone who attempted to become a tyrant or helped to set up a tyranny, and was as old as the crime of tyranny itself, which was provided for and condemned even before the amnesty of Solon. It was confirmed in the Eighth Law of the Twelve Tables, which excluded anyone who had attempted to become a tyrant from judicial pardon; Plutarch, *Sol.*, 19, cf. De Sanctis, *Atthis, cit.*, pp. 141 and 187.

On the day after the fall of the Four Hundred, Demophantus obtained approval for a decree to the effect that all Athenians, divided by tribes and demes, should solemnly swear to kill anyone who attempted to become a tyrant or who helped to establish a tyranny. The oath is recorded by Andocides, *De myst.*, 96-99, and part of it is as follows: "I will slay by word and by deed, by my vote and by my hand,whoselover shall suppress the democracy at Athens, [...] or shall help to |install| a tyrant" (trans. K.J. Maidment, London, 1941).

186. See, for example, Mondolfo, *Nota sulla filosofia presocratica, cit.*, esp. p. 50 *et sqq.*

187. For the political nature of religious offences, see above, p. 000.

such, but rather the disturbing tyranno-monarchical tendencies aroused by the philosophical thought which Anaxagoras had introduced into Athens from the frontiers of the empire, and of which Pericles, the disciple and protector of the metic philsopher, was the perfect incarnation.

9. The conviction of Anaxagoras thus brought to light the elements of a conflict, which was already keenly felt[188], between Athenian democracy, as an ethical ideal, and the political systems put forward as a result of philosophical thought; and this happened at a time when the fate of democracy, opposed by Spartan oligarchy, hung in the balance, and when Pericles himself was suspected of tyranny.

The conflict was to become more bitter and irreconcilable during the disastrous, interminable Peloponnesian war, when the mystical and religious influence of Pythagoreanism grew more powerful, altering the meaning of the ancient Delphic precept so that it was taken as an exhortation to know the divine within man[189]; the Pythagoreans also put forward a new ethical and political ideal, connected with the new conception of man propounded by Philolaus in Thebes and by Archytas in Tarentum, on the principle of geometrical equivalence, that is the prevalence, of quality over quantity, of the ἀγαθοί over the κακοί[190], and favouring the form of a composite aristocratic-

188. From the time when Athens had to face up to the Persian threat, which brought into opposition two forms of political constitution, the monarchical tyranny of Persia and the democracy of Athens, these two forms were always contrasted, one of them being praised as a model to be followed while the other was condemned. Thus, while the Persians called their enemies democrats, Herodot., VIII, 81, the Athenians said the opposite of the Persians, who kept their people in a state of extreme servitude, while the Athenians aimed for the greatest freedom for theirs, Plat., Leg., III, 699e.

189. On the sense given to the Delphic precept "know thyself", in the Orphic-Pythagorean doctrine, cf. A. Delatte, Etudes sur la littérature pythagoricienne, Paris, 1915, p. 69; Pettazzoni, La Religione, cit., p. 107; P.M. Schuhl, Essai sur la formation de la pensée grecque, 2nd ed., Paris, 1949, p. 251; Jaeger, Paideia, I, cit., p. 194 ff. Mondolfo, Sócrates, Buenos Aires, 1955, p. 31; La comprensione del soggetto umano, cit., p. 469.

190. On the extension of the Pythagorean notion of geometrical equality to include a politics opposed to the democratic principle of the vote, which is based

monarchic government[191]. In comparison with this, all that the Athenians could offer was the sorry spectacle of a corrupt, corrupting democracy, which destroyed all moral values and was the cause of all the miseries of the war.

The effect of Pythagoreanism on Socrates' spiritual development[192] explains his collusion with the Pythagoreans of Thebes[193], who sided with Sparta against Athens, and clarifies the

on arithmetical addition, cf. Schuhl, *Essai, cit.*, p. 377. On the Pythagorean assumption of a God who was a geometrician, a doctrine flowed away through to the Italian humanists, cf. E. Garin, *Storia della filosofia italiana*, Torino, II, 1966, p. 616, *L'Umanesimo Italiano. Filosofia e vita civile nel Rinascimento*, Bari, 1952, p. 232 et sqq., it is useful to recall Florus' speech in Book VIII of Plutarch's *Dinner-Table Discussions*, in which it is pointed as the difference between mathematics and geometry is the same that the difference between democracy and aristocracy, and that God always prefers geometry; cf. Farrington, *cit.*, p. 26 ff.

As for the terms ἀγαθοί and κακοί, it should be noted that, even in Solon and Theognis, because of the "identificazione costante nello spirito greco dei valori politici con quelli etici", Fassò, *cit.*, p. 70, they had more than a moral significance, Farrington, cit., p. 76, since they indicated the two classes of citizens in the polis: the aristocrats (the good) and the common people (the bad), and also, by extension, the constitutional forms associated with the rule of each class.

191. At the height of the Peloponnesian war, the contrast between the Theban monarchic ideal and the Athenian democratic ideal was displayed to the spectators of the Dionysia by Euripides, *Suppl.*, vv. 403-454. In this work, Euripides, the friend and disciple of Anaxagoras and Socrates, sings the praises of his democratic native land, but on the other hand the criticisms expressed by the Theban herald are identical with those of Socrates concerning Athenian democracy, according to Plato, *Apol.*, 22d; *Prot.*, 319d; *Alc. M.*, 113d, and Xenophon, *Mem.*, III, 7, 6.

192. The influence of Pythagoreanism on Socrates has been particularly emphasized by Burnet, *EGP, cit.*, p. 320 et sqq.; GP, cit., p. 152; Plato's *Phaedo*, Oxford, 1911, 1956 ed., *Introduction*; by A.E. Taylor, *Varia Socratica*, Oxford, 1911, I, p. 1 et sqq., and by G.C. Field, *Plato and his contemporaries*, 2nd ed., London, 1948, p. 175. For Plato, see also Schuhl, *cit.*, p. 376 et sqq., and for the relationship with Archytas, esp. Timpanaro Cardini, *Pitagorici, Test. e Framm.*, II, Firenze, 1962, p. 265.

193. The fact that Plato included the Theban Pythagoreans, Simmias and Cebes, among the characters in the *Phaedo*, 61d, indicates that the friendship with Socrates, Xenophon, *Mem.*, I, 2, 48, began several years before the end of the war, and consequently that close relations had been maintained, even during the war, between the Thebans and the Athenian.

197

meaning of Socrates' criticism of democratic institutions and systems, and, more importantly, of the celebrated champions of democracy[194]; it also explains the behaviour of Socrates' disciples towards Athenian democracy, which was destroyed by Critias, fought against by Alcibiades[195] and Xenophon[196], fled from by the Socratics on the death of their master[197], and rejected by Plato in his ill-fated ventures in Sicily[198].

Taking these considerations into account, the conviction of Socrates, like that of Anaxagoras, can be seen to be an episode

194. For Socrates' critique of democratic institutions, see the previously cited passages, *Apol.* 22d, *Alc.* M. 113d, *Prot.* 319d. For the critique of the politicians, see *Gorg.*, 515-526b; *Alc. M.*, 118d-e, 120b; *Prot.*, 319e; *Meno*, 93a; *Theag.*, 126d.

195. On Critias, see the fragments edited by Battegazzore, in *Sofisti*, IV, *cit.*, esp. 14 (88) A 1, and the extensive explanatory notes; Untersteiner, *I Sofisti*, Torino, 1949, p. 376 *et sqq.*

It is still worth consulting the very full discussion by Grote, *History of Greece*, VIII, *cit.*, pp. 314-383; for the relationships with Socrates, see again Grote, *cit.*, VII, p. 48 *et sqq.* An echo of Polycrates' *categoria (Hurubert, Le pamphlet de Polycrates et le Gorgias de Platon*, in "Revue de Philologie", V, 1931, pp.20-77) is found in Xenophon, *Mem.*, I, 2, 12, whose relationship with the pamphlet of Polycrates is examined in A.H. Chroust, *Socrates, Man and Myth. The two Socratic Apologies of Xenophon*, London, 1957, p. 44 et sqq. For Socrates' responsibility in the eyes of the people at least, for the conduct of Critias, see Aeschin. *c. Timarch.*, ch. 34, p. 74, who reminds the Athenians that they put Socrates to death because he was the teacher of Critias.

On Alcibiades, his friendship with Socrates and his attitude towards Athenian democracy, see Grote, *cit.*, VII, esp. p. 41 *et sqq.*, and the excellent study by Hatzfeld, *Alcibiades*, Paris, 1951.

196. Cf. Grote, *cit.*, IX, 1852, p. 240 *et sqq.*, and J. Luccioni, *Les idées politiques et sociales de Xénophon*, Paris, 1947, and for the relationship with Socrates, Luccioni's *Xénophon et le socratisme*, Paris, 1953.

197. In spite of Stefanini's assertion, *Platone*, I, 2nd ed., 1949, p. 22, that "dopo la morte di Socrate, Platone fugge non le rappresaglie della città che aveva ucciso il Giusto, ma la città deserta da colui che le aveva dato un'anima e une speranza di salvezza", the fact is that the Socratics were eager to depart, Maier, *Socrate*, I, *cit.*, p. 10; none of them had distinguished himself by his services to the city, Gomperz, *Pensatori Greci*, I, *cit.*, pp. 519-520, and the fact that they fled to Megara, ruled by an oligarchic government, also reveals something of the Socratics' feelings about the restored democracy.

198. See the study by J. Luccioni, *La pensée politique de Platon*, Paris, 1958, which gives a good account of Plato's experience and the reasons for his radical critique of democracy.

in the conflict mentioned above; in other words, the legitimate defensive action of Athenian democracy in the face of the mortal danger to which Socrates and the Socratics constantly exposed it[199].

We shall not, therefore, allow ourselves to be deceived by the later, disingenuous, idealization of the absent-minded philosopher, detached from the world, the ideal model for the θεωρητικὸς βίος[200], which implies the absurd notion of a philosophy which is not at the same time political commitment, and of which Anaxagoras[201], no less than Socrates, is supposed to have been one of the chief upholders. Against this idealization we must set the image of the philosopher involved in a living

199. For the ethical and legal justifications of the accusation against Socrates, and for his conviction, see below.

200. W. Jaeger, *Ueber Ursprung und Kreislauf des philosophischen Lebensideals*, Berlin, 1928, p. 393, observes correctly that "alle geschichten, die die älteren Philosophen zu bewussten Bekennern des Ideals des θεωρητικός βίος machen, stammen entweder unmittelbar aus der platonischen schule oder sie sind unter dem Einflusse des platonischen Ideals in der nächsten Folgezeit entstanden". But the origin of the ideal of the βίος is to be found not so much in the Platonic ethic which "mehrere entgegengesetzte Lebenstypen aufstellt" and which culminates in the "Wohl des besten Lebens", Jaeger, *cit.*, p. 392, as in the deliberate transformation of Socrates' personality, as a result of which the teacher of Critias and Alcibiades, Xenophon, *Mem.* I, 2, 12, 47; whom Plato consulted because he was eager to devote himself to a political career, Plato, *Epist.*, VII, 342c; the only person with a proper conception of politics, *Gorgias*, 521de, *Alcib. I*, 105c; the ruthless critic of democracy, *Apol.* 22d, *Alc. I*, 113d, *Prot.*, 319d, and of its champions, *Gorgias*, 515c-526b, *Prot.*, 319e, *Alc. I*, 118de, 120b, was represented in the *Apology* as devoid of all learning, *Apol.*, 19e, 21d, 22d, 23b, 33b, and therefore chosen by the god of Delphi, *Apol.*, 21a ff., to whom he was supposed to have sacrificed all that he held most dear and all of his wealth, *Apol.*, 23c, 37b, 38b. Thus the ideal of the βίος made its first appearance at the same time as the *Sokratesdichtung*, O. Gigon, *Sokrates*, Bern, 1947; *Les grands problèmes de la Philosophie antique*, Paris, 1961, chs. VI, IX: both of these phenomena arose out of the same deliberate attempt to produce a literary image of the teacher of Critias and Alcibiades which showed him as totally uninterested in politics and therefore not responsible for the behaviour of his disciples towards the city.

201. The idealization of the personality of Anaxagoras, as a supreme example of a life dedicated to pure φρόνησις, is in Aristot., *Eth. Eud.*, A 4 1215b 1 & 6; A 5 1216a 11 ff.; Jaeger, *cit.*, p. 400. The anecdotal material is in Diog. L. II, III, 7, 10, 13 = DK 59 A 1. Cf. Jaeger, *cit.*, p. 390.

human society, and interested in political life rather than in the problems of God and the world, assuming that the latter can ever be divorced from the problems of mankind. In fact, these spellbound observers of celestial phenomena, vague inventors of verbal artifice, and unarmed moral preachers were not only physicists, metaphysicians and dialecticians, but were, above all, legislators and politicians, with interest in the real world. This is true of Anaxagoras and the Ionian naturalist, as it is of the Pythagoreans, the Eleatics[202] and Protagoras, and even more so of Socrates and his great and varied host of followers[203].

By bringing the philosophers down from the heavens to the earth, we can see quite a different significance in their trials in Attica from that which has been accepted up to now. For all their idealization and transfiguration in the literature, their lives must surely have been consistent with their deaths, which must provide us with an insight into the meaning of the philosophy of, for example, Anaxagoras, Protagoras and Socrates. Otherwise, we are reduced to putting their judges on trial, and instead of Pericles' political adviser, we should find an absent-minded observer of celestial phenomena, or, in place of Socrates ἀσεβής, we should see the innocent image of a religious missionary, entrusted by the god of Delphi with a spiritual mission to the people, an image which clearly has nothing in common with the Socrates who was accused, tried and condemned.

Athens, spring 1967.

202. In my opinion, it is very likely that the Pythagoreanism of Parmenides and Zeno, concerning which Iamblichus, Photius, Simplicius and Strabo are all in agreement, DK 28 A 4, 10, 12, was more political than theoretical in nature.

203. It would not be possible to provide a detailed list of sources, even if limited to the Presocratics, within the space of this note. It is suggested, therefore, that the reader refer to Jaeger, cit., p. 403, where the case is made for the interest in the πρακτικὸς βίος, wherein lay, according to the peripatetic Dichaearchus, the greatness of the ancient thinkers.

ASPASIA OF MILETUS

1. Concerning Aspasia of Miletus[1], nothing but the name is recorded by historians of philosophy, who, while dealing with Anaxagoras[2], refer to the wave of accusations and trials which swept away with the "greatest natural philosopher"[3] of Clazomenae those nearest and dearest to Pericles[4].

1. For Aspasia of Miletus, daughter of Axiochus, the sources are Plato, *Menex.* 225a, 236a-c, 249; Xenoph., *Mem.* 11 6-36; *Oecon.* 3, 14; Plutarch, *Pericl.* XXIV 2 ff; XXV 1; XXXII 1, 5; Clem. Alex., *Strom.* IV, XIX, 122-23; Philostr., *Ep.* 73 (= D.-K 82A 35); Athen. V 219a-220a; XIII 589a; Harpocrat., see Ἀσπασία; Suida, see Ἀσπασία; for the comic poets, Cratin., *ap.* Plutarch, *Pericl.* XIIV 9; Eupol., *ap.* Plutarch, *Pericl.* XXIV 10; Aristoph., *Acharn.* vv. 497-505; Schol. ad *Equ.* v. 969; for the Socratic Aeschines' dialogue Ἀσπασία, see Diog. Laert. II 61; Plutarch, *Pericl.* XXIV 6; XXXII 5; for Antisthenes' Ἀσπασία, see Diog. Laert. VI 16. On Aspasia, see Judeich, in Pauly-Wissowa, *RE*, *s.v.*, 1716-1721; Grote, *HG* VI, p. 132 ff; Curtius, *GG* II, p. 230; p. 394 ff; p. 432; p. 855; Busolt, *GG* II, 505 ff; Bury, *HG*, 3rd ed., p. 409; Glotz-Cohen, *HG* II, p. 578; De Sanctis, *Storia dei Greci*, 4th ed., II, pp. 134, 137, 387; *Pericle*, in *EI* XXVI, p. 476 ff.; Ἀτθίς, 2nd ed., p. 479 f; Cloché, *La démocratie Athénienne* (Paris, 1951), p. 141; V. Ehrenberg, *From Solon to Socrates*, p. 236; Schoemann, *Griech. Altertümer*, French trans. *Antiquités grecques*, 2 v. (Paris, 1884-1885), II, *Appendice*, p. 676; Decharme, *La critique des traditions réligieuses chez les Grecs* (Paris, 1904), p. 160; Derenne, *Les procès d'impiété intentés aux philosophes à Athènes au Ve et au IVe siècle A.J.C.* (Liège-Paris, 1930), p. 18; Dupréel, *La légende socratique et les sources de Platon* (Bruxelles, 1922), p. 263; E.U. Paoli, *La donna greca nell'antichità* (Firenze, 1953), pp. 83-98; M. Delcourt, *Périclès* (Paris, 1939), p. 17 f; Pohlenz, *Der Hellenische Mensch* (Gottingen, 1947), p. 377 f; Afnann, *Zoroaster's influences on Anaxagoras, the Greek tragedians and Socrates* (New York, 1969), p. 29 ff.
    2. For example, Guthrie, *A history of Greek Philosophy*, II, (Cambridge, 1965), p. 268, while discussing the "prosecution of Anaxagoras for impiety", merely states that "the same charge was brought against Aspasia". On the other hand, Zeller, see Zeller & Mondolfo, *La filosofia dei greci*, I, V, edited by A. Capizzi (Firenze, 1969), does not even mention the name of Aspasia.
    3. ὁ μὲν φυσικώτατος Ἀναξαγόρας, according to Sextus Empiricus (= D.-K. 59 B 21).
    4. Concerning the proceedings taken against the members of Pericles' en-

201

Nor do historians of Greek religion[5] and of Attic law[6] really record much more than the name; they all consider that to repeat, in line with the ancient sources, that Aspasia was accused of ἀσέβεια by the comic poet Hermippus and was defended by a weeping Pericles, is sufficient to resolve and close the case of Aspasia, just as, indeed, the contemporary cases of Phidias and Damon, and the representative case of Anaxagoras, have been closed[7].

Political historians[8], however, have more to say about Aspasia when discussing Pericles and the causes of the Peloponnesian war. Yet these, like other historians, have never attempted to investigate fully the offence of ἀσέβεια with which Aspasia is supposed to have been charged; nor have they enquired whether it was possible for an accusation of procuring to be added, as a pretext, to that of impiety[9], or for the tears shed by Pericles in court to suffice for Aspasia'a acquittal on both counts[10]. But if for other historians, the affair has been of minor importance; how important is it to the historian of philosophy to determine the exact nature of the accusation made against Aspasia and to

tourage, and the real grounds for these proceedings, see my essay *On the Trial of Anaxagoras*, in this volume and my book *Socrates. Physiology of a Myth* Amsterdam, 1981; It. ed., p. 263 ff, which also provide an abundant bibliography concerning the matter.

5. See. R. Pettazzoni, *La religone nella Grecia Antica* (Torino, 1953), p. 183 and n. 76.

6. See. G.F. Schoemann, *Antiquités Grecques, op. cit.*, II, *Append.*, p. 676.

7. On these trials, see above, n. 4.

8. Grote, Curtius, Busolt, Glotz-Cohen, De Sanctis, Ehrenberg, *cit.* See n. 1 above.

9. According to Schoemann, *op. cit.*, II, p. 676, and to Decharme, *op. cit.*, p. 161, who follows him word for word, the accusation of procuring was "imaginée à l'effet de prévenir défavorablement le tribunal".

10. Plutarch, *Pericl*, XXXII 5, follows Aeschines in stating that Aspasia was saved by Pericles' tears rather than by his arguments, while Athenaeus (*Deipn.* XIII 589e) takes the same information from Antisthenes, Ἀσπασία. But although it was customary to appear in court in Athens with weeping and grieving friends and relatives in order to soften the hearts of the judges (Plat., *Apol.* 34c), it is hard to imagine a man such as Pericles weeping before the court. In my opinion, it is very likely that this idea derives from the imagination of Aeschines and Antisthenes, who freely altered Pericles' speech in defence of his παλλακή several decades after it was made.

establish Pericles' role in her trial, and the outcome of the trial, from which Aspasia emerged acquitted and Pericles humiliated? This is what the present enquiry is intended to establish, taking as its starting point the need to clarify the historical and cultural situation in Athens in the years immediately preceding the outbreak of the Peloponnesian war. In this period, philosophy, and consequently free scientific research, which had come to Athens with Anaxagoras thirty years earlier[11], were finally banned from the city, as a result of trials intended to drive away those philosophers who had brought philosophy to Athens and who had celebrated its triumph in the house of Pericles[12].

2. What was the crime of which Aspasia was accused?

According to our source, Plutarch[13], Aspasia was accused by Hermippus[14] not only of ἀσέβεια[15], but also of προαγωγεία[16],

11. On Anaxagoras' arrival in Athens and his introduction of philosophy into Attica, cf. my, *On The Trial of Anaxagoras*, here.
12. On this subject, see my *On The Trial of Anaxagoras* and my *Socrates. Physiology of a Myth, cit.* It. ed. p. 263 ff.
13. Plutarch, *Pericl.* XXXII 1.
14. On Hermippus, see Dover in *OCD, s.v. Hermippus.* The fragments of Hermippus' comedies have been collected by Meineke, *FCG* II, 388 ff.; Kock, *CAF* I, 224 ff.; Edmonds, *FAC* I, 284 ff. On Hermippus' use of iambics as well as comedy as weapons in his attacks, see A. Lesky, *A history of Greek literature*, English ed., (London, 1966), p. 421.
15. The concept of ἀσέβεια is defined in ps.-Aristot., *De virt. vit.*, 1251 a 30; Polyb. XXXVII 1c. On *Asébeia*, see Caillemer, in Darenberg-Saglio, *s.v.* On the ἀσεβείας γραφή, see Tahlheim, in *RE, s.v.*; Paoli, *Studi sul processo attico* (Padova, 1933), pp. 16, 58 f., 86. On ἀσέβεια as the legal ground for the prosecutions for impiety in fourth- and fifth-century Athens, see Decharme, *op. cit.*, 141 ff; Derenne, *op. cit.*, p. 9 ff. Cf. also A. Momigliano, *Empietà ed eresia nel mondo antico, Riv. Stor. It.*, LXXXIII (1971), IV, pp. 771-791; K.J. Dover, *Greek popular morality* (Oxford, 1974), 246 ff.; I. Rudhart, *La définition du délit d'impiété d'après la législation attique, Museum Helveticum*, XVI (1966), p. 87 ff.; challenges the indeterminate nature of the concept of ἀσέβεια. On the civil nature of the offences of ἀσέβεια, see Glotz-Cohen, *HG, cit.*, II, p. 249; Pettazzoni, *op. cit.*, p. 184; Nilsson, *Greek piety*, (Oxford, 1948), p. 78; Maier, *Sokrates* (Tübingen, 1913), p. 489; Gernet-Boulanger, *Le génie grec dans la réligion* (Paris, 1932), p. 346; B. Snell, *The discovery of the mind*, Eng. ed., (Oxford, 1953), p. 248.
16. On προαγωγεία, Aesch., *c. Tim.* 14; Plat., *Theaet.* 150a. Cf. *RE, s.v.*, col. 29. For the προαγωγείας γραφή see Glotz, in D.S. *s.v.*, who gives as an ex-

for having procured freewomen for Pericles' pleasure. Plutarch, however, does not say what the offence of ἀσέβεια consisted of; neither have the historians enquired into this.

The possibility of Aspasia's having suffered under the severities of Diopeithes' ψήφισμα[17] for taking part in the discussions and professing the views of Anaxagoras, which some authorities have accepted[18], may definitely be ruled out. Diopeithes' ψήφισμα, which, in any case, came at a later date than the accusation against Aspasia[19], introduced an ἀγὼν τιμητός[20], dependent on εἰσαγγελία[21]. By this procedure, if the metic of Miletus, said to have been defended in court by Pericles,

ample the one against Aspasia, although Paoli, *La donna greca*, *cit.*, p. 174, n. 52, has doubts as to its existence.

17. On Diopeithes, see Swoboda, in *RE*, IX, cols. 1046-1047. On the ψήφισμα introduced by him into Attic law, according to which anyone who did not believe in the gods or who propounded doctrines concerning celestial phenomena was to be brought before the popular assembly, see Plutarch, *Pericl.* XXXII, 2. Cf. Decharme, *La loi de Diopeithès*, in *Mélange Perrot* (Paris, 1903). On the novelty of the ψήφισμα compared with the ancient γραφή ἀσεβείας see *On the Trial of Anaxagoras*.

18. Cf. Grote, *HG*, *cit.*, VI, p. 135. A. Momigliano, *Empietà ed eresia*, *cit.*, p. 778, is also of the opinion that Aspasia was accused under Diopeithes' decree, and that the same decree provided the legal grounds for the accusation against Socrates.

19. This is made clear by Plutarch's account, *Pericl.* XXXII 1, which dates the proceedings against Pericles' circle to the time of the blockade of Megara (Plutarch, *Pericl.* XXXI 1-5; *Thuc.* I 67). Curtius, *GG* II, 345 ff., 370 ff., however, puts it after the accusation against Phidias, but before that against Anaxagoras, XXXII, 2, 5, for which the ψήφισμα of Diopeithes was especially passed.

According to Decharme, *cit.*, p. 161, the trial of Aspasia was later than that of Anaxagoras.

20. On the ἀγῶνες τιμητοί, their special nature and procedural character, see Paoli, *Studi di diritto attico* (Firenze, 1930), pp. 310, 314 ff., 324 ff.; *Studi sul processo attico* (Padova, 1933), p. 59. For the fact that Socrates' trial was also an ἀγὼν τιμητός see my *Socrates. Physiology of a Myth*, cit., It. ed., p. 312, n. 175.

21. On the procedure of εἰσαγγελία provided for by Diopeithes' decree, see Caillemer, in D.S., *s.v.*; Glotz, *La cité grecque* (Paris, 1953), p. 139 ff; Paoli, *Studi sul processo attico*, *cit.*, p. 53. On the explicit provision for the procedure of εἰσαγγελία for offences of ἀσέβεια see Caillemer, in D.S., *s.v.* ἀσέβεια and Thalheim, in *RE*, *s.v.* ἀσεβείας γραφή, cols, 1529-1531.

acting, evidently, as προστάτης[22], was acquitted, then Hermippus would have had difficulty in escaping the counter-penalty of ἀτιμία[23], a danger which always threatened those who accused others unjustly or illegally, or who failed to obtain a fifth of the jury's votes in favour of the accusation. If Hermippus was not punished by ἀτιμία then neither the counts of the indictment or the outcome of the trial must have been different from the above. This also applies to the accusation of procuring.

Both Schoemann[24] and Decharme[25] are of the opinion that Hermippus, as was the custom with Attic orators, added the accusation of προαγωγεία to that of ἀσέβεια with the sole purpose of predisposing the court unfavourably towards Aspasia. This would imply that Pericles was incapable of resorting to all the objections available under Attic law at that time in order to ward off an unjust or unfounded accusation, which was, moreover, clearly intended to harm him through his metic protégée[26]. If Pericles did not resort to these procedures, but appeared in court to defend his παλλακή[27], then this again implies

22. On the nature and function of the προστάτης see P. Monceaux, in D.S., *s.v. Prostátes.* On the fact that Aspasia, as a metic in Athens like Anaxagoras but unlike the Athenian Socrates, did not have the right to defend herself in court, see Glotz, *Cité grecque, cit.,* p. 287; chacun [in the courts] doit parler pour son compte, sauf les incapables, femmes, mineurs, esclaves, affranchis et métèques qui sont représentés par leur tuteur légal, leur maître ou leur patron". Cf. also Clerc, *Metikoi,* in D.S. Therefore, the function of the προστάτης was not limited to that of presenting metics to the Demos and inscribing their names in the demotic lists; I have already pointed this out in *On the Trial of Anaxagoras.*

23. Anyone who incautiously presented a γραφὴ ἀσεβείας was liable to be punished by ατιμία, according to Andoc., *de myst.* 33, 53, or even by the maximum penalty, according to Pollux VIII 41, if the charge was not proven or was not supported by a fifth of the jury's votes: see Caillemer, in D.S., s.v. *Asebeia.*

24. Schoemann, *Antiquités grecques, cit.,* II, p. 676.

25. Decharme, *cit.,* p. 161.

26. This is also accepted by De Sanctis, *Atthis, cit.,* p. 479, in whose opinion the accusation which Aspasia had to face in the court was "ingiusta", and "calunniosa".

27. Aspasia was, in fact, not Pericles' second wife, but his concubine, παλλακή (see Judeich, *RE,* col. 1717; De Sanctis, *Storia, cit.,* II, p. 137; Flacelière, *La vie quotidienne, cit.,* p. 26), whom Pericles could not marry because of his own law on citizenship, cf. Aristot., *Ath. Resp.* 26, 4; Paoli, *Uomini e cose del mondo antico* (Firenze, 1947), p. 99, n.l; Ehrenberg, *The*

that either the accusation or the outcome of the trial was not as given above.

On which offence could Hermippus' accusation have been based, if on acount of it Aspasia could be brought before the court, yet be acquitted, thanks to Pericles' defence, without the charge rebounding on the incautious accuser?

It was not, at any rate, the ἀσέβεια provided for by Diopeithes' ψήφισμα, since impiety, punishable under Diopeithes' decree, could not form the basis of an accusation against Pericles' protégée, simply because not believing in the gods, τὰ θεῖα μὴ νομίζοντας[28], was an offence which could be committed by Athenian citizens, who, as adherents of the State religion, were subject to the ψήφισμα, and not by foreigners, who were free to believe or disbelieve in the Athenian gods. Aspasia was a metic in Athens[29].

It seems implausible, too, that the accusation against Aspasia was based on the offence of μετάρσια[30], which was introduced by the same decree and of which Anaxagoras was accused and convicted, since neither Archelaus, the Clazomenian's Athenian pupil and his successor in Lampsacus, nor any other member of Pericles' circle was charged with it.

It is even less likely that the offence was προαγωγεία[31], since it appears frankly inconceivable that Aspasia, Pericles' beloved

Greek state, 2nd ed (London, 1969), p. 39. Aspasia was a ξένη from Miletus, a city which did not have the right to ἐπιγαμία, and therefore she could not marry an Athenian citizen without running the risk of being sold as a slave, ps.-Dem., c. Neaer. (LIX) 16; Paoli, *Uomini e cose*, p. 125.

28. This was the first of the two offences introduced into Attic law by Diopeithes' ψήφισμα: disbelief in the state gods, which implied an extension of the ancient concept of impiety from the sphere of religious ritual to that of dogma; cf. *On the Trial of Anaxagoras*. On the different meaning that the word νομίζειν in Diopeithes' decree took on, compared with the γραφή ἀσεβείας,see *On the Trial of Anaxagoras*.

29. On the non-applicability of Diopeithes' decree to metics, who could not be accused of disbelief in the city gods of Athens, since they were not adherents of the state religion, see *On the Trial of Anaxagoras*.

30. The second offence defined by the ψήφισμα: λόγους περὶ τῶν μεταρσίων διδάσκοντας was introduced into Attic law so that Anaxagoras could be charged. see here *On the Trial of Anaxagoras*.

31. See n. 16 above.

companion for many years and the mother of his son[32], could have rendered herself liable to the charge of procuring by obtaining freeborn girls for Pericles' pleasure.

Since, in the light of the facts and of the law, it is difficult to see what Hermippus' accusation could have been based on, we may hypothesize either that it was not a judicial accusation at all[33], or that, if it really was a judicial accusation, it was made in a different way and based on different grounds.

3. Our sources do not tell us why or when Aspasia left her native Miletus[34] for Athens. It is probable, however, that she arrived there in about 450[35], since her union with Pericles, who had meanwhile divorced his citizen wife[36], must have commenced around 445[37], if Pericles the Younger was born of this union before, and not after, 440[38]. He was already active in Athenian political life in 410-9[39], and was a strategos in 406, being con-

32. See n. 38 ff. below.

33. In my opinion, it is not improbable, taking into account the remarks made about the grounds of the accusations and the outcome of the trial, that Hermippus accused Aspasia on the stage rather than court, just as Aristophanes was later to accuse Socrates. And just as Plato was to defend Socrates from Aristophanes' accusation, speaking of the comic poet as another, older κατήγορος, *Apol.* 18b-c, so may Aeschines have done, and, in polemic with Aeschines, Antisthenes, Ασπασία, see Diog. Laert. VI 16; Dittmar, *Aeschines, cit.*, p. 31 ff., dramatizing the accusation of Hermippus in a λόγος Σωκρατικός and being a logographer himself, inventing the scene of the defending Pericles weeping in court. Plutarch, in other words, may have been misled by his source, who probably used considerable licence in recalling the accusation and defence of Aspasia. Similarly, Plato freely reconstructed Socrates' defence, while Polycrates was later to invent the prosecution speech. This hypothesis should always be borne in mind when discussing Aspasia.

34. Plutarch's sources all appear to have been in agreement, ὁμολογεῖται, on the fact that Aspasia was Μιλησία γένος, *Pericl.* XXIV, 8.

35. Cf. Judeich, in *RE, s.v.* Aspasia, cols. 1716-1717, i.e. after the promulgation of Pericles' law on citizenship, Aristot., *Ath. resp.*, 26, 4; De Sanctis, *Atthis*, p. 479, n.l.

36. Plutarch, *Pericl.* XXIV, 8.

37. Cf. Judeich, in *RE, s.v.* Aspasia, cols, 1716-1717; De Sanctis, *Storia*, II, p. 137.

38. Judeich, *cit.*, col. 1717.

39. Judeich, *loc. cit.*; Curtius, *GG*, II, 768 f., 772, 777 f.

demned subsequently with the navarchs of the Arginusae[40].

We may reasonably conjecture that, on arriving in Athens, Aspasia was received as a guest by Pericles, to whom she had, perhaps, been introduced and recommended by some Milesian friend.

If, as related by Plutarch[41], following the Socratic Aeschines[42], it is true that Pericles defended Aspasia in court, then Pericles must have defended her specifically as Aspasia's προστάτης[43]; being a foreigner in Athens, she, like Anaxagoras, would not have had the right to conduct her own defence[44].

If Pericles acted as προστάτης in the trial initiated by Hermippus, he must have received the beautiful Milesian on her arrival in Athens, as suggested above, and had her name entered in the demotic lists, thereby becoming her protector and legal representative, and, if need arose (as indeed it eventually did), her defender in court[45].

Above all, this means that, as Aspasia's προστάτης, Pericles assumed the responsibility for the moral and civil conduct of the Milesian metic, making himself her guarantor before the people as soon as he sponsored her inscription in the civic lists[46].

In my opinion, this consideration alone should suffice to counter the belief, still prevalent today, that Aspasia came to Athens to carry on the trade of hetaera[47], openly leading a

---

40. Cf. Xenoph., *Hell.* I, VI 29; I, VII 16.
41. Plutarch, *Pericl*, XXXII 5.
42. Plutarch, *Pericl.* XXXII 5.
43. See n. 22 above.
44. Ibid.
44. "Tout métèque devait avoir un prostate, intermédiaire entre lui et l'Etat, son patron devant les magistrats et les tribunaux" (Monceaux, in D.S., *s.v. Prostatés*). For the ἀποστασίυ δίκη or γραφή to which a metic was liable if he did not place himself under the legal protection of a citizen as soon as he arrived, see Aristot., *Athen. resp.*, 58, 3.
46. The responsibility borne by the προστάτης for the conduct of metics appears evident, both from the very function of προστασία and from the proceedings against Pericles' metic friends, which, according to Plutarch, *Pericl.* XXXII 2, had the precise aim of implicating Pericles in the accusation and conviction of the metics.
47. The tradition that Aspasia carried on the profession of hetaera and brothel-keeper in Athens, in spite of her union with Pericles, derives from the

dishonest, shameful life and training young free girls to profit from immorality, as Plutarch states, following the words of the comic writers[48].

It is quite unthinkable that a man of Pericles' standing should welcome a foreign prostitute into his house, making himself morally and legally responsible for her conduct, and should repudiate his citizen wife out of preference for such a woman. Admittedly, the comic writers have wrought havoc with Aspasia's reputation; but it is well known that these writers' insults were expected to be outrageous, to add to the merriment at the festivals for which the comedies were intended[49].

It should also be remembered that these slanderous attacks date from later times, namely from the end of Pericles' political career, or from after his death[50], when Pericles' adversary Cleon was in power, and the populists held sway. They cannot be dated earlier than this, because, from the time of Aspasia's arrival in Athens (and in spite of her illegal union with Pericles)[51] to the

comic poets, from Hermippus, *ap.*, Plutarch, *Pericl.* XXXII 1, who accused her of προαγωγεία, to Cratinus and Eupolis, Plutarch, *Pericl.* XXIV 9, 10, and Aristophanes, *Acharn.* 524 ff., *ap.* Plutarch, *Pericl.* XXX 5, who supposed that the blockade of Megara and the outbreak of the Peloponnesian war were due to Aspasia's anger at the rape of two prostitutes, πόρνα δύο, by Megarian youths, anon. fr. 122 = Kock, III 431. See also Athen. V 219a, 220e-f; Hermesianax, *ap.* Athen. XII 599a. On the hetaerae and their situation in Athens, see Paoli, *La donna, cit.*, p. 89 f., 91ff.; on Aspasia's not being a hetaera, p. 93 and n. 61.

48. Plutarch, *Pericl.* XXIV 5.

49. On this subject, see my study in this volume and notes 165, 166, 167 *Socrates between the first and second Clouds.*

50. The accusation of Hermippus can, in fact, be dated to around 432, i.e. at the time of the blockade of Megara, according to an explicit reference in Plutarch, *Pericl.* XXXII 1, *Thuc.* I 67, when Anaxagoras was also accused; Aristophanes' *The Acharnians*, was, however, performed at the Lenaea of 425, four years after Pericles' death, while Eupolis' *Demoi* was performed 16 later in 413/2. This is also the possible date of Cratinus' lost comedy from which Plutarch, *Pericl.* XXIV 9, records two verses against Aspasia. In this context it should be remarked that Cratinus called Aspasia a concubine, παλλακή, a term which had no connotation of moral disapproval in 5th century Athens, but merely indicated an inferior social status, that of foreign women united *more uxorio* with Athenian citizens who could not legally marry them. To translate παλλακή as "prostitute" or "courtesan" is to give the term a pejorative significance which it did not originally possess.

51. See n. 27 above.

time of the all-out political struggle, fifteen years later, in which the circle of Pericles' friends was broken up, her behaviour, although of an audacity unheard of in Athens[52], was, as far as we know, never subjected to public censure.

Meanwhile the great love of Pericles[53], and the admiration and respect of Socrates and his followers[54] provide the best eulogy and the strongest refutation of the centuries of slanderous assertions about Aspasia.

There must have been fairly general respect for Aspasia in Athens even after the attacks of the comic writers, since the son of this foreigner was, exceptionally, granted the right of citizenship[55], and eventually supreme military command[56].

Evidently, the reasons for Aspasia's move from Miletus in Ionia to Athens must have been quite different from those put forward by the comic writers and accepted by Plutarch, and, in any case, must have been such as to provide grounds for Pericles' love and Socrates' respect.

4. While the comic writers smeared Aspasia's name with the most scurrilous slanders, thus prejudicing later generations against her, a different literary tradition, deriving from the Socratics[57], gives us a picture of Aspasia which reveals in her

52. De Sanctis, *Atthis, cit.*, p. 479, n.1, has rightly noted that "agli occhi degli Ateniese, fedeli alle tradizioni patrie, per la stessa libertà del conversare con uomini, essa [Aspasia] appariva uña etèra: proprio come oggi, agli occhi di un turco, o di un arabo, è un'etèra la donna musulmana che vada col viso scoperto".

53. Plutarch, *Pericl*, XXIV 7, 8, 9.

54. See Plat., *Menex.* 235e; Xenoph., *Mem.* 6, 36; *Oecon.* 3, 14; Hermesianax, *ap.* Athen. XIII 599A; Plutarch, *Pericl.* XXIV 2, 5, 7.

55. Plutarch, *Pericl.* XXXVII 5.

56. Xenoph., *Hell.* I, V 16.

57. Cf. Plat., *Menex.* 235 ff.; Xenoph., *Mem.* II 6, 36; *Oecon.* 3, 14; Aesch., Ασπασία *ap.* Dittmar, *Aeschines von Sphettos, cit.*, ch. 1, *Die Aspasia Dichtung der Sokratiker*; Antisth., *ap.* Diog. Laert. VI 16; cf. Dupréel, *La légende, cit.*, p. 264. That "chez Eschyle et chez Antisthène, le personnage d'Aspasie est bien plus importante que chez Platon" has been pointed out by Dupréel, *cit.* On the ironic nature of the preface to the *Menexenus*, cf. Plutarch, *Pericl.* XXIV 6, Dittmar, *Die Aspasie*, in *Aeschines, cit.*, ch. 1, p. 1 ff. and the justified objections raised by Taylor, *Plato*, 5th ed. (London, 1948), p. 41 f.

political wisdom[58] the true reason for Pericles' love[59] and for the frequent visits of Socrates "together with his pupils".[60]

Plutarch, too, gives a similar picture, together with that drawn by the comic writers, even though the picture of Aspasia as a hetaera and brothel-keeper is superimposed, in the story of the priest of Delphi, on the Socratic picture of her as an expert in political eloquence, thereby blurring the immage.

In my opinion, Aspasia when young (although indeed not very young) must have been introduced and recommended to Pericles precisely because she was, as all sources agree, an expert on political eloquence[61].

We know, moreover, that Pericles had received Anaxagoras of Clazomenae in Athens in the same way, keeping him at hand as τῆς πολιτείας σύμβουλον[62] throughout his long political career. The musicians Damon of Athens[63] and Pythoclides of Ceos[64] were political advisers, as well as Protagoras of Abdera[65], who had come to Athens to practise the art of politics (πολιτικὴ τέχνη)[66], and, subsequently, Aspasia, who taught political elo-

---

58. Taylor, *Plato, cit.*, p. 42, has correctly pointed out that "the remains of the *Aspasia* of Aeschines of Sphettus, make it clear that the view, which underlies the proposals of *Republic V.*, that 'the goodness of a woman and that of a man are the same', was a genuine doctrine of Socrates, and that he quite seriously believed in the 'political capacity' of Aspasia".

59. Plutarch, *Pericl.* XXIV 5.

60. Plutarch, *Pericl.* XXIV 5; Xenoph., *Mem.* 6, 36; Hermesianax, *ap.* Athen XIII 599A.

61. In addition to what was said by the Socratics, see Clem. Alex., *Strom.* IV 19, 122-23; Athen. V 219; Philostr., *v. Soph.* II 257 (= D.-K. 82A 35); Plutarch, *Pericl.* XXIV 5.

62. Plutarch, *Pericl.* XVI (= D.-K. 59A 32).

63. Plutarch, *Pericl.* IV (= D.-K. 37A 4); Isocrat. XV, 235; Plat., *Alc. I* 118c. On Damon of Athens, see my *Socrates. Physiology of a Myth,* it. ed., cit., pp. 239, 244, 263ff., 267 ff. and *passim.*, in which the history of Damon' relationships with Pericles and Socrates is reconstructed and the question of his condemnation reconsidered.

64. Schol. Aristot. [fr. 401 Rose] ap. Plutarch, *Pericl.* IV; Plat., *Alc. I* 118c, *Prot.* 316e.

65. Diog. Laert. IX 50 (= D.-K. 80A 1); Plutarch, *Pericl.* 36 (= D.-K. 80A 10).

66. Plat., *Prot.*

quence to Pericles and Socrates[67], and also arrived in Athens in about 450 B.C., that is to say at the time when men outstanding for their virtue and learning were coming together in Pericles' house — men such as Herodotus of Halicarnassus, Hippocrates of Cos, Parmenides and Zeno of Elea, Prodicus of Ceos, Hippias of Elis, and Hippodamus, a Milesian like Aspasia; these, together with Sophocles, Euripides, Phidias and Socrates, were to help make Athens the soul of Greece, when Pericles was the soul of Athens[68].

However, with the arrival in Athens of the metic philosophers with their different intuition of man, and therefore of God and the world, the result of philosophical and religious speculation on the distant Aegean and Italian shores, the soul of Athens was no longer that of the Marathon generation, mourned by Aristophanes[69], just as the soul of Pericles was no longer that of the choral dancer celebrating victory over the Persians[70].

It is a fact that, just as the προστάτης τοῦ δήμου[71] was turning into the undisputed prince of Athens[72], so within Periclean Athens the rough-and-ready manners and the severe mentality of former times were changing, native traditions were weakening, and the old gods were being neglected, while there was a relaxation and, eventually, the disappearance of the tension which had kept Athenian democracy steadfastly opposed to the two detested enemies, tyranny and Persia[73].

67. Clem. Alex., *Strom.* IV 19, 122-2: "Aspasia of Miletus [...] was made use of by Socrates in the sphere of philosophy, and by Pericles in the sphere of rhetoric". Cf. Athen. V 219E; Plutarch, *Pericl.* XXIV 5, and n. 58 above.

68. Glotz-Cohen, *HG*, II 2, p. 170: "Il [Pericles] fut l'âme de sa Cité en un temps où cette Cité fut l'âme de la Grèce".

69. Cf. Aristoph., *Nub.* 986.

70. In 472, Pericles, the son of the victor of Mycale and Sestos, Xanthippus, Herodot. IX 96-106, Glotz-Cohen, *HG*, ii 2, p. 94, in other words the son of the man who had annihilated the Persians and freed Greece from the barbarians, had led the chorus of Aeschylus' tragedy, Plutarch, *Them.* XV, which celebrated the victory over the Persians and praised both Athens and the whole of Hellas for the triumph over the barbarians. See my *Socrates. Physiology of a Myth.* It. ed., p. 111, ch. II, esp. p. 265 ff.

71. Aristot., *Resp. Athen.* XXVIII 2.

72. Thuc. II 65, 9; De Sanctis, *Atthis, cit.*, p. 467 f., who writes, justifiably, of a princedom set up by Pericles in Athens.

73. Aristoph., *Thesm.* 335 ff.; Isocrat. IV 157 f.; on this subject, cf. mv

In fact, everything that had once been regarded with horror as possible approval of tyranny or Persophilia was now becoming quite fashionable and commonly displayed.

Indeed, no scandal was created in Athens by Anaxagoras' book *On Nature*, which, in the doctrine of Noῦς, celebrated the supremacy of the Mind which is omniscient and omnipotent, the supreme organiser and regulator of the universe[74], thus providing a theoretical basis for and virtually justifying the political actions of Pericles, who was, with reason, compared with Pisistratus and named a tyrant[75]. Moreover, the unheard-of freedom of Aspasia's manners was, over a long period, to be the object of admiration and interest for the Athenians, who saw in her behaviour, free from preconceived ideas, a living example of the superiority of Persian education to that of Athens[76].

Protagoras, educated by the magi[77], laid down or adapted a constitution on aristocratic principles for the Panhellenic colony of Thurii[78] at Pericles' request; while Damon the musician pro-

Socrates. Physiology of a myth, It. ed., cit. pt. III, ch. II, esp. 270 ff. and the notes thereto. On the decree against tyranny successfully proposed by Demophon on the fall of the Four Hundred, which is clear evidence of a relaxation of the hostility towards tyranny in the Athenian mentality, cf. *op. cit.*, p. 278 and notes thereto.

74. See my *On the Trial of Anaxagoras*.

75. Cf. Thuc. II 65, 9; Plutarch, *Pericl.* VII 8; De Sanctis, *Atthis, cit.*, p. 477; Cloché, *La démocratie Athénienne* (Paris, 1951), p. 108 ff; Ehrenberg, *From Solon to Socrates*, p. 230 & 238; M.A. Levi, *Grecia e Persia fino ad Alessandro Magno* (Torino, 1970), 300 ff., esp. 314 f.

76. For the praise of Persian education as compared with Athenian, see Plat., *Alc.* I 120 ff.

77. On Protagoras' education by Persian magi, see Philostr., *v. Soph.* I 10, l ff; Untersteiner, *I Sofisti*, 2nd ed., (Milano, 1967), 2v., p. 15 f. & n. 7, accepts "come autentico l'incontro con i magi che educarono Protagora παῖς"; cf. Capizzi, *Protagora. Le testimonianze e i frammenti*, 2nd ed. (Firenze, 1955), p. 225. Recently Guthrie, *His. Gr. Ph., cit.*, p. III, pp. 262-3, has also found in Philostratus confirmation of the date of birth of Protagoras as 490 B.C.

78. Diog. Laert. IX 50 (= D.-K. 80A 1). On the aristocratic nature of Protagoras' constitution, cf. Untersteiner, *I Sofisti, cit.*, p. I, p. 17 ff. & nn. thereto, and Capizzi, *Protagora, cit.*, p. 232, who finds more evidence in favour of "la tesi di Lana che Protagora adottasse a Thurii le leggi di Caronda, con qualche influenza di Zaleuco, attuando cosí il programma ateniese di un compromesso fra la democrazia e la tradizione aristocratica pitagorica", a program which, I might add, corresponded exactly to the political program which Pericles

vided an astonishing example of medism or Persophilia by having the Odeon built, in the form of the Persian king's field tent, in the heart of Pericleans Athens[79], and Prodicus of Ceos, transforming the quality of an act into the virtue of the agent[80], presented the fanatics of all times with the doctrine of the "best person", already professed by the Persians in an aberrant form of anthropolatry[81].

It should come as no surprise, therefore, to learn that in this climate of openness towards the Persians, who were looked on no longer as the established natural enemy but as the bringers of a new civilisation, the admirers of oligarchically governed cities were coming out into the open in increasing numbers, while the number of pro-Laconians was also growing[82], and it no longer seemed a crime to praise the Persians[83].

Since the supporters of this dangerous involution in Athenian thought, which showed itself in practice in the rule of Pericles, were precisely those metic philosophers who had become the

followed in Athens. For my hypothesis concerning the condemnation of Protagoras, seen in relation to the turbulent events of the history of Thurii, and seen as one of the psychological repercussions suffered by the Athenian as a result of the colony's hostile attitude in the Peloponnesian war, see my *Socrates. Physiology of a Myth*, It. ed. cit., p. 271, n. 23.

79. Cf. Plutarch, *Pericl.* XIII; Paus. I 20, 4; Glotz-Cohen, *HG*, II, 2, p. 182 f., p. 531.

80. On Prodicus' doctrine of ἐπιμέλεια and the way in which it was interpreted and adopted by Socrates, see my *Socrates. Physiology of a Myth*, It. ed. p. 140 ff. & esp. nn. 130, 131 to p. 341.

81. I believe that this neologism, "anthropolatry", ["antropolatria" in the original. — Translator], which I cannot find recorded in Tommaseo-Battaglia, was coined by Silvio Spaventa, who used it in one of his pieces later collected under the title *La politica della Destra*, ed. by B. Croce for Laterza of Bari, which I read in my youth but cannot obtain at present. I prefer to use this term because it pre-dates and is more suitable than the over-used cliché "cult of personality".

82. Cf. F. Ollier, *Le mirage spartiate*, 2v. (Paris, 1932-1943); on the Athenian admirers of Sparta, cf. esp. p. 144 ff.; with reference to Socrates, cf. p. 231 ff. More will be found on the laconism of Socrates and the Socratics in my *Socrates. Physiology of a Myth*, It. ed. p. 285 ff. & throughout pt. III, ch III, pp. 281-317.

83. An example of this is the *Alcibiades I*, where, in a comparison with Athens, the Lacedaemonians and the Persians, especially the latter, are praised. Plat., *Alc. I*, 121A ff.

teachers and counsellors of the Olympian[84] of Athens, they became the target of the political reaction which swept them away in a series of trials, motivated in a contingent way by inter-factional strife, and at a deeper level by Athenians democracy's spirit of survival despite the insidious presence of the tyrannical tendency which had entered Athens along with monotheism and naturalistic monism[85].

5. Whereas Greek women were expected to be educated in such a way that they would attract the least possible comment, whether favourable or unfavourable[86], Aspasia attracted too much of both kinds of comment.

Her very arrival in Athens from Miletus in Ionia, which had always been open to Median influence and had only recently freed itself from Persian domination, must have caused a sensation if, as is likely, she arrived in the centre of a colourful entourage of exotic slaves.

The fact that Pericles himself became her προστάτης[87], offer-ing the Milesian his personal protection, must surely have amazed the Athenians, who would never have expected such an honour to be given to this unorthodox young metic.

When, finally, Pericles repudiated his lawful wife, "a lady of his own class and kinship"[88], for the sake of a union with this foreigner, although he could have maintained relations with both

---

84. He is called Περικλέης Οὐλύμπιος by Aristoph., *Ach.* v. 530, who por-trays the wrathful Pericles as Olympian Zeus, hurling thunderbolts and shaking all Hellas with his thunder. See also Plutarch, *Pericl.* VIII, and ps.-Plutarch, *cons. ad. Apoll.* 33, p. 118E (= D.-K. 80B 9).

85. On this subject, see also the two concluding paragraphs of *The Trial of Anaxagoras* and pt. III, ch. III of my *Socrates. Physiology of a Myth*, It. ed., where the question is re-examined in greater depth.

86. Thucydides (II 45) makes Pericles himself say this in his epicedium for those who fell in 439. Xenophon (*Oec.* III 13; VII 5) says that women should "see and hear as little as possible before their marriage". On the education of Greek women, see U. Paoli, *La donna greca nell'antichità* (Firenze, 1953); the still useful Picard, *La vie privée dans la Grèce classique* (Paris, 1930); Pohlenz, *Der hellenische Mensch* (Gottingen, 1947), p. 377 ff; Flacelière, *La vie quoti-dienne en Grèce au siècle de Periclès* (Paris, 1959).

87. See n. 22 above.

88. Plutarch, *Pericl.* XXIV 8.

of them without causing any scandal[89], Aspasia must have become a legendary figure in Athens and beyond.

Furthermore, in a society in which women, shut away in their homes, were virtually non-existent[90], the beautiful Milesian introduced a way of life resembling, in its freedom, that permitted only to the hetaerae[91]; she would boldly allow herself to be seen out of doors[92], and would freely receive Pericles' guests[93], conversing with them as a "cultured woman possessing great political awareness".[94]

According to all the sources, Aspasia was particularly skilled in rhetoric and political eloquence[95]. Socrates described himself as her pupil in this art[96], and Pericles was certainly taught by the Milesian, who refined not only his oratory[97] but also his manners, freeing them from all prejudice[98]. Later on, Lysicles, "a dealer in sheep-meat", was also a pupil, and thanks to Aspasia's teaching "rose from his poor and humble state to a high position in Athens".[99]

89. Cf. Flacelière, *La vie quotidienne, cit.*, p. 96. The scandal consisted not in living with a metic woman, but in repudiating a wife who was a citizen: "C'était d'avoir renvoyé de chez lui une Athénienne pour donner sa place à une étrangère" (ibid.), whereas, according to Athenian custom, Pericles would have been quite free to keep both his Athenian wife and his metic concubine.

90. Cf. esp. Paoli, *La donna greca, cit.*, p. 3 ff; Flacelière, *La vie quotidienne, cit.*, p. 75 ff., 87 ff.

91. On the hetaerae, their situation, education, and function in Greek society, Paoli, *La donna greca, cit.*, ch. V, *Le cortigiane*, p. 83 ff.

92. "La donna greca non va cercata in piazza o per le strade", writes Paoli, *La donna greca cit.*, p. 6.

93. Plutarch, *Pericl.* XXIV 5.

94. Plutarch, *Pericl.* XXIV 5.

95. See, Plat., *Menex.*, 235e; Clem. Alex., *Strom.* IV 19, 122-3: "Aspasia of Miletus was made use of by Socrates in the sphere of philosophy, and by Pericles in the sphere of rhetoric". Plutarch, *Pericl.* XIX 5, 7; Philostr., *v. Soph.* II 257 (= D.-K. 82A 35): "It is said that Aspasia of Miletus also refined the language of Pericles according to the manner of Gorgias".

96. Plat., *Menex.* 235e. On the presumed ironic nature of the *Preface* to the *Menexenus*, see above, n. 57.

97. See Philostr., *v. Soph.* II 257 (D.-K. 85A 35), cited in n. 95 above.

98. Plutarch, *Pericl.* XXIV 9, records, for example, that Pericles never failed to embrace and kiss Aspasia whenever he entered or left his house.

99. Plutarch, *Pericl.* XXIV 7.

However, while the freedom of the Milesian's manners caught the imagination of the Athenians and formed the subject of surreptitious gossip, Pericles' deep love and the admiration and respect she earned from those with whom she conversed[100] at least kept the Athenians' tongues in check, even if they could not impose complete silence. In fact, before the beginning of the Archidamian war, when Pericles' fortunes were clearly declining, no-one, not even the comic poets, dared to criticise the manners of Aspasia, although she was the most admired, the most visible and consequently the most vulnerable of the circle of metic philosophers that had gathered about Pericles.

While these learned metics from the furthest frontiers of the empire were surreptitiously introducing into Athens ideas and tendencies to subvert the deep-rooted ideal of ἰσονομία[101], which, since Solon's time, had formed the basis of Athenian democracy, Aspasia herself was ostentatiously displaying Median customs and manners[102]. The strong contrast between her manners and those of the Athenian women must have caused comparisons to be made between the Median style of education, symbolised by

---

100. Plutarch, *Pericl.* XXIV 2.

101. On *isonomia*, "the fairest of names", Herodot. III 80, 6, which signified justice through equality as the ideal measure of government by the people before the word "democracy" became current, cf. Ehrenberg, *RE*, Suppl. VII, col. 293. There is a good definition of *isonomia* in Nilsson, *Religiosità greca* (Firenze, 1961), p. 71 f.; see also Fassò, *La democrazia in Grecia*, 2nd ed. (Bologna, 1967), p. 38. Ehrenberg, *The Greek state*, 2nd ed. (London, 1969), p. 51, has shown clearly how the increasingly distinct antithesis between *eunomia* and *isonomia* reflected the antithesis between the two forms of political organization in Sparta and Athens respectively.

102. It will not be forgotten that Ionia, already exposed to Median influence, fell under Persian domination in 489 with the fall of Miletus, Herodot. V 31 ff.; Glotz-Cohen, *HG*, II, II, p. 26; Levi, *Grecia e Persia, cit.*, p. 63, and was not free from it until 479; Herodot. VIII 59-70; Glotz-Cohen, *Histoire Grecque*, II, pp. 90-92, 94-95, who considers that Aspasia may well have had a Median education, in an environment where loyalty to the Medes was still substantial. Afnan, *Zoroaster's influence on Anaxagoras, the Greek tragedians and Socrates* (New York, 1969), has the laudable aim of focusing attention on Aspasia's medism, but contains a mass of second-hand information interspersed with unbelievably elementary mistakes, such as making Aspasia and Thargelia contemporaries, *op. cit.*, p. 30.

the intelligent, cultivated, refined, self-confident Aspasia[103], and Athenian education, which rendered women ignorant and awkward[104]. Such comparisons were entirely favourable to the Milesian and to the ideal of behaviour represented by her, at a time when Athens was prepared to accept everything from the Medes that had previously been detested.

It is highly likely that Aspasia was not only the living example of a Median way of life previously unheard of in Athens, but also a keen propagandist for, or actually an agent of the Medes in Athens, just when Periclean Athens was becoming open to the Median tendencies and models put forward by Pericles' friends and advisers.

Certainly, Plutarch[105], following Aeschines[106], states that Aspasia modelled herself on one Thargelia[107], "an Ionian woman of former times [...] of noble and refined manners and highly intelligent", who, during the Persian wars, "persuaded all those who loved her not to oppose the King's designs", thus sowing in Athens "the seeds of the Median faction"[108].

From what has been said, it seems reasonable to conjecture that Aspasia, like Thargelia, was operating on behalf of the Medes[109],

---

103. It was precisely these qualities that convinced Delcourt, *Périclès* (Paris, 1939), p. 77, *ap.* Flacelière, *La vie quotidienne, cit.*, p. 96, that Aspasia was a hetaera: "Aspasie", writes Delcourt, "était trop brillante pour être une honnête femme". A strange way indeed to judge a woman by another woman.

104. In addition to what has already been said, above, n. 86, concerning the ideal of Greek womanhood, and admonition of Euripides to the women of Athens is noteworthy: "una moglie saggia deve considerarsi la schiava del proprio marito", Eurip. fr. 549 N², *ap.* Paoli, *La donna*, p. 98, n. 82, as an illustration of the difference between the upbringing of Aspasia and that of a Greek woman. The fact that Euripides was a misogynist does not detract from the significance of this remark.

105. Plutarch, *Pericl.* XXIV 3.

106. V. Dittmar, *Aeschines von Sphettos, cit.*, I, *Die Aspasia Dichtung der Sokratiker*, p. 118 ff.

107. On Thargelia of Miletus, see Philostr., *ep.* 73 (= D.-K. 82A 35) Athen. XIII 608 f (= D.-K. 86B 4); Hesych., *s.v.* Θαργελια; Suida, *s.v.*; Plutarch, *Per.* XXIV 3-4. See the close portayal of the Milesian in Curtius, *GG*, II, p. 59; also Bury, *CAH*, v. 5, p. 175; Glotz-Cohen, *HG*, II, II, p. 578; Dittmar, *Aischines, cit.*, p. 18 ff., 27.

108. Plutarch, *Pericl.* XXIV 3-4.

109. The gathering of intelligence for an enemy and the making of propagan-

and was in fact sent to Athens for this purpose by pro-Median groups in Ionia and placed close to Pericles, who fell in love with her, thus furthering her designs. It is a fact that Aspasia not only inspired and advised Pericles in his conduct of government, but also actively intervened in public affairs, as for example in the Samian war, which she is said to have instigated in the interests of Miletus[110]. Aspasia's influence both on the formation of Pericles' character and on his political decisions must have been a matter of general knowledge, if only in the form of surreptitious gossip among the Athenians. But when Thucydides, son of Melesias[111], returned from exile and, supported by the popular front rekindled the struggle against Pericles, sweeping away his friends and advisers with a flood of accusations and trials, the comic poets, as may easily be imagined, were unleashed on Aspasia, Pericles and their illegal union[112], making up for their long period of silence with savage insults, and eventually going so far as to drag Aspasia before the court.

But if Damon was accused of supporting tyranny[113], and Anaxagoras was accused of medism[114], which has been alleged to be

da in favour of an enemy or an opposing faction were commonplace in classical Greece; in fact, recent studies have shed light on both the vast extent of these activities and on the use of refined techniques; cf. L.A. Losada, *The fifth column in the Peloponnesian war* (Leiden, 1972); D.Y. Mosley, *Envoys and diplomacy in Ancient Greece* (Wiesbaden, 1973); AA.VV., *Propaganda e persuasione occulta nell'antichità* (Milano, 1974); F. Adcock & D.Y. Mosley, *Diplomacy in Ancient Greece* (London, 1975).

110. Plutarch, *Pericl.* XXV 1. The fact that Pericles set up a democratic government in Samos, καταστήσας δημοκπατίαν, *cit.*, XXV 3, does not invalidate what has been said in this study concerning the monarchical and tyrannical tendency of Pericles' government; Athens under Pericles was also, nominally, governed by the people, but was in fact governed by one man, Thuc. II, 65.

111. On Thucydides, son of Melesias, and the campaign which he led against Pericles both before and after his exile, particularly at the time of the trial of Anaxagoras, and his participation in the trial, see *On the Trial of Anaxagoras*.

112. See nn. 27-86 above.

113. On the grounds for the exiling of Damon, see my *Socrates. Physiology of a Myth*, It. ed., p. 267, n. 56 f.

114. Cf. *On the Trial of Anaxagoras* and *Socrates. Physiology of a Myth*, cit., p. 266 and n. 52.

equivalent to instigation to tyranny[115], then what was the offence with which the comic poet Hermippus could have charged Aspasia, the most beloved and therefore the most influential of Pericles' circle of learned metics, and, like Thargelia, the most ardent and active propagandist of Median ideals in Athens?

6. After all that has been said, it is surely difficult to escape the conclusion that Aspasia, like Damon, Anaxagoras and finally Pericles himself, was accused of medism, for having instigated Pericles to tyranny.

Moreover, the evidence of Plutarch's account itself, with its repeated references to Aspasia decidedly un-Greek and particularly un-Athenian behaviour[116]; with its mention of Thargelia, also a Milesian, who was Aspasia's model and the first agent of the Median faction[117]; with its remark about Aspasia's reputation with Cyrus the Younger, who called the most beloved of his courtesans Aspasia[118]; and with its description of Aspasia's unconcealed and powerful influence on the formation of Pericles' political personality[119] and of her intervention in public affairs[120], makes such a conjecture extremely plausible. This view is further supported by a consideration of the historical and cultural environment of Athens in which Aspasia lived and worked[121], and in which Hermippus' accusation took shape.

This accusation was certanly not that of impiety and procuring, from which she was saved by Pericles' tears, according to the tale told by Aeschines, on whom Plutarch relies[122]: in Plutarch's account, the only reliable fácts are the date of the accusation[123] and Pericles' presence in court[124].

115. Crat. *ap*. Plutarch, *Pericl*. III 7 (= fr. 86 Kock).
116. Plutarch, *Pericl*. XXIV *passim*.
117. Plutarch, *Pericl*. XXIV 3, 4.
118. Plutarch, *Pericl*. XXIV 11, 12.
119. Plutarch, *Pericl*. XXIV *passim*.
120. Plutarch, *Pericl*. 2, XXV 1.
121. See above, 4. Cf. *Socrates. Physiology of a Myth*, It. ed., chs. II & III of pt. III, p. 251 ff.
122. Aeschines *ap*. Plutarch, *Pericl*., XXXII 5, cited above.
123. Plutarch, *Pericl*. XXXII 1; i.e. at the time of the blockade of Samos, 432, see Thuc. I 67.
124. Plutarch, *Pericl*. XXXII 5, see above.

The very fact that Pericles, not in the guise of συνήγορος[125], but rather, as has been said, in his special role of προστάτης[126] carried out the legal defence of the Milesian metic, plainly gives the lie to Plutarch and his source, according to whom Hermippus could have brought Aspasia to court to answer a general accusation of ἀσέβεια, to which the further charge of προαγωγεία could have been added as a pretext[127].

It is hard to believe that a man in Pericles' position would not have made use of all the prestige which he still enjoyed in Athens and all the exemptions provided by Attic law, in order to protect the woman he loved from trial on a groundless and outrageous charge, which, whatever the outcome, would discredit him.

As I have remarked elsewhere[128], the damage done by those trials of the metic philosophers of Pericles' circle consisted in the fact that Pericles, in his position of προστάτης, was made to account for the behaviour of his metic friends and advisers, which was publicly condemned by the court in spite of his defence.

If, therefore, Pericles was unable to prevent Aspasia's being brought before the court, and was himself obliged to defend her, the accusation against her must have been soundly based and the case skilfully conducted.

This also implies that Hermippus would not have prosecuted Aspasia simply in order to gain renown by initiating a sensational trial; he was already well-known in Athens and outside because of his victory at the Great Dionysia in 435[129]. Nor would he have wanted to risk unpopularity by doing this; he would have been exposing himself to the wrath of Pericles and the hostility of the majority faction by going to court with an accusation which would

125. On the institution of συνήγορος, which altered the strict rule in Attic procedural law, according to which each party had to defend itself, by introducing to the trial a defender who was not acting in a professional capacity "ma in quanto ha un diretto interesse personale alla causa che si discute", see Paoli, *Uomini e cose, cit.*, p. 126. In the case of Aspasia, Pericles could not act as συνήγορος, because Aspasia was a foreigner in Athens, and therefore needed a προστάτης, see n. 22 above, to defend her in court.

126. See n. 22 above.

127. Plutarch, *Pericl.* XXXII 1, *cit.*, see above.

128. Cf. my *On the Trial of Anaxagoras*.

129. See K.J. Dover, *OCD*, 2nd ed. *s.v. Hermippus*.

have struck at Pericles himself through the medium of the Milesian metic. He would have been even less willing to expose himself to the severities of ἀτιμία[130], by frivolously making an accusatiòn which he could nor substantiate in court.

It is also hard to believe that Hermippus, a comic poet, would have prosecuted Aspasia because he was shocked by her manners. The comic poets enjoyed total licence in the theatre, and are unlikely to have been intolerant in real life[131].

A comic poet like Hermippus who, instead of softening his attack on manners with humour, showed himself to be so shocked by Aspasia's private behaviour that he prosecuted her for it, would have lost all his credibility as a comic poet. If, in spite of this, Hermippus did denounce Aspasia to the popular assembly, then he must have discerned in her behaviour not just the makings of a scandal, but something more serious, which he could reasonably consider to be a clear danger to the city. He therefore reported on this danger to the popular magistrates, thereby accepting the responsibility of proving the truth of the matter, but without running the risk of serious sanctions should he be unsuccessful. The comic poet must have found this to be a most timely precaution when none other than Pericles took up the defence. And, as we know, although Aspasia was acquitted, Hermippus was not indicted.

From this fact, essential for an understanding of the nature of the proceedings against Aspasia, it may reasonably be deduced that Hermippus' accusation concerned a matter that was still ἄγραφος νόμος, for which the judge, as was often the case in Attic criminal legislation, had first to define the offence and then the deed which constituted the offence[132]. This could not be so for

130. On ἀτιμία as a counter-penalty explicitly prescribed for anyone who unjustly accused others of ἀσεβεία see Caillemer, in *D.S.*, *s.v. Asebeia. Atimía*, the loss of civil rights, was still hereditary in 444-43, see Glotz, *Cité grecque* (Paris, 1935), p. 302.
131. On the function of comedy and the freedom which it enjoyed, see infra my study *Socrates between the first and second clouds*, cit., p. 47 ff. and n. 166.
132. Paoli, *Studi sul processo attico*, p. 87, observes "che corrompere la gioventù sia reato di empietà in Atene non lo aveva stabilito il legislatore; furono i giudici di Socrate che con il loro voto stabilirono che quel fatto costituiva reato e giudicarono poi, con una posteriore votazione, della pena applicabile al reato".

the γραφὴ ἀσεβείας[133], nor for the γραφὴ προαγωγείας[134], both of which offences were defined exactly, and for both of which not only judicial procedure but also the penalty for wrongful accusation were precisely laid down; but it could well have been so for the offence of medism, since judges were required to pronounce from time to time both on the definition of the offence itself and on the deeds that should be accepted as constituting the offence[135].

133. For the γραφὴ ἀσεβείας see Thalheim, in *RE*, *s.v.* Ἀσεβείας γραὴ, cols, 1529-1531. On the highly imprecise nature of ἀσεβεία, as a result of which "qualunque fatto poteva, mediante l'uso di quelle azioni, essere giudizialmente perseguito", see Paoli, *Studi sul processo attico, op. cit.*, p. 86. J. Rudhart, *La définition du délit d'impiété d'après la législation attique, Mus. Helv.* 17 (1960), p. 87 ff., does not provide convincing arguments for his identification of the γραφή ἀσεβείας with Diopeithes' ψήφισμα, which later extended the concept of impiety to cover dogma as well as worship, i.e. belief in the gods as well as the practice of worship; cf. *supra. On the Trial of Anaxagoras.*

134. Cf. Aesch., *c. Tim.* 14; Plat., *Theaet.* 150A.

135. The term Μηδισμὸς had a great variety of meanings for the Athenians of Pericles' time; it could signify not only an inclination towards the Medes, often also known as "Persophilia", Thuc. I 95, 135, but also plotting with the Persians or siding with Medes or Persians, μηδίζω, Thuc. III 62-62; Xenoph. *Hell.* III 1, 6, so that even half a century after the victory over the Persians the Thebans had to answer a charge of Persophilia, Thuc. *loc. cit.* It could also mean favouring tyranny, cf. Aristot., *Resp. Athen.* XVI 10, or favouring the establishment of a monarchic-tyrannical government like that of the Persians, cf. the well-known *Logos Tripolitikos* related in Herodot. III 80-83, in which Megabyzus describes government by the masses as stupid and insolent, while Darius exalts monarchy as the supreme form of government. Opposition to the Persians, in the form of the opposition of democracy to monarchy, is a constant theme in classical literature, and is to be found in Plat., *Leg.* III 693d; Isocrat., *Paneg.* (IV) 157-8, and again in Plutarch: cf. Fassò, *La democrazia in Grecia*, 2nd ed. (Bologna, 1967), p. 251 f. Another common meaning of the term μηδισμός was to behave in a Persian manner, μηδιστί, or to adopt the fashions and customs of the Persians, to act in a Median way, in other words, just as Aspasia did. But siding with the Persians or acting in a Median way were never in themselves offences; similarly, a pro-Laconian stance was never a crime, even during the Peloponnesian war. In the minds of the Athenians of the 5th century, who saw their opposition to the Persians as the opposition of democracy to tyranny, medism came finally to be identified with tyranny, Aristot., *Resp. Athen.* XVI 10, cf. A. Levi, *Commento storico alla* Resp. Athen. *di Aristotele* (Milano-Varese, 1968), I, p. 178, according to whom anyone who attempted to make himself a tyrant or to help establish a tyranny was punished by *atimía*. And

Since the offence of medism[136] was not precisely defined, Hermippus would not have brought a proper γραφὴ before the court, but would have used the procedure of προβολή[137], aiming for a "jugement préjudicielle et à sanction purement morale"[138]; by means of this procedure, any citizen could, in the public interest[139], bring before the popular assembly an accusation intended to result, not in a judicial decision, but in a declaration, based on a vote, as to the legality of a deed, and also intended to sound out public opinion as to any indictment that might be made[140].

since the law on tyranny was as ancient as the crime of tyranny itself, being confirmed in the eighth law of the Twelve Tables, which excluded those who had aspired to tyranny from pardon, (Plutarch, *Sol.* 19; cf. De Sanctis, *Atthis, cit.*, pp. 141, 187), Athenian democracy, spontaneously identifying the crime of tyranny with that of medism (Aristoph., *Thesm.* V 335 ff.; Jacoby, *Apoll. Cronich. Philolog. Unters.*, p. 428 & n. 7) found in the law on tyranny the necessary legal precedent for the offence of medism, for which, according to Isocrates, *Paneg.* (IV) 157, the Athenians often imposed the death penalty. The Athenian aversion to tyranny, which was also experimented with in the Peloponnesian war, was so great that, immediately following the fall of the Four Hundred, Demophontus had a decree passed which obliged all Athenians, divided into their clans and demes, to take a solemn oath to kill anyone who attempted to become a tyrant or who helped to establish a tyranny. The oath is referred to by Andocides, *de myst.* 96-99, which I quote here in part, in the translation by Fassò, *La democrazia in Grecia, cit.*, pp. 112-113: "darò morte con la parola, col voto e con la mia stessa mano, se mi sarà possibile, a chi abbia rovesciato la democrazia in Atene [...] o abbia contribuito ad instaurare la tirannide". Cf. my *Socrates*, cit. It. ed., p. 278 & nn. thereto, and in general pt. III, ch. II, pp. 251-279, in which the identification of medism with tyranny is observed in the behaviour, and in the subsequent condemnation, of Pericles' friends such as Anaxagoras, Protagoras, Damon, Aspasia, and later Socrates.

136. Which, as has been pointed out, was identified in Pericles' time with that of τυραννίς, cf. Aristot., *Resp. Athen.*, XVI 10, and was consequently loathed and, on occasion, punished. Later, medism was also associated with Demophontus' decree against tyranny, issued on the fall of the Four Hundred, cf. *Socrates. Physiology of a Myth*, It. ed., p. 278 & n. 101.

137. On the procedure of προβολή see E. Benecker, *RE*, cols. 43-48, *s.v.*; Glotz, in D.S., *s.v.*

138. Glotz, *s.v. Probolé*, in D.S., *cit.*

139. "Il n'eut pas fallu cependant que le plaignant fût seul intéressé dans l'affaire qu'il déférait à l'Assemblée, il était bon que la chose publique fût en jeu" (Schoemann, *Antiquités Grecques, cit.*, 1, p. 448).

140. Schoemann, *cit.*, I, p. 448-449; Glotz, in D.S., *s.v. Probolé, cit.*

If, however, the popular assembly rejected the accusation, thus refusing to define the offence and the deed constituting it, "le plaignant n'avait rien de mieux à faire que de l'abandonner"[141] without incurring any penalty. According to Glotz, "le caractère exceptionnel de la προβολή se marque encore par un dernier détail: l'accusateur débuté de sa plainte et qui n'obtenait pas un cinquième des suffrages, n'avait pourtant pas à payer l'amende ordinaire. Sur ce point il était couvert par l'approbation préalable du peuple"[142].

This would appear to have been the case with Hermippus; namely, that he did indeed accuse Aspasia before the popular assembly, and so obliged Pericles, as προστάτης, to defend his metic protégée; but that, on being defeated at this initial stage, he abandoned any further legal action, as he was entitled to do, without suffering any counter-sanction or loss of favour among the people. If this is the case, as all the evidence indicates, then in Plutarch's account of the prosecution of Aspasia the offences of ἀσέβεια and προαγωγεία, with which she is supposed to have been charged, as well as the tears shed by Pericles in defence of his protégée, must be the inventions of Aeschines[143]; not, however, Pericles' presence in court, necessitated by his special role as the patron and legal defender of the metic. Meanwhile, the hypothetical accusation of medism would, through the procedure of προβολή, fully account for the fact that Hermippus was not indicted following Aspasia's acquittal.

If Aspasia was accused of medism by Hermippus, her trial would no longer appear to be an episode of interfactional strife under the pretext of religion, as is generally believed, but rather an aspect of the strong reaction of Athenian democracy against the dangerous, subversive, monarchic and tyrannical tendencies which, during the rule of Pericles, emanated from his friends and counsellors, among whom Aspasia was the most beloved and therefore the most influential[144]. But if this reaction was to result in the outlawing of Aspasia and the rest of Pericles' metic

141. Schoemann, cit., I, p. 449.
142. Glotz, s.v. Probolé, cit.
143. See n. 33 above.
144. See, again, pt. III, chs. II & III, of my Socrates, cit. It. ed.

counsellors, this would mean the outlawing of philosophy too, or rather, of the free scientific research which had been introduced into Athens thirty years earlier by Anaxagoras in particular[145], and in general by all the learned metics who had come from the distant frontiers of the empire. These metics imported into Athens a monistic and monotheistic civilization[146] which, undermining Athenian democratic pluralism, was to give rise to the harsh conflict between the supporters of the opposing ideals of the "one" and the "many"[147], or, in other words, of "monarchy" and its transparent synonyms, and "democracy"[148], a conflict which ultimately divided the city. This conflict continued after the Pelopponesian war, and Socrates — also accused of being a "teacher of tyrants"[149] — was to be its most fearless protagonist and most illustrious victim[150].

London, spring 1976

145. Cf. *On the Trial of Anaxagoras* in which the question of the arrival of the Clazomenian in Athens is re-examined, showing how the banishment of Anaxagoras signified the prohibition of free scientific research in Athens.

146. For the profound influence of Oriental civilization on the development of the Greek philosophers, see the book by M.L. West, *Early Greek philosophy and the Orient* (Oxford, 1971), which brings to light the existence of Oriental elements in the thinking of presocratic philosophers.

147. The excellent study by M.C. Stokes, *One and many in presocratic philosophy* (London, 1971), is, unfortunately, only a logical and semantic investigation, and does not take account of the powerful ethical and political significance which these terms had for the early Greek philosophers.

148. The opposition of the terms "one" and "many" in civil life in 5th-century Athens, as expressions of opposing ethical and political ideals of monarchy and democracy, is studied more thoroughly and, I think, elucidated, in my book *Socrates*, It. ed., Part III, esp. chs. VI & V.

149. Polycrat., *ap.* Liban., *Apol.* 60. Cf. *Socrates*, cit. It. ed., p. 301.

150. Socrates' μισοδημία, and the reasons for the condemnation of the Athenian master on the same charge as that faced by Critias, Alcibiades, Plato and Xenophon, are subjected to a lengthy analysis in my *Socrates*, cit. It. ed., Part III, esp. ch. III ff.

226

INDEX OF NAMES

100, 119, 147, 189, 190, 198
Gorgias 32, 34, 104, 118, 216
Grote, G. 41, 48, 50, 58, 80, 132, 147, 170, 198, 201, 202, 204
Guardini, R. 48, 62
Gulley, N. 8
Guthrie, W.K.C. 20, 148, 161, 168, 170, 174, 201, 213

Hackforth, R. 60
Harpocration 201
Hatzfeld, J. 44, 45, 58, 116, 117, 198
Hegel, G.W.F. 2, 28, 50, 80, 83, 103, 124, 126, 127, 128, 147, 151
Heidhues, B. 97
Heine, H. 123
Helios 108, 175
Hellas 157, 168, 171, 175, 189, 212, 215
Herder, J.G. 124, 125, 126, 127
Hermann, C.C.F. 150
Hermesianax 209, 210, 211
Hermippus 180, 182, 186, 201, 226
Hermodorus the Platonist 15, 23, 58
Herodotus 30, 74, 150, 152, 156, 157, 158, 166, 182, 212, 217, 223
Hesychius 218
Hicks, R.D. 151, 152, 153, 161, 164
Hiestand, M. 48
Hild, G. 136
Hildebrand, K. 11, 51, 79, 103, 131, 132, 133
Hippocrates 212
Holwerda, D. 89
Homer 168
Humbert, J. 26, 29, 36, 54, 60,

61, 66, 115, 119
Hussey, E. 148
Hyperbolos 76, 94, 97, 98
Hyppodamus 212

Ionia 156, 184, 215
Irenaeus 148
Isarco 85
Isocrates 20, 211, 223, 224

Jaeger, W. 31, 42, 48, 50, 51, 58, 67, 71, 115, 118, 130, 132, 189, 190, 196, 199
Jamblicus 200
Joannidis, Th. 5
Joel, K. 26, 29, 39, 50, 52, 147
Jonsius, J. 165
Jowett, R. 55, 68, 71, 168
Judeich, W. 201, 207

Kahrstedt, U. 174
Kiesow, F. 56, 60
Kirk, G.J.-Raven, J.E. 149, 150
Kock, Th. 27, 45, 88, 136
Koechly, H. 113
Kuhn, H. 32, 48

Labriola, A. 29, 41, 48, 50, 80, 130, 132
Lampsacus 154, 187, 206
Lana, I. 213
Lanza, D. 148, 150, 151, 153, 155, 156, 158, 159, 161, 171, 187, 192
Laterza, G. 214
Laurenti, R. 148, 156
Leon of Salamis 54
Lesky, A. 207
Leslie Peck, A. 154, 177
Lessing, G.E. 41, 42, 126, 131
Levi, A. 27
Levi, M.A. 213, 217, 223